Long Shadows in Cyprus

Long Shadows in Cyprus

A Green Line Odyssey

M. J. W. CLARK

T

Troubador Publishing Ltd
Unit E2 Airfield Business Park
Harrison Road, Market Harborough
Leicestershire LE16 7UL
Tel: 0116 279 2299
Email: books@troubador.co.uk
Web: www.troubador.co.uk

ISBN 978 1 80514 455 7

British Library Cataloguing in Publication Data.
A catalogue record for this book is available from the British Library.

Printed and bound by CPI Group (UK) Ltd, Croydon, CR0 4YY
Typeset in 11pt Minion Pro by Troubador Publishing Ltd, Leicester, UK

MIX
Paper | Supporting
responsible forestry
FSC
www.fsc.org
FSC® C013604

In grateful memory of Flt Lt John E. Clark
1932–1999

Contents

Maps and other images can be found around the centre of the book

Review the past for me,
let us argue the matter together;
state the case for your innocence.
Isaiah

Introduction

... I stepped from a surface of new and uneven tarmac onto a trail of soft and pleasant sand, a move from asphalt into Eden. It was obvious that every step along the lovely, deserted track would lead down to the Mediterranean, each sway forward delivering the torso into the gentle aid of gravity ever downwards towards the sea...

... I knew I would be taking those steps. My journey was a requirement, a pilgrimage. Instinctive. The origin of this book is more profound than sharing a journey or desire to write a memoir about my boyhood in Cyprus, or my adult journey across it. The reason for the trek lay deep within my subconscious, even though it took half a century to finally embark upon it. Every step was deeply cathartic, yet still insufficient to fully fathom the mysterious waters left behind by passing from childhood into adulthood. These weren't bitter waters, quite the opposite. I floated in the warm Mediterranean as a boy and *flew* over landscapes of coral lying under a firmament of liquid sky. Living on the island of Cyprus had changed me forever, leaving something tangible that beseeched the bowels more than the brain and I wanted to find out why…

… It all started with a laundry basket… that is, my experience of Cyprus started with a laundry basket. Or to be more exact, my first *taste* of Cyprus started with a laundry basket. In 1970, my father, a navigator on Vulcan aircraft in the Royal Air Force (RAF), flew to RAF Akrotiri in Cyprus, on exercise, and that's where the bootlegging took place…

Anyone who's flown on an airliner knows you have a weight allowance for your luggage, but if you have a moderate level of autonomy over a large nuclear bomber the weight limit is… well, generous. Consequently, during my childhood, my father would return from corners of the globe with extraordinary quantities of booty, all carried home in the cavernous bomb bay of the Vulcan. The facility was never tested to the max, but I'm certain that if my mother had been desirous of, say, an enormous American wardrobe, then my father would have obliged and even filled the furniture with canned goods and perhaps an outboard motor. Personally, I had been in receipt of an American toy rifle that didn't look like a toy, so the boys in my Lincolnshire village queued to look at the exotic item with its brass-coloured bullet. Had I ventured onto the street with it today, it would be about thirty seconds before the call was put in to an armed response team.

Cyprus must have stimulated a more poetic number of purchases for my father and, like a returning spy from Eshcol, he filled a large wicker laundry basket to the brim with all manner of citrus fruit. When the hamper was set down on the carpet of our lounge, we stepped back to see if Ali Baba might emerge. Fortunately for us, Her Majesty's Revenue and Customs officials had either not been at RAF Scampton to spot the contraband, or they'd been duped by the domesticity of the basket, and the prohibited fruit entered the country. *Had* any contamination taken place with the fruit trees of England, I suspect it would have been a beneficial cross-pollination; the specimens of Cypriot fruit were enormous! The peel fell away easily from fragrant oranges too big to hold in my small hand and the grapefruit were astonishing in their vibrancy of colour and juicy weight; and all delivered from Cypriot tree to Lincolnshire child in less than eight hours – better than any supermarket supply chain. From the evidence on display that morning, Cyprus must be paradise. I suppose that's why my mother was so excited when she announced Dad was to be posted to Cyprus, and his family, including an eight-year-old me, were to be housed at RAF Berengaria near Limassol. Like thousands of other British Forces personnel and their families I developed a love for Cyprus which has remained with me all my life. Yet, despite two years living on the island (1970–72), I knew very little about the hinterland of this 'jewel of the Mediterranean'.

The island's location, so close to Asia but still offering European ports in the eastern Mediterranean, has produced a long and turbulent history. Cyprus was an important player in the Classical world and a way marker for sailing crusaders in the Middle Ages; it's been a land desired by many countries ancient and modern. Today it exists in a state of division following a Greco-Turkish war in the summer of 1974, but signs of unrest were evident long before the July of that year.

In December 1963, the Commander of British Land Forces – Cyprus, Major General Peter Young, attempted to extinguish a fire of intercommunal violence on the island. His method was to draw a line of demarcation across Cyprus that would serve to separate the two factions of Turkish and Greek Cypriots. Apparently, a green chinagraph pencil was tactfully selected from a choice of colours to draw the agreed line, whilst red and blue were discarded owing to their inclusion in the flag colours of the opposing sides.

Although Cyprus received its independence from Britain in 1960, the island still has two Sovereign Base Areas, with the Royal Air Force and British Army maintaining a sizeable military presence on the island – post-independence.

This book revolves around my desire to learn a little more about Cyprus by walking along the entire length of the Green Line, although the last British governor of the island famously said, 'Anyone who says he understands Cyprus has been misinformed.' The Green Line is two green lines, one north and the other south, and, between the two, a no man's land is patrolled by the United Nations. This Buffer Zone, as it's known, varies in width, from just a few metres in central Nicosia to several kilometres in various places along its 190-kilometre length. It runs west to east across the entire island, separating the Republic of Cyprus, in the south, from the Turkish Republic of Northern Cyprus (TRNC) in the north. The Turkish Republic of Northern Cyprus is not officially recognised as a country, which means it continues to struggle economically. In writing this book, and under advice from a Turkish Cypriot academic, I have, almost entirely, referred to the TRNC as Northern Cyprus.

This book is written with a particular interest in the events of 1974, when a coup d'état was launched by Greece in an attempt to annex Cyprus to the Greek mainland, despite a United Nations ruling that no such unification should take place. In response, the Turkish military landed in the north, with what they called an 'intervention', launched to protect Turkish Cypriots, and so, vicious fighting ensued. Thousands died.

Today we often travel from dot to dot, with the space between passing as a blur or momentary landscape sliding by a car window. I needed to strain sinews in a sacrifice of sorts, to pay for the privilege of seeing hidden corners of Cyprus with a currency paid out in steps – 380,000 of them. In the summer of 2018, I fulfilled my plan to follow the Green Line and record the detail of my journey. The reader will be my welcome companion, sharing what I saw, whom I met and how I felt. I want to say a little more about this… I am not going to mention any names, but as a fan of many established travel writers I have been shocked to discover that some famous books contain 'embellishments'; I want to assure you that this book contains only things which actually happened! Also, in an effort to carry the reader with me across the island, this is a very detailed description of what I encountered; it's more a stream of consciousness but expressly not an abstract one. So please, slow right down and enjoy the walk. Also, I read, recently, a book by a famous travel writer whose account of an entire region of Arabia was dispensed with in a tiny paragraph. I felt this was a shame, as it's the minutiae of a country which I find most fascinating. I want to be informed about how other people operate through the supposedly mundane. It may be familiar to the stranger, but it is often intriguing for me.

This is the story of three journeys. Firstly, across space, as I cross the island on foot. Secondly, across time, as I recall my life on the island as a boy – made easier by the fact parts of the island, familiar to me as a child, are frozen in time; in Nicosia there are car showrooms containing vehicles with only delivery mileage on their odometers, brand new 1970s vehicles covered in half a century's worth of no man's dust. Abandoned coffee cups remain, their contents long-since evaporated, following rapid evacuations in the war; it is a window into the exact living spaces of a time when my own conscience and mind were awakening. Finally, this is a journey within the mind as I attempt to reconcile the experiences I had in Cyprus as a boy with how they influenced me as a man. It is the hope of the author that the reader might identify with what I discover about myself. Having left the island two years before the conflict of 1974, I was interested to see a little of how the island has suffered and if there were any signs of recovery or a desire for the island's reunification or a rapprochement.

The best map I could find was a National Geographic 1:165 000 scale, and although it lacked the accuracy of British Ordnance Survey maps, it did provide a reliable guide. I also spent hours studying satellite images of the entire walk and had been informed by Captain Peter Vanek, of the United Nations Peacekeeping Force, that he was 'pretty sure' (!) that all the landmines remaining after the war of 1974 had been removed, or were now safely fenced off. Because of this ambiguity, my route across the island followed roads as near to the Green Line as possible. I rarely launched out 'cross-country' as it were. Also, I walked in June when temperatures are high and my reliance on water would mean frequent stops for rehydration, so civilisation and shops needed to be reasonably nearby.

As for place names, I have used (as far as I am aware) Greek place names when in the Republic of Cyprus and Turkish names when in Northern Cyprus, though references to former place names have been made when necessary. I have also used the spellings found on my map – a decision born out of a need for some consistent method to employ with regard to names and how they're spelled, as I encountered many different spellings.

I walked east to west, from the coast near Paralimni to Kato Pyrgos via Nicosia – a total distance of around 200 kilometres – allowing for various detours. I slalomed my way across the island, crossing from one republic to the other as much as possible to compare the two countries. I wild-camped overnight, though from what I've read, wild camping is discouraged south of the Green Line, but I started no fires and took very great care not to damage anything. My days consisted of two walks: firstly, from dawn to circa 10am, and an evening walk starting in the late afternoon and ending around 9pm. To recount my experiences of Cyprus as a boy I've included '*One Day*' sections to each chapter, inserting them between every morning and evening walk. In a way, these memoirs of 1970–72 'break the fourth wall' as they differ in style from the journals of the 2018 walk, but that's deliberate as I was trying to regain the mindset of my eight-year-old self and the wonder at all I was seeing. I'm a published film writer, but this is my first book and I love poetry so, as I say, I'm afraid I do err on the descriptive, but I'm trying to take you with me and share the journey.

M.J.W. Clark – Swaton Village,
Lincolnshire, UK, April 2022

Sonnet 74

Anatolia wept her waves of plenty,
Dreaméd limbs well kept in temporal mettle,
Her sighs – the wind and tears the clouds did envy,
Take sea; tight sails t'wards fair lands to settle,
She crofts with Troodos her forbidden mate,
Their bed, soft moss 'neath Cypress shady leaves,
Rid borders their bright quay to heaven's gate,
Our lovers kiss to steal from evil thieves,
Unblessed the children's graceful, melded names,
Aphrodite's rock dipped in blood-warm waves,
Provides black salt sky and asterisk games,
Cut short by war which dug their offsprings' graves,
The minarets, the bells, the siren's song,
Anatolia, Troodos and how you're gone.

M.J.W. Clark – *Memories of Cyprus 1970–72*

1

Republic of Cyprus

The Coast Near Paralimni
to Deryneia

Tuesday 5 June 2018

I had caught a bus from Nicosia to Paralimni and had been set down amongst the tourist shops and restaurants in the afternoon sun. The pavement and road beside the bus stop were a concrete crucible of heat, with the belching exhaust of the coach adding an almost appropriate black smoke to super-heated air.

Paralimni lies just south of the Buffer Zone and, following the conflict of 1974, the town had received a considerable influx of Greek Cypriot refugees. Within minutes of my arrival, I was to discover clear evidence that the effects of a war fought nearly half a century ago were still evident today, and within days I would find my sensibilities assaulted and challenged by stories still lingering from the past.

On my back I carried all I needed to survive several days on the road, and alongside the crowds of tourists, who were wearing just enough to avoid arrest, I looked as conspicuous as a hiker in Paralimni. So, it was with a mixture of acute self-consciousness and the need for a long, cold drink that I scuttled off towards the quieter end of town. I selected what looked to be the least frequented end of the least frequented bar and sat down in the welcome shade of a merciful awning. A few moments later, Nicos, the owner, approached me to take my order. Nicos was about forty years old and looked to be wearing his lime green T-shirt with some reluctance. The fact that Nicos had instigated the colourful uniform didn't seem to matter, he had the bearing of a man who would rather be doing something else. He scratched his short, dark beard and looked at me with a pair of soulful eyes. 'Yes please?' he said, flipping a grubby tea towel onto his shoulder and fixing me with a serious look.

'Hello,' I said. 'A bottle of water and a large fresh orange juice. Thank you.'

'You don't want nothing to eat?' he asked, broaching his disappointment.

'No thank you,' I answered. 'Maybe in a while, I'm waiting for the sun to go down…' Nicos, who had revealed his identity via the indiscretion of his personalised T-shirt, disappeared behind a tall stainless-steel bar. A few minutes later he returned with my order and the drinks were placed before me with obvious disapproval of my economy. I tried to encourage him. 'What time of day does it start to cool off a little?' I asked this sounding like I was ignorant of the Mediterranean climate, which I really wasn't, but it gave Nicos the role of 'informed host' and I watched to see how he'd respond. After a few seconds of silence, he looked out at the brilliant street still shimmering in the sunlight.

'Maybe seven o'clock, today is very hot,' he said.

'Seven?!' I exclaimed. 'I was hoping to be heading for the coast long before that…'

'Where are you going?' asked Nicos, who was now looking more relaxed – and definitely more Greek.

ng for the east coast,' I said.

go there?' persisted Nicos.

'I'm walking across Cyprus, along the Green Line,' I replied, and noticed a change in his face.

'Why are you doing that?' said Nicos. 'My family were refugees in '74.'

'I'm going to walk on both sides of the line and see what I can learn,' I said, hoping for a level of magnanimity from Nicos.

'I can tell you that all Turkish peoples are shit,' said Nicos, without a trace of excitement in his voice. I didn't reply, but it didn't matter because after uttering his absolute he'd spun on his heels and retreated behind his shiny bar to regroup.

Over the next hour or so I whiled away a little of the anger from the sun and spent enough at Nicos' bar to help with the early sales receipts. Nicos allowed me to charge my plethora of batteries and, at about 6pm, I gathered up my kit, wished him goodbye and stepped out onto a road which felt far too hot to be hiking on.

Before I could start my walk, I had to find my way to the eastern end of the Green Line, which was on the coast just a few kilometres northeast of Paralimni. I was in the Famagusta district, located in the southeast of the island with the Green Line running horizontally just to my north. Either side of the line the United Nations patrol a no man's land known as the Buffer Zone and I wanted to start my journey as close to this area as possible. My intent was to wet my boots in the Mediterranean somewhere near the Buffer Zone before turning around and walking west for 200 kilometres. I estimated it would take me about five days to reach Nicosia and around another five to reach my destination, which was the small fishing village of Kato Pyrgos in the northwest of the island.

I had originally intended to start my walk on Wednesday 6 June, but an eagerness to get started had combined with a desire to reclaim some of the time I'd spent sitting on the bus from Nicosia, so I found myself starting my journey that evening as opposed to the following morning. This meant any

3

progress I made in a westerly direction that day was a bonus, and consequently my pace out of Paralimni was languid and leisurely. After a period of gentle ascent, I located a 'B' road and spent a few minutes gazing at the eerie sight of abandoned buildings and hotels in Greek Varosha, the southern quarter of Turkish Famagusta. The structures were unlit but still clearly visible across a valley between Paralimni and the old resort town. It dawned on me then just how much money must have been lost in the war of 1974. Greek Cypriots who owned hotels in the town, and who'd made an enormous investment, must have lost everything. The banks which had loaned money to the owners would have been forced to write off huge debts without a hope of anything to liquidise. In other parts of the island, Turkish Cypriots lost money too. Sobered by the sight I turned right and started along a descending road towards the coast.

The copyright on my National Geographic map was registered in 2012, which was only six years earlier than the time of my walk, yet a network of smaller tracks and trails presenting themselves in the actuality were not recorded on the chart. Nevertheless, with the aid of a compass, I kept heading obliquely northeast until I reached an area of new developments. My memories of Greek villages are brimful of charming houses which all seemed to have been built with some romantic element in mind – rural villages which grew organically like the vines cultivated to shade and cool verandas. Curved and wonderfully asymmetric buildings of daub and timber, or stone picked from the ground and carefully assembled to deliver a house made-of-hill. Generations of villagers, whose dwellings were aligned to face the sea or catch the shade of a great tree, had not considered efficiency an essential component of design. The net result would be a delightful collection of houses, barns and gardens which existed as a body, with streets and fields as vital as limbs and, somewhere in the midst, a whitewashed church as the heart. Intersecting lanes were built gently onto natural undulations, and to walk through a village was a walk over the ancient contours of the land on which it was built. There was an absence of tarmac, narrow streets were mettled with stones, and every little hamlet had a communal gathering place where the passing day might be mused over with glasses of wine produced from presses just a stone's throw away. So far, on my evening's walk, I'd seen none of these charming aspects on display. I cut through a collection of bland and featureless structures whose windowless state made them look like surreal skulls painted by Dali. The space between the buildings existed for privacy; nothing was built for community, these were holiday dwellings made for no more than fourteen nights of temporary residency. After a few turns through the complex, I stepped from a surface of new and uneven tarmac onto a trail of soft and pleasant sand – a move from asphalt into Eden. It was obvious that every step along the lovely, deserted track would lead down to the Mediterranean, each sway forward carrying me ever downwards towards the sea.

The early evening atmosphere was utterly serene, and everything my eyes found to gaze upon seemed at rest and tranquil. I enjoyed the brightness of a swathe of Mediterranean reeds bordering the quiet trail; the tall, green stems nearest the track were gilded by a still hot sun already dividing the sky into quarters of bright gold in the west and muted lilac in the east. I touched the reed stems and my mind drifted to a memory of boyhood Cyprus; in a quiet corner of the grounds of Kolossi Castle near Limassol, there existed a tiny oasis. In the middle of a growth of reeds, a cool, dark pool was home to the tiniest of frogs and each was vividly coloured. Kolossi was a popular playground for me and my siblings and, no matter how hot or dry the day, the water in the concealed pond always contrasted with its deep, dark water providing an alternative world to gaze into.

My journey would truly start when I reached the sea, so I was just a few minutes from the true beginning of my walk.

I was as excited as a child about the adventure that lay before me. The sense of freedom I felt, as the sandtrack guided me obliquely eastwards, was palpable to the depths of my core and it tickled the tummy. I think the origin of the thrill was the immediate feeling of an absence of responsibility. Any parent or guardian knows the constant demands of a family, and attentive parents of kids, even of kids in their twenties, know full well the call to pick up, drop off, feed, clothe, advise, or listen to essays. However, on this journey, all these pressures were gone, and I was starting to wonder exactly where in the brain loved ones go when we are alone. Where in the cerebral cortex do they wait for us when they are not immediately part of the landscape? I was wandering along with the close-sightedness of a child. My world was suddenly shrunk to my immediate surroundings, and this reduction in distractions caused my adult brain to seek out the subconscious agent behind why I was undertaking this journey. I was the returning salmon seeking out fetal headwaters, the sacred haunts of cold-mouthed childhood. I was attempting to *'regain the happy highways where I went'* (A.E. Housman) and though I knew this to be impossible, parts of the island presented as a *Mary Celeste* begging to be boarded. The advance of time changes our scenery, the familiar morphs into the unfamiliar, but in certain parts of this island the rapid evacuations of 1974 had enshrined the mundanities of life under half a century of sacred dust. It was a less hot version of Pompeii with a Vesuvius of war covering streets and houses in an ash of abandonment. At certain points along my route across the island I would have the strange privilege of placing my adult self into the unadulterated scenery of my youth. I would view myself in the rarest of mirrors. The island's no man's land was a museum of patinated articles held in my memory for fifty years. I wanted to come close to the undisturbed infrastructure and measure my changed self against what was unchanged; I wanted to compare the boy I was with the man I had become. For me, this was not an expedition into nostalgia, it was the checking of the wake of a life.

I rounded a corner and was shocked to read an ominous sign which forbade the taking of photographs; I walked on. There was thick and tall vegetation on both sides of the track forming a dense, green corridor twisting its way ever eastward... then I stopped suddenly at the sight before me... I felt an apprehension taking hold. Just in front of me, and to my right, a barbed wire compound came into view. It had the look of an active military post and, as I walked on nervously, I saw machine-gun dugouts with camouflage netting covering bulky equipment beneath. There were a few military vehicles and a lookout tower occupied by two Greek Cypriot soldiers. The silence was broken by laughter as the pair eased the boredom of maintaining a military presence not far from a Turkish Cypriot mirror post. I was certain that at any moment I would be challenged and forced to turn back. Had I accidentally stumbled into the Buffer Zone? Perhaps naively, for this journey I had obtained a UN-blue bandana in the vain hope that it might prevent a nervous guard – either Greek or Turkish – from using my head for target practice. Maybe these guards thought I was a UN inspector of sorts, I don't know, but I walked on unchallenged and rounded another bend where my heart started beating even more quickly. I was now certain I was in trouble...

I was less than 400 metres from the sea, but between me and my planned 'wet-boot-start' was a major problem. Right next to the shore I could see a cluster of low buildings all painted a familiar white, and written clearly on the walls were two unmistakable letters: UN! The sight of the compound confirmed my suspicions; somehow, I had walked right into the middle of the Buffer Zone! By now, I suspected I was being observed by both Greek and Turkish lookouts. A post-walk study of satellite images of Paralimni clearly showed this UN outpost on the coast complete with helicopter landing pad. I was learning very quickly that the Green Line and Buffer Zone are mostly spaces of invisible demarcation. In Nicosia, the Green Line is obvious; impassable structures of concrete and barbed wire clearly define forbidden areas. However, not far from any of the agreed crossing points from the rural Cypriot Republic into rural Northern Cyprus the barbed wire soon fades. Illegal crossings might be made quite easily, *if* you're willing to risk being shot at by soldiers manning the lookout posts on either side of the Buffer Zone, or stumbling into the few fenced-off areas where landmines remain. I recalled my conversation with the taxi driver who had dropped me off at the bus station in Nicosia. When he learned that I was going to walk across miles of 'occupied Cyprus', he told me, with some certainty and a strange kind of cheerfulness, 'They still shoot people, you know!'

… From where I stood, I could see in the distance, and to my left, an austere-looking watchtower in Northern Cyprus and the UN compound straight ahead. Just behind me, to my right, the Greek Cypriot soldiers' conversations were still within earshot. I was in the epicentre of a tripartite entanglement, yet, according to my map, I was supposed to be well south of the Buffer Zone. I soon discovered that, over time and in some places, the Buffer Zone had been adjusted, and wondered if this might be one such example where the Green Line had moved further south making my map inaccurate.

The UN's military wing is a multinational organisation which, as far as I had witnessed, operates with great efficiency and professionalism. At Foxtrot Gate, near Nicosia airport, I'd decided not to be flippant or jovial with any of the Argentine soldiers; they appeared to be serious people and, of course, I was British! Before I started my journey across the island, I had visited Nicosia airport by special arrangement with the UN; the decaying terminal infrastructure now lies abandoned deep inside the Buffer Zone. In conversation with my UN guide I discovered the day-to-day administration and maintenance of the Buffer Zone can be extremely complicated.

Right then, I wondered whether, at any minute, a UN jeep would be dispatched to arrest me for trespassing and my walk would be over before it had begun! But something wasn't right…? As I walked on, as nonchalantly as possible, nothing stirred from within the UN compound; as I drew closer, I realised with some relief that this station, numbered 146, was unoccupied and in a state of some dereliction. I felt a little uneasy as I stepped over the rusty barbed wire perimeter of the outpost. A few steps more and I looked down a shallow cliff into the sea below. Like a great, somnolent creature the sea returned my gaze with a kind of disinterest. There below me was a breathing kaleidoscope of greens and blues changing shade as the gentlest of waves washed over a rocky seabed. The sun was low in the sky behind me and, as if intent on countering my perception of tension in the Buffer Zone, the sea became flat calm under expansive skies of lilac and pink. A few lines of cloud gathered up the gold of the descending sun and shared it with the surface of the water. There was no doubt about it, the Mediterranean was as beautiful in the Buffer Zone as anywhere! It was utterly peaceful…

… I had scrambled down a deeply rutted track from the UN outpost to stand on perforated rock resembling a kind of sponge made of pumice. I looked back at the compound's broken fence and was shocked to see an enormous sign facing south declaring 'UN Buffer Zone – NO ENTRY!' I felt a little embarrassed that I'd made such a miscalculation this early in my expedition, but I soon learned that local fishermen and farmers regularly transgress the lines of division with a kind of studied immunity.

I had bought a drone to record aerial shots of my walk and decided to shoot footage from over the sea towards the shore. The little aircraft was so easy to use, so steady in flight, that I was confident, even as a novice pilot, I wouldn't lose the expensive piece of kit to the sea. I hurriedly recorded some film with the drone flying low over the water to find its owner standing resolutely on the beach. I kept imagining myself being interrogated and my precious drone being hammered to a pulp by a displeased border official – but I got away with it. I quickly packed up the drone before bending a knee to wet the sole of my right boot in the eastern Mediterranean... I watched as the water darkened the dusty tread of my boot. I stood and looked out to sea for a few moments before turning and choosing a more southerly trail to take me back inland away from contact with soldiers. After weeks of planning and assembling all manner of kit it was finally happening; I was walking the Green Line.

The area between the beach and the inshore tarmac road was given over to small agriculture and there were, perhaps, a few hundred metres of small fields growing root vegetables or given over to an untidy collection of fruit trees. As I climbed up from the beach, a concerned fisherman, who had obviously been watching me, pointed in the direction of the UN sign and politely informed me, with common, local mispronunciation, I was still in the 'Puffer' Zone! The elderly gentleman looked to be made of coastal flotsam, with breakers of white hair and whiskers made from sea surf. He had a kind face with skin as brown as the dark sand he was standing on and a smile which entreated and disarmed, though there was something in his eyes I couldn't fathom. He wore a dark blue T-shirt perforated with so many holes it looked more like a fishing net than a top. His khaki trousers had been hacked off at the knee and his weather-beaten feet were sliding out of a pair of ancient and inadequate flip-flops. I acknowledged my navigating error.

'Yes. I know. I'm sorry, I thought I was further south.' The fisherman was pointing at the sign again.

'Over there, good,' he said, waving at a beach road forming a crescent heading southwest behind a shallow escarpment of sandy rock. I nodded my understanding.

'Thank you very much.' I smiled and walked further south and west, away from the 'Puffer' Zone and deeper into the Republic of Cyprus. The old man seemed intent on displaying his own special level of immunity from military intervention and wandered off deeper into the restricted zone; I watched him zigzag his way down to the water. If Hemingway had been charged with casting a Greek film based on his famous novel, then surely this man was perfect to star in *The Old Man and the Sea* – no costuming necessary...

My plan was to walk from the coast near Paralimni to the crossing point at Pergamos in the Dhekelia, British Sovereign Base Area. From there, I would cross into Northern Cyprus and make my way northwest to Nicosia, where I would cross back into the Republic of Cyprus taking a half-way break for a good look at the ancient city's historic quarter. From Nicosia, I would track west, crossing back into Northern Cyprus at Astromeritis, then I'd head towards my westernmost crossing, just east of Kato Pyrgos. My route across the island would be mostly flat, as I'd be traversing the Mesaoria plain which makes up most of central Cyprus. Only the last dozen kilometres or so would see me winding my way through the steep hills which are the last remnants of the Troodos mountains; the range peters out near the small fishing village of Kato Pyrgos. I had highlighted a route on my map which stayed reasonably close to the Green Line, without straying too far from civilisation.

I planned to rise at dawn and walk until around 10am each morning before taking to the shade as the day became too hot for hiking. In the late afternoon I planned to begin a second daily walk, ending whenever I felt tired enough to pitch my tent and turn in. The reason for staying close to villages and towns was purely because I needed lots of water! Daytime temperatures in Cyprus, in June, can regularly hit 40°C, and carrying a twenty-five-kilogram rucksack in those temperatures dehydrates a person with alarming speed. Had it been possible, I would have loved to take cross-country routes all the time, but I needed to drink up to a litre of water per hour. As one litre weighs one kilogram, hacking into an unbeaten path would mean carrying as much as ten kilos of increasingly warm water. Pragmatism overruled romanticism, so I'd chosen a route with many watering holes and to launch into corner-cutting adventures only occasionally. Whenever I found myself with no obvious reference point, I would use a compass to guide me across the 'outback' to a village with a shop and a fridge full of cold water.

Officially, wild camping is forbidden in the Republic of Cyprus, but I would arrive and depart in the dark. I would light no fires and take great care not to cause damage to crops or property. Exactly how many times I'd need to camp was something of an unknown quantity because I was uncertain about how I'd cope in the heat, how long I'd be on the road and how much progress I'd make each day.

... I found the 'B' road on the inland side of the fields and made my way back to the highway leading to my first waypost which was the town of Deryneia, a walk of about six kilometres from the beach. This was much less than I planned to walk on any given day, but it was late, and it would soon be dark, however, I was half a day ahead of my planned schedule. Tomorrow would see me setting off from a point west of Deryneia with something of a head start.

I joined a larger road heading north, and tracing its path on the map revealed that the route used to lead to Famagusta, but its pathway across a valley into the old tourist town had been rudely interrupted by the Buffer Zone. The map showed an intransigent 'No Entry' sign marking the point at which the road had been closed to traffic and pedestrians for many years. The nearest crossing point into Northern Cyprus lay approximately ten kilometres west of Famagusta, but even then, the most direct, easterly road to the town was also closed to traffic. To reach the town one needed to circumvent the Buffer Zone's restrictions by first heading west to the village of Frenaros, where you could take a road north for eight kilometres, and finally turn right to descend into Famagusta.

For me, the slightly uphill road from the perimeter of Paralimni was alienating, as it seemed to be a thoroughfare best suited to me being *in* a car as opposed to me trying not to be hit by one. The kerb stones of a busy roundabout were painted black and white in places, which seems to be the preserve of either racetracks or ex-colonial roads long lost from the British Empire.

I circled a large, multi-exit junction and found that I was on the outskirts of Deryneia; a reflective blue sign informed me that I was travelling along the E305. The expressions on the faces of passing motorists made me feel like a newly landed alien and I felt sure I was the only backpacker in all of Cyprus.

Deryneia is a large village and caters for tourists with an interest in local history, especially those curious to hear a Greek Cypriot perspective of the 1974 conflict. There is a cultural centre and folk museum, but unfortunately my arrival was several hours after these had closed for the day. From a signposted viewpoint in Deryneia it is possible to catch a better view of Varosha and its abandoned hotel quarter south of Famagusta. In guidebooks, Deryneia and Paralimni are described as being in the region of Ayia Napa, a town I had travelled through on my bus journey from Nicosia. Ayia Napa, for me, is a tacky, 18–30s type resort which embodies the very worst of Cyprus. However, in Deryneia, a few minutes' car journey from the town, I was enjoying a quiet village not far from the throbbing nightclubs just ten kilometres to the south. Even nearby Paralimni, a thriving tourist centre itself, lacked the enforced glitter of its tawdry neighbour. To be fair to Ayia Napa, long before it was chosen as the site for the imposition of neon overkill, it possessed the typical simplicity of a quiet fishing village. Anyone seeking out the town's sixteenth-century Venetian monastery will discover a stark contrast to the decidedly non-monastic hordes not far from its high walls and sanctity.

As I entered Deryneia centre, I took note of the names and stock-in-trade of the rows of shops either side of the main road dissecting the village. One boutique boasted the name 'Snob', and I wondered whether this was a very post-modern take on self-deprecation or if something had just got lost in translation on an application to the local chamber of commerce. The village was readying itself for an evening of idleness as I walked past a garden wet from a recent watering; this was an event I was to witness a lot. It is the custom on both sides of the Buffer Zone, in fact all over the Mediterranean, to cultivate shade-giving plants, vines and scented creepers on or near the porches of houses. Every evening, at about 6pm, the locals emerge from shuttered rooms to water their gardens and patios before sitting in the cool of the day with a kind of studied quietness unique to this part of the world. The dowsing of tiled verandas or pavements is to reduce the latent power of the sun still stored in infrastructure long after the sun has retired. Some verandas or front gardens were so well covered with verdant growth I didn't notice the concealed occupant until the last minute, whereupon they took on the role of a Japanese soldier deep in a Malaysian jungle.

In the centre of Deryneia, across a wide square, I passed the impressive church of the Birth of the Theotokos (or church of the Virgin Mary). It was built in the fifteenth or sixteenth century, and for me it was far more pleasing to the eye than the nearby, and larger, pantiled Agioi Pantes or All Saints' church. The church of the Virgin Mary looked exactly right with its honey-coloured stones and simple architecture. In the dimly lit square it looked like a film set where medieval worshippers might arrive on horseback at any moment.

As I left the village, I noticed a curious standoff. The main road passed between two cafés poised on either side of the street;

they were just yards apart divided only by the kerb and about five metres of highway. They were so close, the men sitting in the one café could easily have a conversation with the occupants of the other without needing to raise their voices. It was fascinating to muse on the exact criteria locals employed in deciding which café to use, given it looked, essentially, like one snack bar with a road running through it.

I would discover, on this journey, that both Greek and Turkish Cypriots carefully memorialise important events in local or national history, and, on both sides of the Buffer Zone, the populations of towns and villages had often come together in their respective communities to erect statues. South of the Green Line these tend to be effigies of Archbishop Makarios, and north of the line they usually favour Mustafa Atäturk. Makarios (1913–77) was a fiercely nationalistic figure and, secretly, very pro EOKA (National Organisation of Cypriot Fighters). In 1960, Makarios became the first president of the new Republic of Cyprus and many of the local memorials feature pictures or busts of the cleric. Mustafa Kemal Atatürk (1881–1938) was the first president of the Republic of Turkey and had done much to shape and develop a modern, more secular Turkey. However, both these men were not professional contemporaries; Makarios was only in his twenties when Atäturk died in 1938. Despite these differences, wherever the lives of men lost in the war of 1974 are remembered, Makarios and Atäturk are never far away from their Greek or Turkish 'sons'. I would learn the 1974 conflict was a thoroughly nasty affair with atrocities committed on both sides, and in some cases hatred still had power to poison years after the war had ended.

For example, in 1996, not far from the centre of Deryneia, an ill-conceived plan was hatched for a sizeable gang of bikers to travel from once-divided Berlin, across Europe, to a still-divided Cyprus. Once on the island, Greek Cypriot bikers were to swell the numbers of the Berlin contingent. The idea was to commemorate the twenty-second anniversary of the division of Cyprus and to protest at what was seen as 'occupied' land. Despite great efforts to halt the protestations by UN Secretary-General Boutros Boutros-Ghali, a determined but reduced number of bikers ignored his pleas, and in skirmishes near Deryneia, twenty-four-year-old Tassos Isaac, a Greek Cypriot protester, was brutally beaten to death in the Buffer Zone. According to the autopsy, Isaac died from multiple-blunt-instrument trauma to the head, and video footage of the murder shows three Turkish policemen were clearly involved. The UN produced a detailed report of the incident and the events leading up to it; the details made it obvious that some authorities had lost control, and some authorities were pleased that control had been lost.

Unaware of any of this at the time of my visit, I walked on under sodium lights until the buildings of Deryneia were behind me. I located the E305 road tracking southwest towards the village of Frenaros and began looking for a suitable place to camp. Just then, I became aware of my homeless state. Overhead a few light clouds formed a mustard-coloured canopy as the sodium lights tinted everything below with a sickly yellow. I was suddenly a vagrant wanderer without a fixed abode and, to someone used to a solid roof or an organised campsite, I found myself a little bothered about my vulnerability.

The road out of town seemed to switch abruptly from urban to rural, and the benefit of street lighting ended just as quickly. Under the last streetlamp a pair of discarded shoes suggested that their owner had been raptured for daring to leave the village limits. A street sign gave the distance to Frenaros as five kilometres, and across the road a pair of oversized tennis rackets, complete with ball, were floodlit to mark out the location of the local tennis club.

It was now too dark to walk safely, so I started to look more earnestly for a place to set up camp. I was quite apprehensive about the process of pitching my tent because I was looking for somewhere with flat and soft ground but also secluded and safe. I have wild-camped many times in England and have always managed to avoid being disturbed, but I have less cautious friends who have pitched their tent, arranged their gear, and reposed themselves in unbooted comfort only to be moved on by a disgruntled farmer or zealous policeman. Stealth is to be applied to all elements of the wild camp and it begins with the purchase of a tent which is not Day-Glo orange or stripy pink. Once you are in possession of an earth-coloured residence it is equally important to pitch it out of sight, thus avoiding Messrs Plod and Giles!

Although the sun had long since disappeared, the evening air was still as warm as breath. I was scanning left and right, and every now and then a small building would loom out of the darkness. It was then I noticed Greek Cypriots favour a four-legged alarm system, because every set of farm buildings, garages or outhouses was guarded by boisterous canines. Once disturbed, the barking would go on for ages! I decided that in future, having disturbed many such alarm systems, I would avoid camping near buildings of any sort. On my left, a recently harvested field reflected just enough light for me to make out a ghostly collection of circular straw bales; I thought pitching my tent to the rear of one of these might be ideal. I crossed the road, double-checking to see if I was being observed but, by then, I would only be visible with a powerful spotlight. I chose a bale near the edge of the field and rested my rucksack against its cylindrical wall. I unclipped my tent and fed the two aluminium poles into the tent's sleeves. In about three minutes my little house was assembled. Once erected, it could be carried in one hand and manoeuvred easily to the most suitable spot before being pegged down. Within another two minutes I had crept into the solace of my dwelling and was pleasantly boot-free.

Taking my boots and socks off was to become a daily joy, and having a two-man tent meant I had enough room to set up an extremely comfortable bedroom – with a self-inflating sleeping mat, pillow, quality sleeping bag, reading light and refreshments close to hand.

It was still too hot to sleep inside my sleeping bag, so I used it as a mattress and lay back to examine my map. I was delighted to see my progress from the coast could be seen clearly on the chart. I took a fine black marker pen and carefully marked my route so far with little chevrons forming a neat line from the coast to just east of Frenaros.

My mind drifted over the events of the day, from waking, packing, and leaving the Cleopatra Hotel in Nicosia, walking across town to the bus terminal, arriving in Paralimni, escaping trouble in the Buffer Zone, the deserted UN post, reaching the sea, my drone footage and walking west for the first time; according to my reckoning I had about 190 kilometres to go!

Outside, on the distant road, an occasional car sped by; inside, I was snug and had everything I needed for a relatively comfortable night. What would tomorrow bring? What might I see? Who would I meet? I had no schedule, no deadlines, just the open road and complete freedom to explore it.

My mind returned to the old man by the sea and his enigmatic gaze. I was searching for a word to describe his eyes; as I submitted to tiredness and my own eyes began to close I saw his eyes again. The old fisherman was carrying something deep within and I settled on 'weariness'. He carried loss.

A few moments before I turned my headlight off, I checked my rucksack thermometer; it was reading 27°C. Before long I fell asleep – still, very definitely, on top of my sleeping bag.

The Bright Frogs of Kolossi

Bright jewels coloured by God – awaiting my return,
Yellow diamonds or pulsing emeralds yearning in the reed bed,
Little frogs of Kolossi permit us to catch you,
Bring you to our faces and marvel at your cress-seed eyes,
Fearfully made – shining bodies,
Flawless skin shone again by kind water,
Find your ancestors blessing the palm of Berengaria,
She delivers them to the king for a monarch's smile,
Take to the space of black water,
Weightless as a star, hung on nothing,
The gowns of the princess; shamed by your robes of light,
Lie in wait for my century; ancient light now arriving,
Bright frogs of Kolossi.

M.J.W. Clark – *Memories of Cyprus 1970–72*

2

Republic of Cyprus

Deryneia to Dhekelia Sovereign Base Area

Wednesday 6 June 2018

The great travel writer Freya Stark said, '*To awaken quite alone in a strange town is one of the most pleasant sensations in the world. You are surrounded by adventure.*'

When my tent had lit up with early sunlight, I awoke with Freya's words forming in my mind. I felt that today would be an adventure, and thanks to yesterday evening's walk, I was already about ten kilometres into my journey along the Green Line.

Outside my tent, the only evidence that I was not the first soul to witness the dawn was a lone yet persistent cockerel with an innate alarm set to 'way-earlier-than-first-light'.

I dressed quickly, carefully packed my rucksack with my 'day kit' nearest the top, and prepared my feet for a long walk. I took great care to lubricate my toes with ointment and ensured that both liner and walking socks were put on without stowaway stones or seeds. I laced my boots and applied sunblock to areas of exposed skin. I'd bought breathable clothes which were cool to wear and easy to wash and dry. After neatly packing away my night gear, I stepped into the dawn. It was a fresh morning with a clear sky pierced here and there with a few stubborn stars reluctant to yield to daylight.

I took a good look at my campsite. I had pitched my tent near the edge of a newly harvested wheat field, and the entire enclosure had a uniform covering of spiky stubble. On the other side of the nearby road stood a farmhouse, and because I did not want to arouse any kind of misplaced suspicion, I packed my tent quickly, so, to anyone catching sight of me, my appearance was that of a walker and *not* a camper.

The eastern horizon was silhouetted against a faint pink light, as the sun had not yet broken cover. To the west, the direction I was soon to be headed, the land was caught between night and day as if my presence had caught the land undressed and in a state of surprise. The field was growing lighter by the minute, though there remained a shroud of mist near the ground. I have camped many times in England, where the day begins with the unpleasant separation of occupant from sleeping bag. The air always feels damp, and the cold penetrates the skin and muscles whatever the season. In Cyprus, I was to experience no such unpleasantness. I didn't need to spend a few minutes of vigorous walking to establish a blood flow, the air outside my tent was already room temperature with every passing minute ushering in more warmth; all around was the promise of a lovely day. Overhead, the vacant sky had now split in two, white to the east and pale blue to the west. A row of cypress trees was standing to attention and exchanging a uniform blackness for hues of dark green as their ranks began to glow in the rising sun. The field's stubble took on the form of close-cropped hair, and it was dewless and dusty with patches of dark red soil. I stood in the stillness of the dawn and took in the wonderful scenery until it started to feel like I had become a figure in a French impressionist's painting. It almost felt indecent to move, as if an unseen Monet might chastise me for impeding his genius.

Having assessed the threat from any displeased farmer as minimal, I decided to grab some drone footage of my first campsite and set up my aircraft for flight. The machine was a Mavic Pro, and was controlled via my phone; this also provided a monitor for the onboard camera. It was oddly comforting to see the thing take off so steadily with its coloured lights glowing warmly as it hovered just a few metres above the ground. Looking at the monitor I saw myself from on high and I looked to be a very conspicuous component in an idyllic setting. By the time I'd finished taking the drone shots and completed a GoPro piece to camera, the sun had revealed its burning rim and the quiet field was coming alive.

As if someone had thrown a switch, a scraggy flock of sheep in a nearby field suddenly started bleating. I finished my film with the words, 'I wonder what I'll find out today?' I didn't know then, but my day would turn out to have a very upsetting event.

The morning was just begging to be walked into; every turn of the road would be new to me, just like Freya had suggested. I was so anxious to be on the road that I had to discipline myself to carefully check my campsite for anything valuable which might be left behind; this procedure became an essential part of my morning routine. The last thing I did before starting my walk was carry out what I called a 'precious-check'. I had often witnessed many walking companions striding off and inadvertently abandoning all manner of expensive equipment. All *my* kit had been carefully selected to make me as self-sufficient as possible; I'd even attached small solar panels to my rucksack.

I made straight for the road, turning left to head southwest towards Frenaros. There was a thrill in stepping from the soft field onto the road surface and finding an increase in purchase as my boots gripped the tarmac granting me better speed.

The farm beside the road still showed no signs of movement. I checked the time; it was 5am and my thermometer was reading 19°C.

As I settled into a comfortable stride I thought of the poet and novelist Laurie Lee. When a young Laurie left his Gloucestershire village of Slad, he was headed, as I remember, for the nearby town of Stroud, a journey he'd made many times on the local bus. This time Laurie was leaving his much-loved, childhood village for good and so, without any deliberation and completely automatically, he *walked* out. I understand why; a sacrifice of physical effort needed to be made when, finally, the time came to put distance between himself and his '*land of lost content*' and '*the happy highways where [he] went*' – to slightly misquote A.E. Housman. For me, I *needed* to walk across this island; even a bicycle was out of the question, I wanted to be more atavistic. My speed would be that of ancient man, the pace at which mankind had viewed the earth and hunted in its forests for thousands of years. At this most natural of speeds the immediate surroundings come into sharper focus with a natural high definition and, compared to being in a car, everything seems to appear in slow motion.

This theory was proven when I passed several plastic road markers with bright red reflector strips; passing these in a speeding car it would be unlikely anyone would have noticed what I was fascinated by. I was witnessing a truly bizarre mini spectacle, which, I must confess, I was entirely ignorant of at the time. In a cluster on the top of each post were hundreds of tiny snails. As I studied the horde, I noticed still more snails were making their way up a vertical climb to join the party. I walked on and noticed that other such heights were similarly occupied... Gateposts, stakes of iron fencing and lamp posts all had identical snail-clusters at a uniform height of about a metre above the ground. Subsequent research showed that the clusters are known as 'grappes' and it's a strategy which snails employ to avoid dehydration which is more likely for the creatures when they're near to hot surfaces like Cypriot earth in June!

The morning air, though warm, still had a welcome freshness to it and before long I reached the outskirts of Frenaros. On a low wall a display of untidy graffiti clawed at the eyes with dark blue spray paint proclaiming, 'FREEDOM FOR FAMAGUSTA' and 'ANORTHOSIS'. I thought this might be a clever corruption of the word 'enosis', the word used to describe the dream of Cyprus' union with Greece, here being applied to a union with the 'occupied' North. However, as it turned out, the interpretation was more prosaic; 'Anorthosis' was just the name of a local football team.

Frenaros is not a village you can find much mention of in most Cyprus guidebooks. I passed a verdant lime tree warming in the morning sun and entered the village on a raised pavement bordered by an impressive row of tall and dusty pine trees. The sun, even at that young hour, had dispensed with any early ambiguity and now pierced the shadows of the trees with patches of intense light. I mused on shadows… The long shadows of the trees had no substance; their existence was caused by light streaming past a body onto the surface of the road. Then I thought about life and its own shadowy nature… *'Life's but a walking shadow, a poor player, that struts and frets his hour upon the stage, and then is heard no more. It is a tale told by an idiot, full of sound and fury, signifying nothing.'* You can always trust Macbeth (Bill) to deliver shade.

… I was walking across Cyprus because I had loved my boyhood on the island, and that happiness beamed brilliant, long streams of light into the relative shade of adulthood and its responsibilities – long shadows of life caused by a penetrating light from carefree childhood. Whatever happened to me here, all those years ago, had benefited me greatly; the man was indebted to the boy, and both man and boy were indebted to the island. Now in my fifties, I was able to look back on an extraordinary life: I was happily married, I had three wonderful children, I had travelled the world as a journeyman musician.

Through my day job I'd visited many tens of thousands of homes – from the humblest to sprawling mansions – and so I'd been privileged to witness life on both sides of the tracks. My life had been interesting and full, but I felt the season of travelling as a musician was coming to an end – though the 'season' had lasted almost forty years. Much of my identity came from my association with an instrument. I'd worked hard at my craft; I had spent thousands of hours studying technique and musicality, yet, in truth, I could claim little more than I'd been a 'useful' musician. However, in mitigation, it is also true that most musicians never become useful; perhaps I should explain, forgive the digression...

... Working musicians will understand; by 'useful' I mean that a valuable musician understands their role in a band and how to find their place. As they mature, they learn the art of playing less – not more. Subtlety is the name of the game. I often centred teaching-seminars on three alliterative and critical components in music: Timing, Tuning and Taste. These three constituents are rarely evident in any one musician and so, sadly, most musicians remain confined to the bedroom, or they very quickly plummet after early public exposure. Was I going to have to learn new crafts? I had recently come across a quote by the Polish poet Czeslaw Miłosz; he wrote: '*When it hurts, we return to the banks of certain rivers*'. Charged with producing an essay on this line, I think I would focus on the adjective 'certain'. Certain-specific or certain-assured? I hoped it was the latter because Cyprus, for me, was a certain river. Seminal. Foundational. Fetal. Definitive. It was ground zero for my life-long way of functioning. It felt natural, as my *musical* river reached the sea, to consider the navigation of former rivers or the formation of new ones. I was going through an unsettling time, having spent so long being carried by the urgency of one exceptionally long river. Was there an element of Forrest Gump in my journey across the island? I recalled Forrest's instinct to run across America as a coping mechanism, to keep moving until something new came along. I understood the Israelites who wept by the rivers of Babylon; I knew why they had hung their harps in the trees. That's another thing about music, real musicians cannot play lightly; every note starts from deep within the core of who they are…

… The road into Frenaros provided a gentle uphill walk which ended at a junction where, thankfully, a corner shop was just opening for business. With the luxury of complete autonomy, I decided it was time for comestibles. I stepped inside and found an excellent selection of quality food – fresh fruit, a small bakery and ranks of freezers and fridges full of thirst-quenching nectar. I replenished my water supply and treated myself to chocolate croissants for breakfast. I augmented this with bottled orange juice and a few nibbles to sustain me until 10am when I intended to shelter from the sun. I emerged from the little market like a polite Viking loaded with spoils and retreated to a low wall where I breakfasted with as much dignity as could be afforded by picnicking in front of early-morning motorists. My meal was functional and speedy; I'd still not walked for an extended period in intense heat, so my mettle was not yet tested. I neatly disposed of my waste in a bin, had my morning ablutions courtesy of a few wet wipes and walked off along a very narrow path deeper into Frenaros.

In the centre of the village there was a bust of a Greek Cypriot fighter called Fotis Pittas. Fotis had been a local schoolteacher who fought the colonials in the 1950s. Local uprisings started in April 1955, and EOKA fighters came together from all over Cyprus to wage a guerrilla war against the British. EOKA is an acronym for Ethniki Organosis Kyprion Agoniston, and it means the National Organisation of Cypriot Fighters. I'd learn more about the hidden and public face of this organisation on my journey and discover EOKA's reputation for violence. On the day I 'met' Fotis he was surrounded by loud songbirds and a few hardy plants squatting on his plinth; he looked like a very noble chap indeed. The writing on his statue informed me that he had died in 1958 after refusing to surrender to British troops who had cornered him in a local barn. Was anyone innocent in Cyprus' history? Nearby, six local men were memorialised in a floodlit monument; two had died just two days into the 1974 conflict, which was sixteen years after Fotis Pittas gave his life in a different struggle.

I left Mr Pittas to his fan club of singing birds and as I entered a more built-up area of Frenaros I passed a dusty and unruly cactus which seemed to have been caught attempting to cross the road. The houses in the village didn't seem to extend too deeply from the main road, which eventually led out into a mixture of farmland and small business enterprises. Before long, the village started to thin out and more cultivated fields came into view. Frenaros was the point at which my hitherto southwesterly track turned directly west towards the village of Avgorou. A signpost directed me to turn right and informed me that I had eight kilometres to walk to reach my resting point. The road from Frenaros towards Avgorou was a very wide affair with an incongruous-looking boat repair shop reminding me that, by car, the sea was never far away. I passed several concrete and glass buildings which seemed to lack any kind of commercial cohesion; some looked to be empty while others seemed to be touting for business in too rural a setting. There were a few large and unfinished concrete structures, a common sight throughout the island. Apparently, taxes or levies are only taken when a building is completed so, in Greek culture, working slowly in stages – as money allows – avoids early payments to the authorities… or so I was told.

On the outskirts of Frenaros an old shipping container had been utilised as a tyre repair shop complete with the flag of the Cypriot Republic flying overhead. A steady, easterly breeze was straightening the flag and providing a discombobulating view of a back-to-front island, as if the land had been presented to a mirror and copied erroneously onto the flag. The ground around the container was typical Cypriot '*bondoo*' which is a colloquialism on the island for the khaki-coloured dirt found covering areas of unadopted, suburban land. In the UK, areas like this would be covered with lush green grass produced by high annual rainfall, but in Cyprus any unirrigated land tends to default to a threadbare expanse of compacted and dusty brown soil or... *bondoo*.

Leaving the last of Frenaros behind me I entered an area of open fields and untidy smallholdings, each with a ramshackle shelter of corrugated metal from which, occasionally, I would watch a hardy farmer heading out into his field to engage in a battle of survival with his baking crops.

To my left, a short way on, there was a field of rather sorry-looking sheep; the flock seemed surprised to see someone walking along the road, and a few braver beasts approached the roadside fence and fixed me with a wonderfully indignant look. Their field had a sparse covering of tough grass, and the herbivores were lazily meandering with their heads down when I left them. The sight of the sheep reminded me so distinctly of my boyhood in Cyprus that I found myself engaged in a fleeting daydream in which I came face to face with a flock I'd met before. The event of fifty years ago replayed in my head... as if these shaggy animals had travelled through time to surprise me in a husbandry version of *This Is Your Life*...

... I was sitting on the back seat of our car, which was zigzagging its way down a series of hairpin bends on a late evening drive home. We hadn't been on the island for very long, so I was enthralled with the strange landscape parading past our car windows. Suddenly a young man appeared on the highway causing us to pull up quickly. His descent onto the road was accompanied by a violent scattering of stones which had been dislodged as he more or less fell onto the tarmac surface. For my parents, in the front, this must have looked like the first move of an ambush, but to my eight-year-old self it just presented itself as an exciting scene from a matinee. The youth who had arrested our car was a teenage version of John the Baptist. If my fisherman friend had been created from flotsam, then this shepherd had been put together with the accoutrements of sheep. He wore a sheepskin jacket, which looked to be the same colour as his dark skin, and he was carrying a large bark-less stick in his left hand. As the seconds passed, we all wondered what was about to happen. The boy's eyes were wide open and his right arm was extended toward us palm down; this hand was being lowered as if we were receiving a command from the bandit to lie down. A few more seconds passed with the shepherd frozen into position… Suddenly a landslide of hill cascaded across the road like a multicoloured lava of brown and white and black. It took a few moments to register exactly what we were seeing, but we realised that the shepherd was only visible from the waist up because he was standing just beyond a flowing river of sheep which was now washing by just inches from our bonnet. The animals were streaming downhill from right to left and ignoring us in their pursuit of an evening's treat of fodder and water… then the woolly tide was gone, and the brigand ran off after his flock, his staff raised towards us in thanks as he disappeared down the darkening hillside…

… Being in no hurry I decided to experiment with the Mavic Pro, setting it up to track me as I walked alongside the road. Sure enough, as instructed, the drone hovered at a height of about six metres and lurched forward as soon as I began to walk; its onboard wizardry was following my shape and wherever I went, it went. Reviewing the footage, I was a little bothered to see the drone's shadow luring me through a crop-less field of blood-red earth, though it lent the pictures a kind of urgency and import.

On the other side of the road there was an abandoned building; it didn't resemble the rough field shelters which were scattered all around but looked instead like a tiny house with doors, windows, and an overgrown vine on its east side. I felt intrigued and crossed the road to take a closer look. I mused on who had woken one morning years ago with an overwhelming desire to build the place and why and how it had become derelict. I was about to move on when something moved in the upper branches of the vine. The movement stopped and I caught sight of an enormous starred agama lizard. It must have been at least forty-five centimetres long with an oversized and angular head. It scuttled off towards the back of the house, and the vine shook with the weight of the fleeing reptile. I dashed round the back in pursuit, but when I reached the rear of the property my arrival disturbed what must have been twenty similarly sized lizards; the place was crawling with them but, with me being seen as a predator, they had all concealed themselves from view in no more than two seconds. No stone or rattled vine branch would move them from their hiding places, so I moved on.

The next few minutes were occupied with memories of the hour or so I'd spent the previous afternoon in Paralimni at Nicos' café. Nicos' parents were refugees from Northern Cyprus and, in 1974, they had been forced south with thousands of others, leaving behind everything they owned. Nicos was a tall man with sad eyes and a tired demeanour, and he did not like 'the Turks'. Given his age – he looked to be about forty – his viewpoint must have formed mostly from things he had been told by his parents. Much of what he told me about 'the Turks' was either conjecture or biased by distrust and suspicion. He didn't seem to have much grasp on the wider geo-political ramifications of what went on and why. Though, no doubt, his parents, bereft of most of their worldly possessions, would have had just cause to despise the dispossessors. These opinions were stumbling blocks in any pathway to reunification, but they were less obvious traits in the younger generation. I'd met a few Greek Cypriots over the last couple of days who were in their twenties, and they seemed to be less intransigent and uninterested in blind nationalism;

in fact they were typically global citizens more interested in interpersonal relations than wider international problems.

The timeline of the 1974 conflict would apparently place the first move with the military junta in Athens. They formed an ill-conceived plan based on a spectacularly blunt piece of thinking and attempted an inept and clumsy coup d'état. Part of the plan was the forced removal of Archbishop Makarios as the country's leader. When referring to their response to the Greek invasion, the Turks I met in the north were all careful to correct any mention of the word 'invasion' and insist on its replacement with what they felt was the more appropriate 'intervention'. And, thinking objectively, they did have a point. For the Turks *not* to have engaged would have meant a very uncertain future for Turkish Cypriots and so they felt their hand was forced. What else would a patriarchal government do *but* come to the aid of its kinsmen? However, the 'intervention' was carried out with a level of efficiency that, perhaps, smacked of long-prepared plans and dog-eared designs on partial occupation.

What troubled me was that the junta in Athens didn't seem to really think the plan through, and it appears arrogant on their part not to have considered the terrible cost to parties on either side of the Green Line. Were there, perhaps, *two* visions of enosis: one Greek and another Greek Cypriot? I should imagine that most Greek Cypriots would have expected an 'enosis' which included Makarios in some figurehead role, after all, Makarios was the public face of EOKA. Whilst the guerrilla leader, General Georgios Grivas, was conducting a clandestine battle from a base in the Troodos mountains, Makarios was very much in league with him, though General Grivas died six months before the Greek coup in the summer of 1974. *My* theory is that the junta feared a popular figure like Makarios might find his way to an even higher office, post-enosis, and end up undermining the junta on the mainland. All over the island, Makarios is hailed as a hero and a deliverer; even if this elevation, which practically beatifies Makarios, is perhaps the result of rose-tinted spectacles, Makarios is still a very much admired figure for most Greek Cypriots.

I turned my mind from political speculation to an enclosure beside the road. The field, like the one I'd camped in, had a large rectangle of green growth in its centre and, running through it, the means by which it achieved such robust health: an irrigation system. Across the great centre of the island most crops must be watered artificially during the summer because the island can stay dry for weeks. Consequently, there are over one hundred dams or reservoirs right across the island, and most of the fields I saw had networks of thick black piping to deliver water.

Geographically, I was on the edge of the great plain of Mesaoria which can only really be appreciated from high in the Kyrenia mountains. The Kyrenia massif rises steeply from the plain in Northern Cyprus and, from within the plain, you cannot gauge the true magnitude of flat expanse you are travelling through. Nearly a year after my journey I stood high in the Kyrenia range and had a God's-eye view of much of the land I'd walked across. From up there I saw my route tracked across a green plateau as flat as a tabletop, and I was sure I could see all the way from the east coast to Nicosia – at least half my total journey.

En route to Avgorou a whiskery gentleman in a beaten-up pickup truck slowed down to offer me a lift. I had seen no other backpackers in Cyprus; anyone walking with a load this size and in June's fiery heat must need help, either psychiatric or mechanical. 'Do you need a lift?' the man said.

'No – but thank you for stopping. I'm not allowed lifts, it's cheating!' I was laughing as I said this to bolster my declination with good humour. The man nodded an understanding, tapped his steering wheel, and smiled at me with a sympathetic turn of his grey head.

33

'OK. Good luck,' said the guy, and he lurched off in a cloud of thick black smoke. I'd been walking for hours now, and I was suspicious someone had been employed to keep moving Avgorou further away from me. My intent was to stop walking, each day, at 10am, and Avgorou was my planned watering hole and resting place. I was pleased my estimated time of arrival wasn't too far out; I was hot, thirsty and my hips and calf muscles ached under the unfamiliar load of a heavy rucksack.

The sky was cloudless and a lovely, unadulterated azure blue. The sun was so hot it felt like its rays were tapping me on the shoulder. The long grass at the side of the road was slowly baking to become like strands of crisp fibreglass and yet the sun was still hours from its zenith. In truth, though, I was deliriously happy. I'd always loved warm weather and I couldn't ever remember complaining that anywhere was *too* hot. Perhaps it was owing to years of walking in the British Isles, where precipitation might come in parallel to the ground like silver darts of icy water, hail or snow. Perhaps it was the gale force winds which might suffocate you, making conversation impossible, but there, on the road to Avgorou, the land was a brilliantly illuminated scene of victory. Why? Because these people had conquered the arid land with the benefit of experience centuries old; they had dug wells, stored water and bred livestock. Stalwart farmers had worked hard to provide thirst-quenching watermelons, oversized strawberries, and oranges as big as grapefruit. There were lemon and lime trees laden with zesty fruit to flavour drinks or add a spark to all manner of cuisine. Their efforts had produced acres of olive and pomegranate trees, or vines heavy with grapes. They had harvested from bees and furnished their tables with rich wines, crisp salads and blocks of delicious feta cheese; this was their conquest.

I passed a walled vineyard of deep green leaves which looked like an enticing place to lie in the shade, but I would rest soon, Avgorou must be near, and a few lemon and lime trees cheered me up with their bright green and yellow fruit. It compared to a scene from a soft drink advert, apart from the fruit not being drenched in water and bouncing in slow-mo for the cameras.

Avgorou is one of the larger villages in the south Famagusta district and, according to available statistics, its population of around 5,000 includes twenty per cent Greek Cypriot refugees from the war of 1974. Looking into the near distance I could make out speed limit signs. I walked on until a lone and very gnarled olive tree rattled its leaves in a slight breeze to applaud my arrival. Everything looked bone dry and dusty, and by now all around was almost shadeless – save any area directly beneath the branches of a tree.

I entered Avgorou passing a few unimpressive houses and incomplete buildings, but in the centre I discovered the local minimarket. Inside it was dark and cool, and there was a delicious hum from pumps circulating coolant in the collection of freezers and drinks cabinets. I decided *not* to jump into a chest freezer and roll around amongst the bags of frozen peas, though I was sorely tempted.

I bought a lemon ice pop, which is something that I rarely consume in the UK given their calorie count. But, so far, I calculated my calorie burn was at least three times my usual energy output. These icy treats were to become a twice or thrice-daily event. They cooled the blood quickly and the sugar brightened the eyes in a similar fashion to how Samson's lion carcass and honey platter improved his chances with the pesky Philistines.

I offset the carbs with a few protein bars, salty snacks and small bottles of water. I had, up to that point, been using a water-camel pouch, but the combination of my body heat and the sun's power made it tepid and unpleasant to drink – though I do appreciate that John Mills and Co would have been incredibly grateful of it should I have met them en route to Alexandria. The water camel was also an unnecessarily heavy item because the frequency of shops on my journey quickly made it redundant. I decided that when I reached Nicosia, in about two days' time, the water vessel would be unceremoniously ditched.

The village of Avgorou had more than its fair share of Byzantine architecture and an EOKA museum just in case anyone was in doubt about the partisanship of the locals. Like many other villages south of the Green Line, Avgorou grew exponentially in 1974 – in fact, the population very nearly doubled!

I've always been something of a self-conscious chap so, like a dog with a bone, I looked for a suitable place to consume my early lunch, undisturbed. I left Avgorou on a quiet country road which, in places, was tree-lined like rural France. A line of pine trees provided a shady arboretum, so I took my rest under their dusty branches. I propped my rucksack up and ensured my solar panels were facing east to catch the sun's full force. This piece of kit had been a boon; I could recharge all manner of electrical equipment while on the move, and fading batteries from a headlight could be fully replenished by the time they were needed again. Similarly, my watch, cameras and phone could all be at a hundred per cent by the end of the day. I felt smug about this self-sufficiency and then immediately felt guilty about feeling smug.

I collapsed, *sans* dignity, in a roadside dip under the trees. I almost impaled myself on a protruding branch. So, I made a 'technical adjustment' with the saw on my multi-tool. I had judiciously selected my gear from many years of learning from walking in the UK. On this trek I was delighted to see I had catered for everything I could envisage needing. I had maps, compass, phone, GPS, GoPro, drone (with spare batteries and propellers), remote controllers, first aid kit, wet wipes, dry soap and detergent, quick-drying ultra-light towel, tent, sleeping bag, multi tool, spare socks, waterproof sandals, sun cream, ointment, journal, pencils and headlight, and more besides. I was proud of my organisation and forethought, and here it was all paying off because it gave me confidence to survive the heat and the lack of a hotel and the luxury of en suite facilities. However, despite all my experience I would still find myself needing to adjust my equipment as the journey unfolded.

I soon discovered that the shade of the tree overhead was diminishing and, before long, the sun had moved to invade my seated position. Within seconds I was starting to cook, but there was no adjacent swimming pool to help me enjoy the sun. I hurriedly moved down the road and found a farm track with flat ground and more shade. Here I improvised a bivouac with my tent and sleeping mat, and within a few minutes I was shaded from the relentless sun – enough to last me the four hours or so that it would take for the sun to be well into its afternoon descent.

I spent the time writing up my journal, napping and rehydrating. With my packed sleeping bag providing a comfortable pillow I felt very content, and whenever my eyes felt a need to close I offered no resistance. After a few minutes of rest, they'd open again, I'd write a page or two in my journal and then take another few minutes' rest, and this is how my afternoon drifted by.

I enjoyed penning my map-route with more black chevrons, and my progress was plain to see. At home in the UK, my wife noted that the blue circle she was monitoring on her phone – which tracked my progress across the island – had moved further west and, thus far, I was *not* lying in a ditch somewhere with the imprint of a car's radiator badge seared into my forehead. A tiny sparrow alighted on a branch just above my head; she was so close I could have blown her feathers. She waited for a few seconds, eyed the intruder below and quickly flew off. The encounter was so unusual, so thrilling, that I choked back an instinct to weep. I investigated the impulse… In 1970, my family was quartered at RAF Berengaria near Limassol and our bungalow was situated on the outskirts of the camp. Beyond the camp's high fence there was an almond grove, and with what I considered to be impressive bravery I had learnt how to circumvent the barrier to explore the mysterious land beyond. The little woodland was a fascinating playground. The ground beneath the trees was always dry and dusty – a moonscape interspersed with nut trees. On one occasion I was startled to look up from a lizard hunt to find myself confronted by Cypriot teenagers who were hunting small birds with catapults; each boy had several dead birds suspended from his belt. I was both horrified and fascinated. I wasn't spoken to, but the boys spoke to each other, and I assumed I was the subject. After a few moments they walked on with their eyes fixed on the trees. I remained routed to the spot, shocked and temporarily paralysed by the meeting. I considered the birds of the air…

… My little camp was, according to the map, either in or near the Eastern Sovereign Base Area. When the Treaty of Independence was signed by the British, Greeks and Turks in 1960, two areas were retained by the UK: one in the west centred around the Royal Air Force bases of Akrotiri and Episkopi, and one in the east centred around Dhekelia where an army garrison was based. These bases occupy around three per cent of the island and provide United Kingdom Forces with an important foothold in the Near East. From here trouble spots might be monitored in the Middle East – with Syria, Lebanon and Israel lying just a few hundred kilometres across the Mediterranean to the east…

*

One Day (1)

One day my mother took us to the beach at RAF Akrotiri. The drive from our bungalow at RAF Berengaria to the base involved passing through a dense area of citrus trees which had the appearance of a plantation right out of Gone with the Wind – save the crops of tobacco or sugar cane. The lovely road tunnelled its way through fragrant copses of greenery, and the open windows of our car admitted the heady perfume of oranges, lemons and limes; it was a glorious assault on the olfactory senses. In Cry, the Beloved Country, *Alan Paton describes an African discovery, 'a lovely road that runs from Ixopo into the hills. These hills are grass-covered and rolling, and they are lovely beyond any singing of it...'* Anyone plunging into the intoxicating womb of loveliness and sweet suffocation of the citrus farm near Akrotiri might know exactly why Alan Paton could find no song to adequately describe his joy.

As I recall, the beaches at Akrotiri, which lay not far from the orange groves, were divided into clubs. There was the sailing club, catering for an upwardly mobile, adult crowd, and there was the rowing club with a more relaxed, family atmosphere.

My arrival onto the beach was full of promise. In England, trips to the seaside came with all the accoutrements and discomforts of commando training, but standing on the warm, soft sand near Akrotiri was an experience obviously afforded by an altogether different planet, or so it seemed. After the liberal application of sun cream (generally not required in Weston-super-Mare), I ran towards the sea expecting the same shock as my feet touched the water... but heaven! The sea was as warm as my flesh and for a moment I wasn't sure my feet were wet at all. The water was so shallow that considerable effort needed to be made to find water deep enough to swim in. This was one of the reasons families chose to spend afternoons around these waters; it was practically impossible for anyone over the age of five to come anywhere near the vicinity of drowning!

I learnt to snorkel in the waters off Akrotiri and spent hours spotting octopus and flat fish lying on the seabed. I became convinced that I could supply my family with seafood if only my mother would buy me a harpoon gun. However, she was equally certain that this would only supply a journey to A&E where my sister would have a harpoon removed from her eye.

At RAF Berengaria, school started early, well before 8am, and by 1pm school was over, and a kind of mass migration began as families loaded up cars and headed for the sea. Such was the air of freedom and recreation in Cyprus that my mother took on the role of an adventurer and carefree shepherdess. Our entreaties to go to the beach were an almost daily event and I cannot recall a request that was ever denied. The afternoons were a deliciously long sojourn on sands of icing sugar, where the water was a constant joy and, whenever refreshment was required, a nearby cabin provided colourful bottles of ice-cold nectar: Orangina, 7 Up, Coca-Cola and, if you could get away with it, shandy. Even when the afternoon was spent, the day was not. Long and languorous evenings were spent barbecuing or visiting kebab restaurants where sizzling meats were served with crisp salads and pitta bread. Afterwards the meal would be completed with the fruit of the season, and we would go home with a heavy box of Turkish Delight. I cannot remember any controversy over the name of the confectionery at the time, although nowadays it can be prudent to call the sweets Greek Delight when south of the Green Line. The slabs of rose-scented food were huge – about twice the size of a matchbox – and it was rare to ever eat more than two pieces.

On occasion, my father might allow us to drink a very weak kokinelli shandy, which was a mix of 7 Up and the sweet, red local wine. I'm not sure whether my memories of a dark, star-filled sky rotating above my head as we drove home are an invention or a reality but… gosh… those days were numerous and very, very good.

Memories of Cyprus 1970–72

*

From Avgorou, the road I was following turned southwest towards Larnaca and then northwest up to the border crossing at Pergamos near Dhekelia. Tomorrow would be my first crossing into the hinterland of Northern Cyprus.

A few days before, I had crossed into Northern Cyprus in Nicosia. I remembered there was an obvious contrast between the two sides of the old town. The Greek side was well lit, and Ledra Street was the location for all the usual western chain shops. After lining up at the border I had crossed through an area of no man's land with unoccupied and shuttered houses – unchanged in nearly fifty years. I spotted a message scrawled on a low wall which read, 'NO ARMIES'. At the end of the short walk through the Buffer Zone, the Turkish passport control came into view. I noted an interesting contrast: the Greek officials were in an area of obvious wealth, but their control booth and its staff were casual and relaxed. The Turkish counterpart was the entrance point to an area obviously lacking in serious investment, but the border control was manned by immaculately uniformed officers who functioned with a more studied discipline. Over the last few years, border crossing points in Cyprus have increased in number and now there are regular access points along the length of the Green Line. I had paid careful attention to stories about supposedly innocent tourists being arrested for spying, with camera equipment confiscated and the owners held in prison for days, weeks or even months. In addition, I had heard conflicting stories about difficulties crossing at certain border points. Consequently, I was nervous about my long-term plans because they involved crossing the border several times as I slalomed my way along the Green Line from east to west.

Also, on foot, a road border crossing is negotiated with more vulnerability because a hiker presents as an entirely visible unit. A walker can be assessed easily without the 'cloak' provided by a vehicle.

My mind returned to the present with the thought that tomorrow I would cross at Pergamos where I would discover exactly what crossing on foot in the hinterland was like. Studying my map and satellite images revealed the route from Pergamos to Ercan airport to be an intriguing prospect. It was the part of my walk I was most looking forward to because much of the area looked remote and unoccupied, so it was a chance to see a side of Cyprus little changed for hundreds of years.

At around 6pm, I packed up my bivouac and carried out my precious-check, the final one-minute-long inspection to ensure I'd not left anything of value to be run over by a lumbering tractor. Happy that I was kitted out at a hundred per cent, I rejoined the road and turned left. After a few hundred metres I found myself at a corner where a large warehouse was sited to provide short-term storage for the many crops grown in the area. Rounding the sweeping left-hand bend, I saw a lovely but diminutive Orthodox church; the whole building was about the size of a double garage and stood in a dusty compound which served to dwarf the building still further. The church was flanked by a large eucalyptus tree on its left side and a dusty green cypress tree to the right. I noticed that a floodlight had been installed and, at some point, an electricity company had placed an enormous pylon right behind the ancient property in an entirely crass manner. This negated any chance of taking an unspoiled photograph. The church was a labour of love. It was obviously created long before building regulations and lacked any kind of strict symmetry. The whole structure appeared to be inclined to the right like a misshapen cake. Atop its entrance, a small stone cross was visible. I wondered about the lives of the people who had built this place of worship and the vastly different world they had lived and moved in. Before the warehouse and the pylons, before the road and the floodlights, before the adjacent eucalyptus and cypress trees, before all these changes, people put up these stones to an unchanging God. Were I able to meet the builders we might both have understood 'Kyrie *eleison*' and our need of mercy, even though our finite lives were centuries apart. I walked on.

The day was still warm and when I had stepped out for the evening part of my walk my thermometer was reading 28°C.

I had penned onto my map numbered target points for each day, but I hadn't accounted for the additional distance I would cover if I chose to walk a little further during the early evening. Having achieved my target distance during the day, by reaching Avgorou, any further progress west was a bonus. I quickly realised that if I kept up a similar daily distance then my journey across the island would be much quicker than expected.

At the time of writing, a reference to my journal reminded me that my hips were aching from the weight of the rucksack, and this was something I needed to deal with at Nicosia, where I would ruthlessly review all my kit. As it was, I was pausing after every hundred steps to let my hips recover; this was not good.

I was now headed for Ormideia, which meant I was tracking southwest towards the bay of Larnaca. I felt a little concerned when the wide, blue Mediterranean came into view. My southwesterly bearing was at right angles to the northwesterly route that would see me headed for Nicosia. But I was confident I would reach campsite number two, just south of Pergamos, before it got too dark.

The road descended into Ormideia, which was a welcome relief, and the first of its buildings were simple houses and bungalows. In a small garden I was slightly disorientated by a metre-high figure of Snow White; I wasn't prepared for a classic Disney welcome. Gaps between the dwellings appeared to my left and a steep bank of scorched earth flanked my left side as I continued into the village. At the bottom of this dip a few boats were gathering dust, and I was reminded that the sea was now only a five-minute drive away. In the centre of the village, I was pleased to turn right and finally head northwest. I rounded a sharp corner to find a car approaching me with two women inside; the windows of the vehicle were wound down and when the occupants caught sight of me, they burst into hysterical laughter. This may be paranoia; their giggles might easily have been the result of a private joke, but it might have been the sight of a dripping wet and florid Englishman walking with a backpack in Cyprus – in June! I smiled to myself and headed uphill and further inland to the village centre.

Ormideia sits on the northeastern edge of Larnaca Bay and has an interesting history. On the outskirts of the village, evidence has been found of medieval settlements, and at some point in the past, a certain St Constantine of Alamanos lived nearby. Apparently, he dwelt in and preached from a cave near the road which tracks northeast from Ormideia towards the village of Achna. Achna now lies in Northern Cyprus and consequently the village is now known as Düzce. St Constantine of Alamanos was a mysterious character, and it's difficult to find out much about him from the dearth of information available, but it's easy to imagine a rustic saint eking out a basic existence in the hills near Ormideia. Today the village centre has the impressive church of Agios Konstantinos Alamanos, which is a step up from a cave, and I wondered what the rustic St Constantine would have thought about it. The church is a two-tone, cream and honey-coloured building dominating the entrance to the village centre. Shops on either side of the wide central road gave me plenty of options for my customary ice and water purchases.

It was the time of day when the locals emerged to water their plants and, as I left the village, plenty of 'Japanese warriors' were emerging from their jungle dens to drench their extensive camouflage. The road to the village of Xylotymvou was uphill from Ormideia and, as the village houses quickly thinned out, I was suddenly joined by an uninvited companion. A thin, mousy-brown dog of dubious lineage started to follow me as I climbed out of the hamlet on a broad pavement beside a newly surfaced road. I am aware of the attachment issues dogs can have with strangers, but I was sure the creature would lose interest after a hundred metres or so. However, 'Slinky', whose persistence had earned him a name, just kept following me and no insistence on my part would convince him to go home. Slinky stopped when I stopped or circled me as I walked along. Occasionally, he crossed the main road only to return after he had exhausted all local sniffing opportunities. This worried me because although Slinky was not my responsibility, I was bothered that he might amble into the path of a passing car. The road between the villages of Ormideia and Xylotymvou was open and flat, and the cars were passing me at a reasonable pace. Slinky persisted in following me for at least two kilometres and I recalled Paddy Leigh Fermor's black dog which he immortalised in his book *The Broken Road*. Paddy's canine companion stayed with him for many miles, and he *also* wondered to whom the dog belonged. I increased my pace to maximum and Slinky increased his; I took one of Slinky's long sniffing pauses to almost jog away and thankfully the dog fell back. Just as I was enjoying a sense of relief, there was a screech of tyres and a yelp. Slinky had been hit by a car! Now I felt awful; the accident was about a hundred metres behind me, and I agonised for a minute about what to do. No objectivity about Slinky not being my responsibility lessened my anxiety. I did not turn back for fear of seeing Slinky looking a lot less slinky. I walked on and listened acutely, using my ears to build the scene… The vehicle stopped… doors opened and closed… I heard voices… a pause… then the vehicle moved off… then the car, a shining 4x4, passed me… The occupants looked like decent people… I assumed they would have assessed Slinky's condition but, apprehensively, I turned to look. The road was empty, and thankfully there was no sign of a disembowelled mongrel, so I was much relieved. I suddenly caught a glimpse of Slinky limping away and a group of boys going after him. I felt sure the youngsters would look after the dog and hoped they would help him home for treatment. I was quite upset that Slinky was hurt, but I decided to build an argument for my lack of responsibility based upon the British Enclosures Act of 1773 and hoped this would be admissible in a Cypriot court.

Shaking off the near horror of Slinkygate I attempted to fill my mind with the beauty of my surroundings. Everything around me was bathed in a lovely golden hue. The sun's rays were being filtered by the dust of the day and the land was warm, quiet and still. To my right a lovely old vintage Bedford truck was slowly rusting in a fringe of long grass; its paint was sun-bleached and pastel-shaded, and just beyond it lay Xylotymvou, my last village before I planned to pitch camp.

Entrance to Xylotymvou was made along a road which looked very French provincial. There were cycle paths and raised, concrete reservations full of marigolds and other flowers of blazing colour. Lovely sabal palm trees provided me with a very Mediterranean guard of honour, and for some reason I started to remember my French classes at school and recalled the textbooks which immersed us into the lives of *'la famille Marsaud'*. I remembered the liberal line drawings of their children buying stamps and baguettes... *'Bonjour madame. Deux timbres s'il vous plaît et une table près de la fenêtre...'* It was obviously a uniquely French tradition to dine at the post office. Exactly what short circuit of the synapses was delivering this cerebral aberration, I knew not, but I was muttering in French like a mad dog or Englishman as I entered the village. I shook off the horror of the Gaulish language (*Je suis très désolé*) and woke up to a well-stocked and high-end sports shop on the outskirts of the hamlet. I was surprised to see this outlet and wondered if it had enough footfall to remain economically viable. Xylotymvou was showing itself to be very upwardly mobile, and at the village's main junction there was an upmarket café or two. If this village had a mayor, I pictured him as an immaculately dressed Greek in a suit complete with a flamboyant pocket square and two-tone brogues on his feet.

Xylotymvou (often spelled Xylotymbou) means wooden tomb and thereby dangles a story...

... Luigi Palma di Cesnola (1832–1904) was an Italian soldier who had found his way to America where he fought for the Unionists and even met Abraham Lincoln. In 1865, Luigi managed to wangle a job for himself as American consul on the island of Cyprus; once there, he spent much of his time excavating historic sites and taking any discovered artefacts away. In those days, paperwork did not seem to be a requirement and the Italian amateur archaeologist used foreign workers to help him uncover around 35,000 antiquities! Some of these were lost at sea when a ship he'd chartered sank with around 5,000 pieces on board. By this time, Palma di Cesnola was an affirmed smuggler of antiquities, and around Xylotymvou he discovered an ancient wooden tomb covered with carvings of Aphrodite and Artemis. The prolific smuggler was able to avoid any kind of prosecution though and ended up as the first director of the Metropolitan Museum in New York. On a plaque in 'the Met', the closest allusion to exactly how General di Cesnola came into possession of his enormous collection is via the use of the ambiguous word 'colourful' when describing his life. 'Thanks' to Luigi, it would seem Cyprus is bereft of many of her treasures.

At the village's central junction, I wanted to take a little-used, single-track road leading directly north towards the Pergamos crossing, but local enquiries proved this was not possible. A pair of young men shook their heads and said, 'No, no, no... not possible... Soldiers! Soldiers!' I was disappointed because I thought this would be a rare opportunity to go cross-country using my compass to take bearings towards the border. The road tracked directly north and had all the hallmarks of adventure, and, for a while, I considered ignoring the advice and taking it, but the sun was now finishing its arc across the open sky and heading quickly for the western horizon. Encouragingly, a road sign informed me that Paralimni was now twenty-nine kilometres behind me.

I was told by locals that the way up to Pergamos was a little circuitous and I needed to leave the village heading directly south, away from the border, where the main road is carried over the A3 motorway. This major highway follows the coast from Larnaca to Ayia Napa. I was sceptical of my instructions, and as my legs and feet were now quite weary, I didn't fancy a major diversion so late in the day. Yet sure enough the road carried me to a sharp right turn where, once again, I could head north. The landscape was very much Sovereign Base Area now, and I passed a deserted bus stop before taking the turn which was immediately adjacent to a very well-maintained compound. Inside were several instantly recognisable white vehicles with reflecting Battenburg patterns and blue lights fixed to their roofs. Inside I heard voices speaking English and I concluded this was a military police compound. The Eastern Sovereign Base Area consists of two British military stations: one at Ayios Nikolaos and the other at Dhekelia. The Base Area is home to an infantry battalion, an engineer squadron and logistic units, but there are civilian employees too; including the dependents of all the personnel, it adds up to a British contingent of around 1,500 people.

I stopped to film the lovely road curving away in front of me; it was as if the track led directly into the descending sun. The horizon was silhouetted against a still-bright skyline with colours appearing like an immiscible film of oil on water; the way forward looked as enchanting and unreal as those drawn in a child's storybook. The sun touching the horizon appeared as a perfectly white spot in a frame of sci-fi red, and the lens on my camera captured a laser beam of crimson which split the atmosphere and stopped at my feet. To accompany the visual overload a lone bird persisted with a rhythmic and chattering call. Nearby, opposite the compound, a large expanse of open ground proved to be an asphalt landing strip of some size. It seemed to be minimally maintained but looked to be active, having signs and traffic lights to stop vehicles whenever an aeroplane was landing or departing.

The evening was now fully dusk, and the retreating sun had lost its fight to resist sizzling into the sea on the other side of the island. I was now looking for a suitable place to pitch my tent and get horizontal. I didn't want to attract attention, so the ideal spot for me was near a copse of trees where I could conceal myself from passers-by and get in and out with relative speed. Before I quit the day's activities though, I had the drone fly backwards in front of me whilst I walked the last few steps of the day. On each of the four arms of the drone, little lights changed colour to advise me of its flight status. In the half-light of dusk these looked intensely bright, and it was comforting that in this very rural setting such advanced technology still worked so reliably.

I left the main road at a farm track, which seemed to be a perimeter road of the ghostly aerodrome, and then carefully crossed a dip in long grass at the edge of a ploughed field. I checked for buildings which didn't promise hours of barking and saw a small group of low trees which provided an enticing bay of green to shield me from the road. I had just set up my tent when suddenly there was the sound of a moving chain followed by the deep-throated barking peculiar to the sort of dog that eats people as an hors d'oeuvre! I was really annoyed that I'd not checked the environs carefully enough and initiated my contingency plan. I hurriedly repacked my rucksack and inspected the ground with my powerful headlight for any vital kit that I might have dropped. Then I picked my tent up with one hand and carried its long teardrop shape some distance from the unseen hound, setting it down behind a large bush which acted as a buffer between me and the road. The distant dog kept up his complaint, but I was now far enough away to deflect suspicion from a curious farmer that I was the cause of Phydeaux's distress and his epic and endless barking.

After crawling into the tent and getting comfortable, and with unshod feet as light as helium, I lay still and listened; the stupid dog kept its protest up for about ninety minutes! I went over the day's events: leaving the field between Deryneia and Frenaros, the Chris Bonington snail packs, my bivouac, and the curious little bird, Snow White, Slinky Knieval the death-defying dog, and the Eastern SBA. I had made great progress and quickly realised I was covering almost twice as much of the Green Line per day as I had predicted. The amount of ground I had covered in my evening walk was as much as I had covered before taking a break. This meant I'd easily reach Nicosia in three days or maybe less. I penned onto my map a line of new black chevrons and observed I had crossed the second fold in my chart.

As I lay still, I became convinced someone, or perhaps a rabbit with zip skills, was attempting to get into my tent. My Vango, super lightweight tent had a useful awning incorporated into its design and this provided about a cubic metre of extra storage space, but it also meant anyone fiddling with the flysheet needed to access a second zip to get to the occupant. Little things like this somehow contribute a sense of security, albeit very modest, and I listened intently before realising the sound was just the awning fluttering in a gentle breeze blowing from the direction of the open airfield. I dwelt for a few minutes on how my border crossing would go tomorrow and if some of the stories about the difficulties of crossing on foot were true. I was camped just a few hundred metres from the Green Line and, if I hadn't been in the Eastern Sovereign Base Area, I would be camping deep in the Buffer Zone. Sometime after this I fell into a light and fitful sleep.

The Hunters in the Almond Trees

I was not looking for adventure it was just a day – hot to be in,
The tall boys came with quarry hung from belts,
Soft-bodied sparrows taken for the palate,
Rolling on the hips of the hunters,
Lifeless and sad to see,
My frown was sprung from fear,
Incapable of disdain; my limits were a child's mind,
No condemnation – just the breaking waters of wrong,
Rude baptism of unblemished skin; dread – newly met,
The hunters in the almond trees.

M.J.W. Clark – *Memories of Cyprus 1970–72*

3

Republic of Cyprus Crossing into Northern Cyprus

Dhekelia via Pergamos to Dilekkaya

Thursday 7 June 2018

I woke early, at about 4am, and decided to lie in for about twenty minutes. I reflected on my night's sleep... I had not slept well. I seemed to be hungry but struggled to swallow anything and, given the huge calorie burn of the walk and low food intake, I wondered why I felt so good. I trusted that my metabolism would start firing like some recalcitrant engine soon after I started walking.

I dressed horizontally because one cannot stand in tents like mine unless you are eighteen months old. I tidied away my bedding and unzipped the tent to face the dawn. It was another beautiful morning and lighter than when I had emerged yesterday. I quickly packed, carried out a precious-check and recrossed the field's border to rejoin the quiet road across the airfield. The whole landscape was extremely quiet, the sky was cloudless, and its great blue canopy matched my sense of freedom. I rehydrated with a litre of water taken in sips, and ambling northwards, began wondering again what the Pergamos crossing would be like. This would be my first proper crossing in the true interior of Cyprus; my only border crossings thus far had been at the busy checkpoints of Ledra Street in Nicosia.

The road was deserted and wound its way north towards the Green Line through the Eastern Sovereign Base Area. The airfield wasn't far behind me and the areas of open fields on either side of the lane were the typical adjuncts of an airstrip. Although the day was in its infancy, the fields round about and the trees and bushes looked primed to warm up quickly. There was no drenching dew to be burned off, and when the sun broke cover, the land seemed to prepare itself for another scorching arc from east to west. The roadside was fringed with bleached grass, and the only sound was the percussive vibrations provided by my boots and the kit on my back. Was I *really* outside? If I stopped walking, I could hear my own breathing. All around, the middle distance was occupied by dark green and domed bushes whose roots went deeper than the faded grasses. In the distance, to the north, the Kyrenia mountain range looked for all the world like the profile of a prone and sleeping giant.

I passed between two military-looking buildings which, at first, appeared to be unoccupied, but closer inspection proved the opposite. The trees at the side of the track were shedding surreal, long morning shadows onto the gritty road surface. It was a very promising start and, though it was early, the air was comfortably warm and fresh with a welcome breeze just gentle enough to caress the skin.

That morning I was especially excited because across the border lay what I thought would be the most remote part of my walk. Before the day was out, I should pass through several remote villages on the other side of the Buffer Zone. I was cautious about how I should conduct myself in the disputed Turkish Republic. When I had met Captain Vanek of the United Nations in Nicosia, he invoked the acronym and told me to,

'Make no mistake – there are tens of thousands of Turkish troops in the TRNC.' I was enthusiastic about *not* getting put in prison or creating a news article back in Blighty, so I stepped on with a resolve to be as shrewd as a snake. My drone was secreted beneath layers of clothing in my rucksack so any prying customs guard might *not* think I was an itinerant spy intent on obtaining aerial intelligence.

The road before me was curving very slightly northeast, and on either side the land was sun-bleached and empty. Over to my left an incongruous but impressive sports stadium stood quiet and empty. Opposite, across the road, a half-fallen tree looked to have been transplanted from *Avatar* with its bleached trunk entirely coloured pink in the dawning light. I spent a minute enjoying its aesthetic excellence; it would have looked perfectly suitable for any art exhibition exactly as it was, with only nature credited as the artist. I identified the unusual tree as a century agave. It had dwarfish and leafless branches, at the end of which were clusters of mysterious seed pods. The tree seems to start its life as a kind of cactus, but then a trunk sprouts from a cluster of thick leaves as if the plant has suddenly changed its mind about its genus.

I was passed by a goat shepherd and a disorderly herd of scrawny-looking beasts; they disappeared behind me with a fading chorus of muted bells. The road swept left to point directly north. I could tell I was close to the border; there were no warning signs but, in the dawn's thin mist, there was another unmistakable indication that I was about to move into a quite different country. As close to the border fence as it was possible to lay foundations, and built as if to provoke with a kind of phallic power, I could make out the silhouettes of a pair of minarets. With every step they were becoming less monochrome, and I could soon discern they were made up of a sandstone base with bright white pinnacles, almost like marble. Between the two towers both versions of the Turkish flag, with the star and crescent, were flying proudly just in case anyone was foolish enough to think the place of worship was an Orthodox church. The Turkish flag links the Turkish Republic to the ancient Ottoman Empire and, perhaps, provides a symbol of equally ancient enmity between two vastly different peoples. To my left a Greek Cypriot wheat field had been harvested with the edge of the field less than a stone's throw from the provocatively situated mosque. Further on, I read a blue, rectangular sign which indicated this zone was a Sovereign Base Area customs checkpoint. It was interesting that the accompanying crest on the notice carried the crown of the British Government, but this crossing was not the tripartite, international cocktail I thought it would be. Because this checkpoint was in a Sovereign Base Area, there were no Greek border officials. Technically this was a move from the UK directly into Northern Cyprus. There were clear signals that NO PHOTOGRAPHY was permitted, and I was getting used to the presence of Turkish writing with its unfamiliar diacritic glyphs attached to some of the letters in its alphabet.

I was now within a few yards of the border control, so I took a deep breath and added more confidence to my stride. The crossing point featured two lines of fibreglass cabins and these housed Turkish officials who entered passport and visa information into computers. I felt a little conspicuous, as I was, very definitely, the only pedestrian at the checkpoint. I walked forward and handed over my passport to a smartly dressed female officer. She was unveiled, like most Turkish Cypriot women, and her long brown hair was worn down framing a pretty face with skilfully applied makeup. She nodded a silent acknowledgement to my utterance of thanks when I said, 'Teşekkür ederim'. My passport was fed into a machine, the details were stored, and it was handed back to me. The officer's brief smile faded from her face before I had time to take the little red book from her hand. I was free to enter, and crossing on foot had proved to be easy.

The barriers of the checkpoint were now just behind me, and I was astonished at just how busy it was in Pergamos at such an early hour. The time data on photographs, taken soon after my crossing, read 6.19am, but a café right next to the checkpoint must have had at least twenty early risers, sitting on a collection of ancient wicker chairs. The men were thick-set, brown as walnuts and moustachioed. In my head I could hear an anthropologist explaining about some complicated diaspora and centuries of cultural development; these gentlemen were very definitely not Greek. They returned my wave with several 'Good mornings', though I had no Union flag attached to my head. How did they know I wasn't German or Danish? I suspected they were taxi drivers whose skill in finding fares ran to keen observation of new arrivals and the colour of their passports.

I entered a cluttered minimarket which stood within a few metres of the checkpoint and endeavoured to buy breakfast. I was suddenly in a hugely different world. The TRNC is not recognised as an official country and therefore sanctions exist which affect its suppliers; consequently, any tenuous familiarity I had with provisions on the other side of the Buffer Zone snapped quickly in this shop. Although I was just a short distance from the Republic of Cyprus, I didn't recognise any of the chocolate bars, cereals, yoghurts or biscuits on display. I bought a few items and went prepared to pay using Turkish lira, but the shop assistant was keen to take my euros instead. Outside, I put a little distance between myself and the intimidating customs officials and paused to furtively photograph a bust of a rather severe-looking Kemal Atatürk. While innocently filming a piece to camera I realised that, with me facing the road and the camera facing me, the footage inadvertently captured an army compound. The base was behind me, and its barbed wire fence sported several signs warning against photography. As soon as I realised my mistake, I abruptly ended my monologue, lowered the camera and sped off as discreetly as possible.

Pergamos must have been a frontline town in 1974, with plenty of open land to its north providing ample space for unhindered, Turkish military manoeuvres. Looking around, I was genuinely taken aback by what I saw. Within a minute's walk of the smart checkpoint, I was confronted with a mixture of tumbledown buildings with rotting doors and windows and overgrown gardens, rife with weeds and full of rubble. The street was lined with jerry-built structures of varying instability. Yet opposite this stood proudly maintained modern houses with satellite dishes and freshly painted walls. It was a mix of the extremes of European housing; the almost barn-like dwellings of the rural east cheek by jowl with the typical modern structures of more developed countries.

My attention was drawn to one of the charming houses on display. Something deep inside me was stirring. It was almost imperceptible, but I was being taken back in time and I knew this would happen the moment I found what I was searching for. I was looking at a single-storey house with shuttered windows and a veranda with a tiny front garden covered with small white slabs. A railing provided a border between the house and public pavement. But it was none of this that provoked an instinctive recognition. What aroused my emotions was something more subtle… it was the patina of the entire house which evoked strong feelings. The shape, style and layout of the house was typical of the Cypriot houses I remembered from my boyhood, but here, almost half a century later, the house remained exactly as it was all those years ago. The 1970s paint had faded, and the overgrown patio area was covered in thick, white dust. The shutters over the windows were muted with peeling, dark green paint and I suspected that I was looking at a house which once belonged to a civilian victim of war. I wondered if a dispossessed refugee had lived here and, perhaps even now, the displaced owner had photographs taken fifty years ago of his smiling children riding bicycles on that very driveway. Maybe the original occupant was sighing over snaps of loved ones enjoying an evening ouzo on this veranda long before the summer of 1974 brought those times to an end.

This was the Cyprus I had come to see. The Cyprus I needed to measure myself against; to superimpose myself against a once-familiar background and muse on the contrasts and comparisons. If my world had changed so much *not* being a victim of war, then how much more so for the people of this island, whether Greek or Turkish? They had endured not only the passage of time, which can be a cruelty, but also an uprooting caused by conflict. Suddenly, the touchstones of life are removed, the reference points are taken away and people are forced to start again with none of their hard-won reputation to relax against. In places like Pergamos, truly ugly things happened – and they happened to people forced to move south *and* north of the Green Line. I had heard sickening stories of brutalities carried out in houses just like this, things that happened to individuals who were not displaced; they were not displaced – because they were killed. Atrocities were committed by people on both sides of the conflict. Despite any level of mitigation, it was destructive for everyone involved. Thankfully, I could move on with no personal ties to Pergamos or its terrible secrets, but there must be many others denied that privilege.

Pergamos now has the Turkish name Beyarmudu, which means the Lord's Pear, possibly a testament to the village's agricultural history. According to data about the village's population, it has grown enormously since the early nineteenth century. Although it *received* displaced Turkish Cypriots from the 1950s up to and beyond 1974, statements have been made to the effect that no Greek Cypriots were displaced from the village during that period. If that's true, then my conjecture was wrong and there must be another explanation behind the long-empty dwellings I had seen. Census data does record the presence of a few Greek Cypriots over time, so I wasn't sure about the validity of such claims or counter claims.

Somehow, in the last century, a contingent of Dukhobors arrived in the hamlet, having been expelled from Russia by an unsympathetic Czar. The Dukhobors were a sect of pacifists who had broken away from the Russian Orthodox Church and had been labelled as heretics. Amongst other confessions of faith, they preferred a spoken and handed-down oral religious tradition as opposed to strict adherence to scripture. They ceremoniously burned any weapons in their possession and became such *persona non grata* to the authorities they were forced to emigrate en masse to countries like Canada. A few obviously didn't get that far and settled in Beyarmudu; how or why they chose such a location remains a mystery.

On the outskirts of the village was an exceptionally large memorial to the lives of many Turkish men who had lost their lives in various circumstances. The dates of their deaths ranged from 1964 to 1974 to 1988. The scale of the crescent-shaped structure was impressive, and I wondered if it revealed something else. This project must have been expensive and, although all human life is priceless, I wondered whether the proportions of the enormous cenotaph indicated a darker machination. Was there a posturing going on that went beyond the memorialising of loved ones? It seems correct to mark the passing of finite lives with a more infinite pile of stones because most humans seem to instinctively understand the soul is infinite. Yet our memorials need to be built with an absence of anger so our loved ones can rest in peace. I hoped there was infinite peace for these men – all unknown to me. I spent a few moments looking at some of the black and white photographs, gazing into the faces of some of the soldiers memorialised there. One of the many displays featured six fallen Turkish men, and two faces stood out by virtue of their obvious youth. One was aged nineteen and the other aged twenty... Looking into the eyes of the younger youth (who, on closer inspection, may not have had his nineteenth birthday) I saw no malice, only innocence and the slim face of someone not

too far down the road from boyhood. His top lip was
with a soft down not yet requiring shaving and his d
seemed open to learning or, just as easily, a command to ng-
– death or glory or, perhaps, I should afford him three: death,
glory and sadness. He had died on 22 July 1974. Just before I
left Cyprus, in 1972, he would have been sixteen or seventeen
and maybe I had passed him in the street with just six years
between us. I tried to reconstruct *my* sixteen-year-old mindset
and the enormous fault existing between *what* I knew and what
I *thought* I knew at that age.

Small conflicts can concentrate the mind because the fewer
the fallen, the greater the attention afforded to each; who would
gather photos for the thousands lost at Passchendaele? For the
bereaved, the sense of loss is exactly equal, whatever the size of
the conflict.

Further on, towards the outskirts of the village, a dishevelled
Turkish soldier emerged from a seemingly superfluous
checkpoint and righted a fallen wheelie bin. I mused on the very
non-military activity, watching the man as he re-entered his tiny
booth. He paid me no attention as I strode past him to put the
village behind me.

Leaving Pergamos meant going deeper into the plain of
Mesaoria where the horizons shrank back and the land was
crushed beneath an infinite sky. Geographically this part of
Cyprus is interesting; the Eastern Sovereign Base Area extends
north like a half-inflated balloon and the deserted road heading
north towards the mountains of Northern Cyprus was flanked
by the SBA on its left. I imagined that if I were challenged by an
over-eager Turkish patrol, I could leap over the rusting barbed
wire at the roadside and proclaim – with just the right amount of
vigour – that, technically, I was on British territory and, if they
didn't mind, would they be so kind as to holster their weapons
and toddle off!

In the distance, just beyond a commercial compound selling

concrete animals and reproductions of Classical and limbless torsos, I spotted an interesting silhouette. A box on stilts with a ladder revealed itself to be a camouflaged and unoccupied lookout tower with the usual signage informing me there was to be no photography. The structure was about six metres high with a similarly camouflaged hut at its base. It stood about thirty metres from the road in a sea of brown grass, and the blazing orb of the rising sun appeared to be, just then, perching like a phoenix on top of the tower. I checked the coast was entirely without armed and uniformed impediment and risked prosecution by taking a photograph.

As I suspected, this landscape was indeed a lovely place to walk. When I studied satellite images of the region it looked enticing. Photographed from space, the whole area presented as a dry land with sun-bleached dirt tracks spreading out as white capillaries or zigzagging like lightning bolts across the plain. The trails twisted and meandered through ancient olive groves and stony fields, gifting the walker with fresh vistas every few steps. I was planning on going cross-country as soon as I had cleared the last of the Eastern SBA's 'balloon' to my left.

Beside the road there were unprotected ruins of unknown origin and age, but they looked rather old to me. One structure was a singular stone wall with the remains of its fellows lying here and there in grassy mounds. The surviving wall was constructed from mud and straw and had a rough archway still visible. I thought about the Egyptians and their Hebrew slaves. The makers of this house certainly didn't know Moses, but they shared the building practices of his adopted homeland. What was happening in the world when these stones were haphazardly put together... the Crimean War, the English Civil War, Shakespeare writing *Henry V*, Magna Carta? I saw these ancient ruins as evidence for the unrestricted access the infamous Luigi Palma di Cesnola enjoyed when he scoured the island looking for treasure as a bootlegging archaeologist. I was certain any excavations around these mysterious structures would produce all manner of interesting discoveries.

Having established that my next village lay to the northwest of me, I took great delight in leaving the road and launching out into a compass exercise. My father, a meticulous and professional Royal Air Force navigator, would have been *very modestly* proud. He had taught me how to align the compass's straight edge to intersect your current position with your target position on the map. Then to rotate the compass dial until its lines were parallel with the lines of grid north, before removing the compass from the map and lining up the magnetic north needle of the device with the fixed north of the compass dial – simple. The arrow on the compass base should point at your bearing, and it's just a case of lining up the direction arrow with an object in the distance and walking towards it. It was always a relief to find the indicator matching up with your natural sense of direction. Occasionally, on more featureless terrain, the direction arrow can surprise you, so you double check by going over the process two or three times before trusting the arrow and making out for a tree or rock a few hundred metres away where the process is repeated.

With a new sense of freedom and caprice I sent the drone up high and allowed it to circle me as I walked through a sparse olive grove growing out of a moonscape. Viewing the footage showed the low morning sun had given me a gigantic shadow of a Tolkienesque tree, magnifying and mimicking my steps along the trail. I was climbing a slight incline, at the top of which I hoped to see my next village in the distance. The various farm tracks seemed to be very artistically and romantically produced; there were no obviously straight paths where the shortest route from A to B might be the objective. It seemed as if a succession of farmers had simply followed the path of an earlier farmer who'd decided that curved paths were far more interesting than straight ones.

I was becoming more skilled at setting up the drone and took some profile footage for use as establishing shots should I produce a video of my journey.

As I walked along, I would occasionally startle a dozing lizard and watch as the reptile ran for cover. The landscape about me was that of a typical Mediterranean olive grove, and it felt wonderful to have my boots on Cyprus soil with the modern insulation of tarmac and hardcore behind me. My desire for the atavistic was suddenly quenched; if the Apostle Paul or a Neolithic copper miner had been forced to walk with me, they may have been spooked by the drone or my polyfibre appearance, but the land would not have caused them any concerns at all. Everything around me was organic, primeval and gloriously unchanged. Looking at the twisted and long-lived limbs of the olive trees caused me to muse on creating a hideout to see how long it would take to be discovered. The shallow hillside was covered in a uniform grey dust covering everything and muting the green of the olive leaves. The deeply rutted tree trunks were as warm as human arms, and each emerged from a sandy ground of churned and rechurned dirt of desert dryness.

I wanted the ashen and dusty path through the countryside to last for hours so I could immerse and lose myself in an imaginary world of Romans and togas, remote villas and cool pools. Perhaps, if I walked far enough into the outback, I'd find Aphrodite or Spartacus. Surely, at some point I'd come across the disciples sleeping in Gethsemane or Jason and his Argonauts foraging for the ship's stores before their journey back to ancient Greece. Or perhaps I'd happen across the fleece of gold hanging from the branches of one of these thousands of trees... then there'd be a great thundering noise and bulls and fiery dragons would appear to defend the mythical treasure.

I was heading for the village of Türkmenköy and, some distance across very rough land, I could see a white minaret on the southwestern side of the village. As I drew near to the hamlet,

I saw that right next to the roughest of goat huts a palatial house was being built with an apparent effort to make it appear as extreme a contrast as possible to its pungent neighbour. With a different kind of comparison, I noticed the mosque beneath the minaret was just a few metres from a disused Orthodox church. At least the locals hadn't sacrilegiously converted the church into a mosque – a practice which had taken place in other parts of the island. I photographed the architectural standoff and allowed my first impressions to form a shallow opinion in my mind. The latecomer was the pristine mosque and though, as I arrived, the muezzin was issuing a call to prayer, no one came. Yet the plaintive song sounded appropriate to me; it resounded as a yearning for embrace, like the desperate cry of a lost child. The undernourished arm of the minaret thrust itself into the sunlight in an attempt to gain a healthy glow. Opposite, the unused Orthodox church stood like a docile horse waiting for its rider to return. The architectural lines of the church seemed softer, and imperfections in its structure smacked of an awareness of the imperfections of its congregation, all now long gone. My heart ached for both communities. My heart ached for the world.

Türkmenköy had appeared out of a quite barren little hilltop with the land all around being made up of scrub bush which might be a survival challenge to the hardiest of goats. But the village itself, a tightly packed collection of aged houses and smallholdings, seemed completely unaware of, or uninterested in, its remoteness.

At a roadside corner, an old Volkswagen Golf sat slowly returning to the earth, a glassless hulk of rusting metal in passive submission to the laws of thermal dynamics. Around another corner I came across a signless shop. One of the large glass windows was cracked and taped up, but there was still the familiar hum of functional fridge motors when I stepped inside. Two plump women were standing behind a cluttered counter

ɣ looked up to see who the intruder was. I discovered
lies were the owners; both could speak a little English,
...___ quite why they looked at me and decided to dispense with
all *other* European lingua, I know not. One of the ladies wore a
lemon-coloured headscarf; she sat down heavily on a wobbly
stool and asked, 'Where you from? Are you from London?'

'No,' I answered, and then I did what I always do all over the
world whenever I have to explain where I'm from. I lifted my
left palm to roughly represent England and pointed to London
which resides near my wrist under my little finger, Manchester
and Liverpool are located at the base of my index finger and
Lincoln is opposite, at the base of my little finger.

'Oh, not London?' they said, looking a little crestfallen.

'No, not London... about 200 kilometres north of London,' I
replied. Had I said I *was* from London I was certain I'd have been
presented with an oral list of Turkish relatives, all perhaps living
in Haringey, that I might know. This is a protocol perfected by
Americans who, upon discovering a newly arrived victim is
from the UK, will assume that the British Isles has one street and
a total population of thirty-seven. Whereupon they'll ask you if
you know James Parker from Wolverhampton? My geography
lesson proved to be a further disappointment for my audience,
so I retreated to spend a few minutes gathering thirst-quenching
goodies from the impressively disorganised store – the snack
bars next to the washing powder, the fabric conditioner near the
toilet paper.

I paid for my goods with Turkish lira and wished the ladies
goodbye. Not wanting me to leave without my knowing they
weren't *really* disappointed that I didn't live in London, the two
women sent me off with a vigorous waving of arms. I squeezed
between the improbable shop-fellows of clothes pegs and
potatoes and made for the door.

I emerged to descend a slight incline leading away to my
right. Dilapidated houses were dark and shuttered to an even

thicker darkness within, and on the untidy verandas I caught sight of roughly washed and damp clothing drying like wrinkled hides in the morning sun. This was almost certainly because the locals hadn't been able to locate exactly where the fabric conditioner was kept in the shop; I'd have checked the frozen veg aisle.

Some of the houses seemed to be on the wrong side of the verge of dereliction. The village was quiet and there were few signs of life until I joined a main road which turned out to be the centre of the village's coffee culture. A good number of senior citizens were sitting under the shade of a simple café awning, and because it seemed a rarity for these village junctions to have any signposts, I sauntered over to confirm my exit road from the village. A friendly gentleman, aged about seventy, with an off-white moustache, insisted I join them. 'Sit. Siiiit.' He almost sang the second request and I willingly complied; you must not refuse to take coffee with a Turk! I received approving nods when I ordered my drink *sans sucre*. My question about the correct way out of the village for Akdoğan was enthusiastically ignored in favour of bringing me a tiny cup of thick black Turkish coffee, along with a peel-top cup of chilled water as an antidote. Had there been a piano playing, and my grand entrance to the café made through swing doors, the music would most definitely have stopped. I was the centre of attention, which I found disconcerting because I didn't want to be taken as supercilious in any way. Especially when my moustachioed friend told me in rather good English that he had worked at the NAAFI in Dhekelia for twenty-eight years. I had to respond by telling the assembled coffee drinkers I used to live in Cyprus and, as soon as I mentioned Akrotiri, I didn't need to say any more. There was much nodding of heads and friendly muttering, with questions about what I was doing. Some of the men drew near to examine my map and the progress I had made. They looked at my line of black chevrons whilst talking quietly amongst themselves in

Turkish; all the while the air was thick with the smoke and scent of Turkish cigarettes.

My chief interrogator went by the name of Ali Kızılşahin, translated as Ali Red Falcon, which we both laughed at. Ali explained what the place was. 'This is boys' futbol club...'

'Football?' I enquired.

'Yes, yes, football,' he replied. After a few minutes I asked him about the conflict and what he thought about the future for Cyprus. He made a noise I took to be an uninterested moan. He shook his head and loudly issued a magnanimous statement. 'Cyprus? Not Greece. Not Turkey!' he paused. His point being that Cyprus was neither Greek nor Turkish. 'Both sides did bad things...' he continued. I nodded my agreement and asked the Red Falcon about the empty houses like the ones I'd seen near the checkpoint.

'Why are the houses by the border empty?' I asked.

'Not enough peoples!' said Ali, with both his palms faced upwards.

'Oh?' I wanted to hear more...

'Here, no jobs, no young peoples.'

'OK.'

'They go away,' he sighed.

'To Nicosia?' I asked.

'Yes, or Turkey,' he replied. 'I have no hope for Cyprus now.' He looked down and exhaled.

'Cyprus was beautiful when I lived here.' I was attempting to lighten the mood. 'Two good years!' I held up a pair of fingers and kissed them. Ali nodded, but his eyes were sad. We sat talking for around half an hour, Ali acting as my interpreter. One of the group was a young man with an obvious learning disability, but as I watched the men in the café, they included him in all their decisions. They praised his efforts and listened carefully to what he said; in return the teenager was uninhibited and moved about with the freedom of a child at home. If a measure of a society is found in how they treat their weakest, then what I had seen at the little coffee house was particularly good – very good for Türkmenköy.

I stood to strap on my rucksack, thanked Ali and his friends and stepped down onto the hot tarmac.

'Good luck with your walk,' wished Ali.

I shook a few hands before disappearing from their sight and making my way down what I hoped was the right road. It headed west, which was good. West was always good.[1] I was tracking towards Ercan airport, and I expected the next few villages would prove to be very much like this one: gentle, unspoiled places promising an unthreatening welcome because they exist in an unusual world not in step with the brash cacophony of modernity.

On the road towards Akdoğan I was lauded with car horns and enthusiastic waving by passing strangers, and I began to relax. The people were friendly, but what happened at Deryneia to Tassos Isaac during the bikers' protest was hard to forgive, and I was sure that pack mentality played a part in the loss of reasoning resulting in the inhumanity which caused his death. Maybe the 'pack' theory was close to the truth; at the time, a few violent Turkish Nationalists were on the island operating under the name 'the Grey Wolves'.

Interestingly, any lone Turk I met seemed quite different from the filmic images of warring Turks marauding across deserts in *Lawrence of Arabia*. In isolation they presented themselves as a gentle, introspective people.

Beside the road, standing in high weeds, there were more ancient buildings, and again the bricks were made of mud and

---

1 I would return early the following year to thank Ali [the] Red Falcon, and I took with me several full-size match balls and some training cones; my wife and I accepted an invitation to be guests of honour at an afternoon match about two days later. Türkmenköy were an excellent side and won the game with ease.

straw. Did the rustic materials make up walls of biblical age?

Further on, a field full of thistles produced an ebbing sea of bright violet and the temperature was now nudging 30°C.

Akdoğan (formerly Lysi) was a short walk from the perch of the Red Falcon, and I passed a Turkish military compound on the main road in. There are many Turkish army compounds along the northern section of the Buffer Zone. The fences are screened off with green or black netting, and I started to develop an interesting theory as to why. Although the cover is ostensibly to prevent outsiders seeing in, I began to wonder if it might also be an attempt to deceive. I suspected only the Turkish Government knew exactly how many Turkish troops are stationed on the island. It must cost a huge amount of lira to keep these bases manned with soldiers, and I thought what if, in exploiting a kind of peace dividend, there were fewer numbers of soldiers than the Turks would have us believe? Was the obscuring of the fences a component in a policy of misinformation? I was probably wrong. I supposed there were UN limits on the size of any Turkish military presence on the island. Perhaps the screening was just part of standard military construction.

There was a significant amount of military activity in Northern Cyprus, and I was passed by dozens of camouflaged jeeps and trucks. Loud explosions could be heard from the Kyrenia ranges where the Turkish army was often on exercise.

Not long after the army compound, I took a left turn off the main road to head into the village centre. The main road bypasses the village to the north as it makes its way towards Ercan airport and Nicosia beyond.

In Akdoğan I struck it lucky when an unlikely photography shop sold me an even *more* unlikely memory card for my GoPro, which had just issued me the message, 'Card Full'. Result! I asked the people in the shop if they knew the best place to eat. Although I was aware this would result in my dining at an establishment run by one of their relatives, I was tired, hungry – and unfussy.

A chair and table would amount to an indulgent luxury after two days of sitting on walls or dirt tracks – apart from my thirty minutes with Ali and Co at the football club.

I was directed to 'our restaurant', the VIP bar, where I found a large man frying onions on a griddle. The sight and smell of sizzling food was mesmerising; I had not eaten anything hot for about seventy-two hours. I felt like ordering a beer, pulling up a chair and just watching him cook for the rest of the day. As it is, I avoided the temptation of alcohol and ordered a chicken kebab, couscous, yoghurt with mint and an ice-cold Coke. A friendly lady with an English accent arrived, and having identified me as English, nonchalantly informed me she was from Stepney Green in London. Her name was Emine, and she was a wonderful host. Emine was a middle-aged lady with vibrant brown eyes, a kind face and a ready smile conducting herself with delightful pragmatism. She wore a red T-shirt emblazoned with the letters VIP and her brown hair was tied back ready for a day's work. She ran what amounted to an Anglo-Turkish enclave of impressive proportions, and her adult children were welcome interlocutors for me. Emine allowed me to stay all day in her restaurant where I was able to run up a tab until I decided it was time to leave. She granted me permission to charge my batteries and to leave my rucksack with her when I went off to film the local Orthodox church which *had* been converted into a mosque.

Emine loved my drone footage, and I showed her my crumpled map with its increasing number of chevrons. She told me about a personal tragedy. She had lost her husband in a car accident and was rebuilding her life in Cyprus. She was of Turkish Cypriot descent, but she was, effectively, a Londoner through and through. I wondered if she kept busy so there was less time to think about her loss.

My food arrived and it was an absolute taste sensation from start to finish, especially the minted yoghurt with its cooling properties to offset the spiced chicken.

71

Normally, in the afternoon, the plan was to retreat to a shady bower, but today there was no need. I wanted to visit the Byzantine-style church in the centre of the village and Emine's kindness made this an easy expedition. Outside, the quiet streets of Akdoğan did their best to shelter me from the scorching heat, but when I reached the converted church it was exposed to the full power of the sun, which was now at an angle yielding no shade whatsoever. I was particularly interested in this church of the Panagia because its conversion into a mosque would not only mean a clash of religions but a fascinating blend of aesthetics too. I was intrigued to see how these differences worked. After 1974 it was stripped of most of its Christian decorations and faced its own radical adjustment – a conversion of use. The building sat on a raised square of grey flagstones which, on the day of my visit, caused the sun to rebound all around making the whole area oven-hot and ultra-bright. The building was sited not far from an unsightly heap of building materials in a nearby builders' yard and, close by, two refuse trucks were parked, passive in the intense afternoon heat. The church was a faux Byzantine structure and seemed to have been built using basic undressed blocks for the most part; the entrance and windows were decorated with Gothic-style arches like those evident in many a European cathedral. The bell tower was ornate and attractive, but the nearby store of sewer pipes offset its beauty with an incongruous presence. Despite its utilitarian setting, the whole upper portion of the building had the look of a medieval crown fit for the head of Richard the Lionheart. There was something more which fascinated me; it seems de rigueur in Northern Cyprus to use places of worship as the accepted place for flying the national flag, and here in Akdoğan there was no exception. The locals had mercifully overlooked the Christian saints carved into the edifice when converting the building into a mosque, yet the Turkish flag indicated its new purpose just in case observers were not aware things had changed inside.

Outside, the stone saints now passively witness daily calls to prayer from the muezzins. If St Paul had strolled into town in ancient times, he would have welcomed the opportunity for debate and, risking a beating to speak here, I see him convening an enthralling discussion just like he did on Mars Hill in Athens 2,000 years ago. Should he have stood where I was standing that day, he would have remained ice cool and said, 'Men of Akdoğan, I observe that you are religious in many respects...' You would need a watertight apologetic to bring your theistic arguments to Paul, though in his day the discussions might have centred on the error of polytheism. Interestingly, within hours I would be walking where he walked when he had crossed the island on a journey from Salamis to Paphos all those years ago – around 600 years before the founding of Islam. I submitted to a sense of being perplexed by the confusing scene and made my way back to the air-conditioned VIP bar and restaurant. I passed a pair of workmen who were engaged in building a very 'relaxed' wall completely without the aid of a spirit level. Further on, a small van was parked outside a shop with two small children and an enormous cockerel on the bench seat. Once again, the village centre was overshadowed by yet another statue of a rather serious-looking Atatürk.

Back at the VIP, I found Emine hard at work preparing for the evening patrons and, later, I took great delight in washing at a proper sink. Before I set out early, at about 4pm, I deployed a heat-beating trick. Given the heat is relentless until about 6pm I soaked my breathable T-shirt in water and put it on soaking wet. The drying process draws heat from the torso and the benefit lasts about twenty minutes by which time the shirt is pretty much dry; although the relief from the sun is short-lived, every little effort helps.

I liked Akdoğan and its community spirit. I made my goodbyes to Emine and set off as if I had emerged directly from a shower by leaving a trail of water droplets along the road.

Above the street the locals had strung lighting in readiness for concerts or festivals and a small stage occupied a part of the village square...

*

One Day (2)

One day the teachers from Berengaria Junior School took us on a bus trip for a picnic. I have no idea where we went, and I could not locate the place today. But I do remember what I saw when we arrived at the mysterious destination. Someone had found a wonderful place and wanted to share it.

As we boarded the bus, I noticed the teachers and their hastily recruited helpers were more excited than we were. In Cyprus everything appeared to be more relaxed, and this attitude extended to education; in England, my uptight school was a Victorian ark of incarceration. The classroom windows were too high to see out of, the walls were just painted bricks, the playground was usually cold and the toilet block detached and of a semi-agricultural standard – barn-like and more fit for animals than children. The headmaster was tyrannical and terrifying but entirely appropriate for his Kafkaesque institution. The whole place was built by minds more fitted for the construction of a hospital or army base, and I hated every inch of its repressive fabric. The authorities had built a little prison and filled it with innocents. However, in Cyprus, my classroom blazed with daylight and any dystopian shadows vanished under the weight of the sun, and its restoring rays were as thick as golden syrup. The children were bronzed and moved with a sense of caprice, our reading cards were bordered with thrilling and sophisticated colours, and each achievement was rewarded with an even more ostentatious border – purple, silver or mustard yellow. At the end of our sunlit day, which seemed to last about five minutes, our lovely teacher, Miss Heathfield, might read from

Prince Caspian *with the entire class falling silent when they heard the name... Aslan!*

On the day of our outing the bus delivered us to a road surrounded by green hills and we climbed the steep banks to eat our sandwiches. The shining slopes were as lush as any in England, but the grass was soft and warm and covered with tiny flowers of white and pink. As if to crown the pastoral setting with garlands of silver, all around, the hill streamed with glistening water cascading over the grass, and bubbling and babbling above and below us, the water chattered away and so did we until after the shortest of times the clock hands sped round and it was time to make our way home.

How great Miss Heathfield's reward must be; to me, she was angelic, delightful, and always kind. She was not an opponent; she was 'for' me.

Memories of Cyprus 1970–72

*

My next village was Yiğitler (Emine taught me it rhymes with Hitler), and once again the exit roads from the village had no road signs because all the locals know where they are going in this part of the world. Emine had instructed me to ask her sister-in-law at the village hardware shop to point out the correct exit road. My target was to reach the vicinity of Dilekkaya before nightfall and from there I was confident I would easily make Nicosia the next day, which would be Friday 8 June – but tomorrow I was in for a major shock!

From Yiğitler I would pass through Erdemli and Kırıkkale before camping just south of Dilekkaya later that evening. The road to Yiğitler began by curving gently west before it straightened to become a beautiful country highway lined on either side with cypress trees and the ubiquitous scorched grass.

I wandered along the quiet road trying to figure out just why I found the lanes and villages so very lovely. I realised it was because they were so peaceful; there are very few cars on the narrow highways in this part of Cyprus, which meant all I heard for ten minutes at a time was birdsong and the sound of the evening breeze in the treetops. There was no threat from rain or cold, and the expansive plain allowed the eyes to wander for great distances to horizons of palm trees, minarets, the spearheads of cypress trees and the occasional small hilltop to my left where the plain had its southernmost edge. Soon Ayia Napa would be throbbing with loud music, but I would never trade my rural idyll for a deafening disco. The 18–30s crowd would return home to answer questions about 'where they went on their holiday' with one word: 'Cyprus' – but that would only be true geographically, not metaphysically.

Cyprus had taught me a lot. In fact, I was certain my two years on the island had been the most vital part of my entire education and that I was not alone in experiencing the benefits. Living an outdoor lifestyle made children adventurous and brave, but the yellow-banded hornets and snakes also taught us to be cautious and sensible. The heat endowed us with automatic hospitality as food and drink were readily shared, as were bikes and toys. The alien environment caused a coming together to survive its common challenges, but our eyes were opened to all manner of beauty in nature. We learned to understand our privilege and to respect and honour our foreign hosts. We learned how to be guests in a land not our own. Most of all, we left the island with storehouses full of eternal treasures. Even now, whatever the depth of grey skies or biting cold of England my mind can always return to the warmth of Cyprus. I might return to the day I wandered alone amongst the warm leaves of my garden in Berengaria and delighted at finding a lovely chameleon in the branches of a tree. I kept it as a pet for a couple of days and found myself to be a celebrity because of it. A more important lesson was learned when I was instructed to return it to nature. I was happy to comply and happier to ditch the weight of celebrity status. A few years later, on my first day at secondary school, made worse by being a boarder, I was clobbered in the playground by the resident school thug. As I was pummelled and roughed up, I honestly thought of Cyprus; the aggressor had no storehouse like mine, and I felt sorry for him.

En route to Yiğitler, another large army compound bordered the roadside. I was impressed and somewhat surprised to see a soldier in a camouflaged sentry box dressed in full combat gear; I waved at him, and he reluctantly returned the gesture. He was fully suited, booted and tin-hatted; my thermometer was reading 35ºC! The sun was still providing a canopy of warm and heavy air even though its crest had dropped slowly from a harsh zenith to become a less punishing version of itself. By the time I reached Yiğitler, the village's minaret was being gilded by a kinder light caused by the sun's rays more robustly filtered through the dust of the day. The shadows of roadside olive trees and telegraph poles were lengthening, and the relative quiet of the little hamlet seemed appropriate in the sieved brightness. All I could hear were birds singing and the echoing bark of a dog. The streets of Yiğitler were a maze of tight twists and turns between buildings with honey-coloured walls. I rounded a corner, where a man sat on a rickety chair opposite a small store on the other side of the trafficless road. He was reading a newspaper. When I entered the shop, my peripheral vision noticed the man fold his paper and cross the street towards me. The shop was his. I bought my usual lemon ice pop and water and paid with Turkish lira.

'Where are you from?' asked the shopkeeper. 'Are you from London?' (*Quelle surprise!*)

'No, Lincoln,' I replied, repeating my palm geography lesson.

'Oh, where you come from today?' he persisted, with genuine interest.

'Akdoğan, but before that, Paralimni,' I said, and waited for a response.

'Paralimni!' he exclaimed.

'Yes.'

'Oooh.' He shook his head with this and the conversation was over. Had our few moments together disturbed the settled dust on memories of an undivided island? The man looked sad and tired and lowered his head with a weak smile. Here was a man carrying the same burdens I had encountered with Ali the Red Falcon earlier that day and the old man near the sea. I was witnessing a generation too familiar with loss.

'Teşekkür ederim,' I said as I collected my purchases.

'Thank you, goodbye,' the man said, and he watched me exit and turn left to head west out of the village.

There were some astonishing sights in Yiğitler. The dwellings had the uniform structure of a film set for a period drama. The streets were so narrow in places that the gaps between the houses had the feel of being 'inside', which made a sleepy cat, resting on a sunlit wall, look like it was reclining at the fireplace of a small home. I could have spent an hour exploring every corner of this enchanted village. There seemed to be something missing though… young people… Everyone I spied was middle-aged or older, which made me worry about the village's future. I passed a roofless building with weeds growing where, perhaps, once stood a table. The table, and those who had once sat at it, were now long gone, perhaps as long as a hundred years ago.

More than 1,000 years after the Apostle Paul walked somewhere near this village, en route to Paphos from the easterly port of Salamis, an inland battle was waged near Erdemli. Isaac Komnenos (1155–96) was a twelfth-century ruler of Cyprus, and he had a fortress at Salamis. Komnenos is recorded as being a violent and somewhat devious character who manipulated and forged his way into gaining control of Cyprus. Princess Berengaria (Richard the Lionheart's fiancée) and Joan of

England, Richard's sister, were shipwrecked in a storm and forced into landing on the island. Subsequently the pair were kidnapped by Isaac – probably in the hope of extracting a king's ransom. However, Isaac miscalculated and, in 1191, he was defeated in a battle by Richard the Lionheart near the ancient city of Tremetousia. Somewhere near modern Erdemli lie the ruins of the town and the site of Isaac's undoing.

Not far out of Yiğitler, a large army compound came into view at the end of a long, straight road; this meant the sentries at the gate were able to watch me approach from several hundred metres away. The base looked different from any I had seen before; the fence was unscreened, perhaps because the inner camp and its buildings were shielded from sight by virtue of its being in the middle of a small pine forest. Again, I waved innocently at the guards, but this time they didn't hesitate to wave back and smile politely. Circling the camp to the left meant that the barbed wire fence was on my right. Looking into the compound revealed all manner of defensive earth works, from man-sized hollows in the ground, just deep enough to conceal a soldier and gun, to large mounds of earth with machine-gun posts covered with camouflage netting and corrugated roofs. I walked for a few hundred metres before the fence turned right abruptly, running for a long distance away from me at right angles to the road. I laughed to myself when I formed the opinion the entire place looked very 'Center Parcs'... Center Parcs but with guns.

In Erdemli, a junction with a very bent signpost declared in Turkish, 'Kırıkkale & Lefkoşa' (Nicosia); this was a joy to me because it was the first time I'd seen a sign pointing to the capital since immersing myself deep in the rural landscape of Northern Cyprus. Nicosia was where I would return to the Cleopatra Hotel and prepare for the second half of my walk. Not all would go smoothly between now and then, but if I kept walking, every step brought me closer to the old town of Nicosia and the assurance of a bed with fresh linen sheets, a hot shower and two days of poolside reading.

With quite some distance yet to go, I could not allow these visions to become too established in my mind, knowing they might exacerbate the relative discomforts of the night's camp which lay somewhere ahead just beyond the village. I asked a small group of Yiğitler locals, sitting at the roadside, if they minded me filming the mangled signpost because they would be in the background. 'Not me!' exclaimed one man in the group. He was aged about sixty and his protestation put his companions into fits of giggles. Remaining straight-faced the comedian followed his outburst with a question: 'Where are you going?'

'Nicosia,' I laughed.

'Ah.' A conversation convened to which I was only an observer. Suddenly a car sped up and lurched to a halt. On the front seat a man was holding a wide-eyed child on his lap.

'He's going part of the way,' suggested the shy sixty-year-old.

'I'm sorry, I have to walk!' I held my hands up in a gesture of thanks and polite declination. I showed the group my map and the progress I had made from the coast near Paralimni. The group made tutting noises and there was much shaking of dark heads before I was waved off as I walked out of the village towards Kırıkkale.

I passed impressive palm trees and piles of tinder-dry palm fronds bleaching at the side of the road. All about was glistening in an evening of warm and rusty light, groups of elegant cypress trees stood like green goddesses and shady houses were fronted with oversized satellite dishes and welcoming patios. Joyous sparrows were darting through the air and feasting on previously joyous insects; everything was unutterably lovely. Occasionally, between the houses, the land opened a little to reveal a square of *bondoo* providing parking for tiny tractors or water carriers on wheels. Behind me the local minaret was, by now, a slender finger of gold shining like the scales of a freshly caught fish, and in front of me a great clump of unruly cactus sat like indignant, green elephant with its dusty extremities spilling out onto the road.

I had, now, experienced three of these evening portions of my day's hiking and I began to look forward to them intensely. I shall never forget those early evening moments: the quiet, the honey-coloured walls shining in the low sun and the gilt-edged trees with the delightful chorus of birdsong. Just being allowed to walk in that lovely circus of life made me smile and sigh with the simple pleasure of being alive. I passed a line of tall eucalyptus trees standing in piles of their own shed bark. Like vertical snakes they had lost their skin and stood with multicoloured trunks of black, brown, cream and white. Outside a modern building, a couple sat reading newspapers; buoyed with the beauty of the day I smiled and said, '*Merhaba* (Hello)'. They nodded with less enthusiasm than my greeting, but the lady stopped reading her paper and panned my exit with a wisp of interest and a gentle smile.

Along a straight road flanked by large fields I saw what appeared to be a hilltop army listening station, and I was still trying to identify its various infrastructures when I reached the outskirts of Kırıkkale. Here a few men sat near a tiny shop; it had little to offer but all I wanted was cold water to rehydrate. When I stepped back outside, after a very brief visit, the muezzin was calling the faithful to evening prayer. A golden Labrador, lying on the roadside, drew my attention and I noticed he was facing southeast, like a good Muslim canine should, at prayer time. I listened very carefully to the muezzin's voice and the turns in the plaintive song. I wasn't sure why, but with the charm and artistry of the day and the divide between Turkish and Greek Cypriots, the music and its minor intervals sounded perfectly right. Usually, the disembodied voices of the singing clerics were fed into crude loudspeakers mounted on the minarets and this made the attack of any phrase bark rudely into the quiet air, yet despite this, the call always sounded soft and sad to me. Unfamiliar intervals cascaded as an expression of need and an understanding of being weighed in a balance and found wanting. The two religions of Islam and Christianity separate like two great rivers. One places the responsibility of holiness on the self, whilst the other declares true holiness an impossibility, claiming righteousness is a gift delivered by the atoning sacrifice of a lowly carpenter. Notwithstanding any debate on justification by faith, the song in the air moved me.

At another unmarked junction, the correct road was pointed out to me by an elderly couple who were strolling in the direction I was walking. The gentleman, an old, thickset man of the land, extended a crooked index finger and I followed its urgency like a faithful dog. I passed a tiny bungalow with both Turkish ensigns draped from its gutters and joked to myself, perhaps inappropriately, that the little bungalow had been Makarios's retirement home. A single-storey anathema. The village of Dilekkaya stood on a slight hillside at the end of another long road, which seemed to be heading directly for the Kyrenian mountains.

After walking for another thirty minutes or so, I started to see lights coming on in Dilekkaya as the expansive plain grew darker by the minute. Perhaps the Troodos mountains far away to the west helped speed the sun's descent? Whenever a car sped by, I was forced to take avoiding action and step into the long roadside grass, which covered very uneven ground. Not wanting to risk an ankle injury, I decided to camp at the first suitable spot. For the next five minutes I watched a tractor moving up and down in a field on the western side of the road; the driver was working under the vehicle's bright lights, and I followed his to and fro movements with interest. On my right, just before a bridge over a dry ravine, there was a freshly ploughed field of sandy earth. At the field's northern edge, a large hawthorn hedge provided excellent concealment from Dilekkaya's descending traffic. In a green, curved harbour of foliage, a stretch of soft earth presented itself as an ideal place to make camp without being viewed by anyone directly west of me. In a minute or two my tent was up, my boots were off, and I was reclining comfortably on my self-inflating mat, with tired feet elevated on my rucksack. Outside, the tractor was still at work; I entertained the remote possibility that the vehicle might cross the road to work my field and I would be found in the morning with my arms and legs protruding from a straw bale or perhaps parts of me would be spread over about an acre of land.

I enjoyed adding a good number of black chevrons to my map and had to completely refold it to reveal my unmarked route for tomorrow's navigation up and into Nicosia. I knew (or thought I knew) that the capital was within an easy day's walk of my location; after Dilekkaya, the roads into Nicosia were major highways.

At home, my wife, Gill, would be noting the 'blue blob' on her phone had now made significant progress on its trek west. I decided that, tomorrow, I'd pause for a long drink at Ercan airport before enjoying the optimum efficiency of a road heading directly west all the way to the heart of Nicosia…

… But tomorrow, all these imaginings would be brutally erased with just a few words. Tomorrow would be a truly epic day!

The tractor clattered on and a glance at my watch showed the time to be 9pm exactly. Agrarian overtime? Inside my cocoon, sleep did not come for hours. I suspected that I finally drifted off sometime well after midnight.

The Chameleon

Peeled from a branch; rudely transplanted,
Passively you looked about,
Overlooking my thievery,
Rocking in deliberation; to step or not to step,
Better than a blackbird,
Crowned by your presence,
Friends bring tribute,
Testing the mettle of your blood,
Trying your colours,
Unfair red – you walked off,
Island creature,
Thrilling alien.

M.J.W. Clark – *Memories of Cyprus 1970–72*

4

Northern Cyprus Crossing into the
Republic of Cyprus

Dilekkaya to Nicosia

Friday 8 June 2018

I woke up in the early hours of the morning and checked my watch. I was anxious that yesterday's weariness might have caused me to oversleep, but the digital display informed me that it was 3.13am. I'd been asleep for just a few hours. I dozed off again and the next time I opened my eyes it was exactly one hour later – almost time to hit the road. I carried out a pre-walk check of the five-day weather report and, according to the data, that day would be the hottest day of the week. When I emerged from my tent a velvet sky offered up no evidence to suggest the forecast might be wrong.

By the time I'd broken camp, performed the essential precious-check and rejoined the road to Dilekkaya it was 5am and the eastern horizon was topped with a lilac band of cloudless sky. The farmer and his clattering machinery had gone, and I had no idea what time he'd finished his nocturnal ploughing.

The little village ahead resembled a sleepy animal using the rising land for a pillow, and to be up so early afforded me a privileged view of a passive collection of dwellings. In the young light of day, Dilekkaya was presented in a monochrome grey with just the odd diamond of light piercing the scene like earthbound stars. I walked on with my attention fixed on the village, and with every step the houses and hillside took on colour and clearer dimensions. I thought about the world turning and returning around the sun – a 365-day journey across an enormous distance in space yet, owing to infinity, it's no distance at all. There I was, approaching Dilekkaya, an infinitesimally tiny dot of humanity on a shallow hillside – totally alone in the world. I thought about the thrill of dawn when you surprise the sun by being dressed for its arrival. It feels like a kind of law-breaking when a diurnal being is placed in a nocturnal landscape, when dusk and dawn are secret passages to observe the mostly unseen. A bright red fox, a majestic deer floating like a boat across a sea of fog, owls caught in headlights, tiny hedgehogs trailing across wet grass like prickly commandos... we catch sight of an alien world. Everywhere feels special at dawn: the temples of Angkor, the forests of Europe, the Rocky Mountains, even the deserted streets of a city. It's as if the absence of humanity brings a transient return to Eden; all is new, and the day is waiting to be unwrapped. The exiled agents of nature creep in like a gentle tide to roam the land for a few hours before the brash cacophony of man and his daylight industry drives them back to their beds and burrows. Yet they take to their dens without complaint. This stillness needs to be joined and enjoyed not disturbed. It's a time to silently observe as a very special guest at a very special banquet of fragile manna. No wonder people write sonnets.

I strode out with a degree of determination which had been absent from previous mornings. I was very confident I'd reach the Cleopatra Hotel by evening, but I knew the day's sun was going to be a formidable opponent. I examined my surroundings... The dry riverbed I had camped beside was broad and shallow and ran parallel with the Kyrenia range; it was entirely without water, and large weeds were now establishing themselves in seasonal defiance along its stony bed. A low bridge carried me over the obstacle and the road bore northwestwards. I noticed the Kyrenia mountains had taken over more of the sky; now the numerous crags and gullies caught the light and took on the appearance of sparkling eyes viewing me with suspicion as I drew nearer. This mountain range was a country within a country; an empire of monasteries and castles, each with a thousand untold stories.

For some reason my phone was dead, and although it was now plugged into the solar charger, nothing exciting was going to happen until the sun was much higher. Any very early spousal monitoring back in the UK would yield no trace of me whatsoever.

Entering Dilekkaya I was surprised and impressed to see two early risers sitting quietly chatting at a small café. The pair of old gentlemen observed my advance up the incline, and I managed to avoid an invitation for coffee by adding more purpose to my gait, as if I were en route to an urgent appointment. A welder's untidy workshop sat alongside a selection of smart new houses and here and there the mouldering ruins of a different age. I took a few moments to create a mental list of the rusty metal items scattered around the little garage. Lengths of steel rod, various steel plates and tyreless wheels, pieces of engine and scavenged appliances. It reminded me of a report I'd watched about Iraq and its response to sanctions and the resulting lack of resources. 'In Iraq,' said the BBC reporter, 'if it's broken, you repair it.' This meant that various shops provided specialist skills for the refurbishment of all manner of things. For example, if an alternator breaks in the UK, we just replace it, but in Baghdad it would be skilfully dismantled, carbon brushes would be repaired, and copper coils rewound. This 'prefabricator' obviously ran a ⸻here locals came to have their cars welded and their ⸻chines brought back to life.

According to local information, around June each year, Dilekkaya hosts a hellim cheese festival. Hellim is a Cypriot cheese traditionally made from sheep or goats' milk with part of its production involving the curds of the milk being pressed into moulds and poached in hot water; this process results in a heat-resistant cheese ideal for grilling. Arabs call the delicacy, hallum, and the Greeks, halloumi; its origin is interesting having been invented by the Arabs and passed on to the Greeks, and from the Greeks to the Turks.

At the top of the hill, Dilekkaya was all but behind me, and the deserted road headed directly and efficiently northwest, which pleased me enormously. Studying my map, I could see that Ercan airport lay to the northwest and that this might be an opportunity for another cross-country adventure. The road out of Dilekkaya bent away from its northwest track and went almost directly north to eventually join a main road running west to east across the plain. I wanted to cut the corner and head directly for Ercan; it was an achievable target, and I was fully stocked with water and an energy drink. Energy drinks can be counterproductive as they dehydrate the body, so they need to be consumed with water in almost equal measure, thus my last few steps along the tarmac road were punctuated with alternating sips from both bottles. Dehydration was a real threat to my performance, and in those conditions, I needed to maintain discipline with a continual check on fluid intake.

After a short distance, just as the buildings of Dilekkaya started to fade behind me, an enticing track presented itself on my left. Closer inspection revealed it headed towards a cattle farm a few hundred metres to the west of me, but I was wanting to trek northwest as much as possible. Any incremental progress in that direction would see me eventually intercepting the main B16 leading west towards Ercan and Nicosia. I stepped off the tarmac and took to the westerly track, but before long I realised the trail was just leading to a collection of farm buildings. Underneath an open-sided barn, a herd of familiar-looking Friesian cattle was standing patiently, and alongside them a couple of stockmen were readying them for milking. I neither wanted a conversation nor a chastisement for trespass, so I performed an impressive leap across a water-filled dyke and scuttled off across a barren field, bearing northwest. Somehow, by going cross-country, I entirely missed my target village of Kirklar, which lay further west of me. As I slogged my way across a soft field, I started to worry I'd step on an undiscovered landmine, but I was sure the traffic of heavy farm machinery would have raked the land thoroughly enough to rule that out. However, there persisted the occasional and vaporous presence of imaginary newspaper clippings sporting pictures of me and my remaining leg. Eventually I found a hard path and joined it heading north; soon a multitude of farm tracks presented themselves so I enjoyed swapping trails judiciously whenever a better direction could be taken.

I used the time to assess my general condition as I sauntered along, because something strange was going on with my metabolism. I wasn't sleeping for long; I was sometimes hungry but when I tried to eat, I struggled to salivate and at other times I wasn't hungry despite vast calorie burns. My legs and hips were aching and sometimes I got into a rhythm of stopping every sixty metres or so. My feet were in good condition because experience had taught me that I could not pay too much attention to my feet when engaged in a long-distance walk. My toenails were carefully clipped, and ointment was applied to lubricate my toes; I used quality liner and walking socks and never economised when buying boots or other essential equipment. Yet I was now determined to reduce my rucksack's weight as soon as possible because this was the cause of my aching hips. Rucksacks are *supposed* to have their weight transferred through the hips, but I was delighted to find my aches disappeared when I tightened my shoulder straps to place more weight on my shoulders. The

rt of my body is packed with muscle from over forty

years of hard work as an engineer and this adjustment, which reduced the weight on the pelvis, caused me no discomfort at all. After a while, my normal walking rhythm resumed, and my confidence returned.

I forced myself to eat some flapjack, consume some energy gel containing caffeine and to sip water continually in the hope my digestive system would reset. Within minutes my whole body started to respond to the input, and I began to turn my attention outward. On my right there was an intriguing fenced compound, but it wasn't a military enclosure. Standing within the fenced area was an ancient ruin and, given the lack of protection provided for other such artefacts, I thought it must be an important site of historical interest. However, it lay too far off to the east to warrant a detour for investigation. In front of me a copse of tall eucalyptus trees stood in relative isolation; the ground beneath them was grassless and flat, a delightful oasis of shade, little frequented by humans owing to its seclusion. I walked through the trees very slowly and, on the north side of the copse, I heard the faint sound of fast traffic for the first time in several days… it was the B16.

I continued to muse on the ancient building which had intrigued me a few moments before; despite its distance from my route making it an unattractive diversion, I wondered what on earth could have been built in such an isolated field. I thought again about Luigi Palma di Cesnola and his unchecked raids on all manner of ancient sites across the island; was this a site which he investigated?

The Ashmolean Museum in Oxford has a large exhibition of Cyprus' artefacts found at archaeological excavations instigated by Sir John Linton Myres. Linton Myres was an Oxford scholar who, to some extent, had collaborated with Palma di Cesnola; Sir John's letters asking Cypriot authorities for permission to dig are part of the Ashmolean displays, so at least he'd submitted his intentions to the proper authorities.

Spending a few hours at the Ashmolean was an overwhelming experience; some of the ancient articles behind the glass in Oxford are utterly stunning. I saw an elaborate earring made up of articulated gold pieces, each intricately carved with very impressive detail. The jewel had a skilfully set garnet and whoever had misplaced this accessory must have been distraught. On display were any number of amphorae and ceramics, each painted with sophisticated and intricate designs and applied with wonderful attention to detail. I saw statues and busts and hundreds of votive figures, each created to invoke blessings on everything from copper mining to wine making. One tablet was covered in Eteocypriot script, as yet still undeciphered! Mysteries of ancient Cyprus lying in plain sight, but they might as well be lying on the surface of a distant planet, for what is on display is a very different world, out of reach and darkly fascinating. The ancient buildings and their foundations are often invisible, but so too are the lives of their unknown inhabitants.

How many secrets were lying undisclosed, how close were my modern boots to treasures just a few feet beneath the soil? Had I just crossed the site of an unknown villa, the family residence of a Phoenician trader or the home of an Egyptian envoy who had settled on the unspoiled plain of Mesaoria many centuries ago? The island had an advanced culture thousands of years before Christ, and the textures of life were leather, stone, ceramics, gold, precious stones and many other kinds of metal. How intoxicatingly spellbinding would it be to silently observe a summer party in ancient Cyprus? To watch the evening breeze move the folds of an ancient garment *before* it was lost to the ground forever, to listen to the cadences of unknown languages. To recognise the laughter and rhythms of conversation which might still be familiar to a visitor from the future. Perhaps the moonlight might leave a streak of silver over the Mediterranean where vessels from Egypt and Rome are moored with holds full of trade goods… and all this, viewed through Doric columns just a few years old.

It was now about 6am and aeroplanes were regularly appearing overhead on their westerly approach to land at Ercan airport. When I reached the road and turned left, a parade of passing aircraft appeared lower and lower as I proceeded west. They were so close the planes' insignia could be read easily, and soon the perimeter fence of the airfield appeared on my left. Over to my right several rising villages abutted the Kyrenia foothills, and I was tempted to leave my westerly track and turn north to visit a village shop. I decided I'd refresh at Ercan as planned and pressed on as the road inclined upwards; I realised that it would be uphill all the way to the airport. I registered some frustration with the approaching airliners because they were still at around a hundred metres in height when they drew level with me. If their speed was around 200 kilometres per hour then the airport-proper was still some way off, even though the perimeter fence had been an inanimate companion for quite some time.

Eventually the terminal appeared as a great, white rectangle of glass and concrete, with an angular control tower standing behind. By now I was extremely hot and, I have to say, a little bothered. Having walked so far in relative silence I was not prepared for the throngs of people milling about in front of Ercan's arrivals and departures building. There was much pushing and shoving, and once or twice my rucksack was collided into, half spinning me round and almost knocking me off my weary feet. I became a teeny bit peeved. These people had been dropped off in air-conditioned cars and had walked about twenty-five metres to an air-conditioned hall; I had just walked at least ninety kilometres in blazing heat – I was an uncredited misfit. Within two minutes I'd had enough of the bustle in the terminal and decided to cross the forecourt to a coffee house opposite the main building. Thankfully there was room to sit in the light-filled refectory, and my irritations subsided by the minute in the cool air and then by the second during a long drink of ice-cold Coca-Cola. I observed just how smart these travellers were; in comparison I must have presented a vagrant-like appearance, having spent the last three days living rough. I had just walked for four hours, and two of those hours were in temperatures of around 35°C.

In the chilled refectory I ordered a sausage sandwich and water to augment my salt-and-sugar-filled soda. I was charged such an eye-watering amount that I double-checked with the assistant to make sure it hadn't been miscalculated. When the sandwich failed to arrive and I approached the counter to enquire about its delay, there was much shrugging of shoulders (de rigueur in these parts); it turned out my order hadn't even been taken! This made the drinks even more expensive, and the adrenaline of shock ignited a desire to return to the road as soon as possible. I made my way to the toilet block, dampened my bandana and shirt to just short of dripping wet, and geared up for the walk out into the midmorning furnace!

Just outside the airport perimeter was a roundabout; it was a roundabout I had been expecting and the one I'd taken the first exit from when I crested the hilltop to arrive at the terminal. But… there was something that mystified me, and it was the beginning of a strength-sapping surprise and major disappointment. I shall endeavour to explain… If the city of Nicosia was a clock face, then, from the B16, main road, I expected to track directly west into the city and hit the suburbs at the 'three o'clock' point – because I was, then, positioned directly east of the centre. But my confusion arose from the fact that the second exit from the roundabout was clearly signposted as a dead end, and this was the road I'd planned to take. Much worse was to come. I knew I was easily within an evening's walk from Nicosia, as the crow flies, but I now found myself heading directly north… away from Nicosia! An enormous road sign, built for speeding motorists

to read, loudly proclaimed that Nicosia was still twe
kilometres away! The sign couldn't have had more impac
been loosed from its position to land violently on my dripping
head. Such was my despair and disbelief I stopped walking and
considered going back to double-check the dead-end signs. But
something suddenly dawned on me... It was the Green Line!
It was the line of demarcation that was preventing my route
back to the cool, linen sheets of the Cleopatra Hotel! In clock-
face terms I had to circumvent more than a quarter of the city's
perimeter and walk from 'three o'clock', anticlockwise round to
about 'twelve o'clock', before I could finally turn south to enter
Nicosia from the north. I was devastated. I had got so close to
finishing the first half of my journey along the Green Line to
ironically become a victim of it. Now, to make the Cleopatra by
evening time, I would have to walk another thirty kilometres!
Although a Friday night arrival appealed, delivering a neat and
full weekend in Nicosia, it would come at the cost of another
thirty scorching kilometres!

I had already walked about fifteen kilometres that morning
and the thought of walking twice that distance again just
didn't appeal. I regrouped and, as I hiked north along the dual
carriageway that circled Nicosia's eastern side, thought about
a contingency plan. I was very much in the land of the motor
car; overhead I was dwarfed by advertising boards the size of
facades from a Hollywood film set... All very *Great Gatsby*, but
thankfully the land was still some way from being like Scott
Fitzgerald's *Valley of Ashes*.

It was already near the time I generally took to the shade. I
was obviously a pitiful sight; a tiny car passed me and stopped
with the hard-shoulder line directly under the centre of the
vehicle. On this busy road this looked reckless, even if it *was*
an act of mercy. Thundering lorries were forced to take action
to avoid hitting the hatchback and this, in turn, caused fast cars
to break heavily in the outside lane. Even more worryingly the

car began to reverse towards me! Desperate to avoid being the indirect cause of mass carnage, I ran forward to speak to the driver, a smartly dressed woman of about forty. She asked me if I wanted a lift and I politely and swiftly declined. 'I'm fine, I'm stopping at the next village but thank you,' I said, waving her on urgently.

'Are you sure?' she replied.

'Yes, yes, I'm resting there, but thanks for the kind offer,' I reassured her and pointed at the village just ahead…

'OK – good luck!' and she was gone. The lady looked Cypriot but had spoken English with almost received pronunciation. I understood why she'd stopped… Anyone seen walking under the relentless sun would look crazy to local people, but I'd planned my rest stop and had enough water to last me until then. But my conspicuous presence on the hectic road obviously made me look vulnerable enough to cause a speedy motorist to pull over.

I took some comfort from the fact that, although I looked ridiculous to locals whizzing by in air-conditioned cars, I was equipped with top quality gear and obviously didn't look too unsavoury. The lady in the car was a very attractive, lone driver; I clearly wasn't a threat! If I *was* a degenerate criminal, I was one with Salomon footwear, Oakley shades and a Berghaus rucksack replete with a solar panel kit!

I was relieved when, after a few kilometres of horrible plodding, I was able to stumble down a steep bank of brilliant white stones to join a dusty track from the highway leading to the village of Balikesir. At least from this place the evening portion of my walk would have me heading west – albeit too far north – but westward towards the big city. I estimated that, in the heat, I was taking on half a litre of water per kilometre and needed to take my rest soon. A note in my diary simply says… 'GAS MARK 6!' (A reference to a high oven temperature – for those not in the know.)

I was still calculating how long it might take me to reach

Nicosia when I finally stepped onto a pristine new pavement in the south of Balikesir. It had taken an age to cover the last kilometre up to the village outskirts. I was on a stretch of road which had been laid to serve a forthcoming development, because the immaculate pathways provided the residents of Balikesir with a route to nowhere in particular. I returned to estimating my distance from the capital. If, with the rucksack and heat, I was averaging four kilometres an hour, it meant walking for about five hours from my usual set-out time of 6pm to reach my destination. *If* I made it… I'd arrive at the Cleopatra Hotel at about midnight! The problem was the landscape around the highway didn't present itself as being a suitable environment for wild camping. Either side of the busy road there were various kinds of infrastructure, and it was obvious that although Nicosia was some way off for a pedestrian, it was just a few minutes away via motorway in a vehicle. I was no longer in rural surroundings. Between Nicosia and Ercan airport there existed a concrete link, which was augmented by new developments and older housing. Certainly, the enchantments of the quiet villages of my journey so far were fading as if I were waking from a lovely dream.

The pleasant memories of my gentle ascent out of the Mesaoria plain were to be further displaced by the thoroughly horrible story of what happened in Balikesir in the August of 1974. It's interesting that many French people return vacant looks when the name of Agincourt is mentioned, a convenient memory blank for a humiliating French defeat at the hands of Henry V in 1415, when he conquered the French despite being hugely outnumbered. However, in the summer of 1944, Oradour-sur-Glane saw many French civilians massacred by the SS in one of the worst actions against non-combatants on French soil. After the war, President Charles de Gaulle ordered that the village be left exactly as it had been found following the atrocity. De Gaulle's move was both sensitive and wise; future generations could visit the village frozen in time, just as it was in June 1944, and see the evidence of what happened for themselves. No attempt by Germany to deny the event would ever look credible so long as the streets and houses of Oradour remained as a clearly visible testimony to the killings. With Balikesir, research under the village's Turkish name doesn't throw up much to be alarmed about. However, its former Greek title was Palekythro, and this name brings with it a terrible story. In August of 1974, the village bore witness to atrocities as bad as those memorialised in Oradour's unchanged streets. Several 'Turkish irregular soldiers' rounded up a few Greek villagers, including women and children, and killed them; around eighteen people died that day. Two brave youngsters, Costas and Petros Souppouris, escaped to tell the world what had happened. Years later, after DNA tests on a mass grave in Northern Cyprus, the boys were able to properly bury five members of their family, including their parents and siblings. The decade leading up to the massacre had seen Turkish Cypriots displaced by Greek Cypriots and then Turkish Cypriots returning... but some returned bent on revenge. This was such an ugly story that it is almost impossible to mitigate other than, at the time, the Turkish regular army might be credited with preventing further bloodshed. I refer to these horrors with full knowledge of similar barbarity in my own country's history. Amritsar in British India echoed with gunfire when a serving British army officer gave an order to open fire on an illegal gathering of civilians... hundreds died. To descend into deep error does not require a lengthy moral decline; the quagmire is only a slip away from what might feel like an elevated road. John Bunyan alluded to this in *The Pilgrim's Progress*.

I was congratulating myself on lugging the rucksack as far as I had in the intense heat when I came across two rough-looking builders working on another very uneven wall construction. I asked in controlled desperation where the village shop was; they watched me and paused before one man said, 'Market?'

'Yes please, market,' I replied. The other man, who had the bearing of labourer, pointed down a narrow street. I rounded a corner to discover, to my embarrassment, that the shop was about ten metres away! I turned back and shouted, '*Teşekkür ederim*'; they both raised their arms and, presumably, said whatever the Turkish is for 'English plonker'.

Inside the quiet shop an enormous man, who was inversely proportional to his tiny store, was sitting behind the counter sorting vegetables. 'Hello, where are you from? Are you from London?' he enquired.

'No...' I replied and, smiling inwardly, raised my left hand in preparation for the famous geography lesson. When I spread out my map and pointed at the mysterious, dead-end road, complaining about the detour, the man muttered four words which confirmed my suspicions. '*No! No! Soldiers! Soldiers!*' I'd heard these words before in Xylotymvou, but this time the negativity had caused me to go a great distance off-track. I was right, I knew the Buffer Zone dissected Nicosia – splitting it in two – but crossing points were few and far between, and entry routes from the east ran into Greek Cypriot territory. For those in Northern Cyprus, this meant roadblocks, barbed wire and all manner of military obstacles! I was a little embarrassed that I hadn't accounted for the Green Line's effect on my progress into the capital. Somewhere in Nicosia's no man's land there are shops, houses and garages which haven't been used since 1974. In one, a few 'new' cars sit rusting in a dusty showroom with odometers showing delivery mileage only, proof that the Buffer Zone has been very well maintained and very well guarded! I'd enjoyed daydreaming about an SAS-type raid with myself as a black-clad Ninja, launching a slick operation in which I enter the forbidden zone, locate the time-locked automobiles and emerge only seconds later clutching a pristine Toyota steering wheel as evidence of my audacity.

Balikesir seemed close to the Kyrenia mountains because the range tumbles south away from the north coast to almost kiss a few villages at the northern edge of the Mesaoria plain. I had tracked right across the enormous flat landscape, diagonally up from Paralimni to Balikesir and the black chevrons on my map were now so numerous that an impressive line showed I had made a significant dent in my overall plan. I had now covered about half the total walk, although that milestone would only be achieved when I climbed the steps to the Cleopatra Hotel.

Outside the little market I collapsed onto the entrance steps and immediately received a full-on attack from tiny, biting flies, probably owing to the presence of two oversized wheelie bins right next to me. I retreated to a disused veranda just metres away and, in the fly-free zone, set up a suburban bivouac of impressive design. As I was going to be there for some time, I unrolled my mat, used the tent pack as a pillow and took off my boots and socks. Having set up the solar charger to rejuvenate my phone and GoPro, I lay down in luxurious shade and broke several world records for the slowest-ever-consumption-of-an-ice-lolly. It was absolute heaven. I was surrounded by a scattered larder containing an ample bag of salted corn chips, a huge bottle of Coke, two bananas and lots of cold water.

I spent what was left of the morning and most of the afternoon observing village life. The shop was very busy, and with no obvious algorithm, a diminutive and vintage tractor seemed to be lapping the village and stopping at the shop every fifteen minutes or so. There was no application of a handbrake. The vehicle's weather-beaten driver, a man of advanced years with impossibly brown skin, simply stopped and lowered a huge hydraulic shovel that arrested the tractor efficiently as it looked heavier than the vehicle it was bolted to.

There was a call to prayer at around 10am and it sounded dreamlike to me as I was hearing it from a state of half-sleep. My walk, from just south of Dilekkaya, had taken about five hours to complete and my early start of 5am had my eyes closing within minutes of lying down. My body was attempting to restore some kind of balance and reclaim the lost sleep of the last few nights.

Across the road from my resting place several coloured doves were departing from or alighting on a red pantile roof. The fluttering of wings provided a soporific muzak to my afternoon's blend of scribbling and dozing.

Balikesir is a village which has a variety of small streets with equally small houses, each appearing to have been built with no thought to central thoroughfares. This means the little village roads twist and turn making a central maze. Further out, more modern buildings have been constructed along more typical, straighter avenues and, for anyone with a car, Balikesir might amount to a super suburb of the capital. I mused on the several villages encountered between Pergamos and Balikesir. They combined agrarian activities of yesteryear with less rural pursuits, so ageing farm machinery was likely to be seen next to a restaurant or taxi stand as village life diversified to survive.

Fortunately, for the whole time I lay on the porch I wasn't moved on at the end of a broom, as an unwelcome tramp might be. As the afternoon wore on, my bivouac yielded its shade to a growing patch of angry sunlight; the floor turned from a pleasant cool shelf to a sizzling griddle. It was time to move. I packed up and set out to look for another place to relax. There were two hours of rest and relaxation to enjoy before it was 6pm; I backtracked a little and relocated to a small play park which looked incongruously ultra-modern. Trusting that I would not appear too suspicious, I took to the lengthening shade of a public WC building. My excitement that the facilities might provide an opportunity for an extravagant wash was quashed when I discovered the loos were locked up tighter than Fort Knox…

*

One Day (3)

One day we went on holiday; a holiday in Cyprus is something of a misnomer because, to a great extent, for me every day was a holiday. My father rented a small cabin cruiser, and we launched out into the Mediterranean to claim inaccessible inlets and tiny beaches for ourselves. My two older sisters, newly returned from boarding school in the UK, were on their summer break and we sat with our legs through the boat's chrome railing as we circumnavigated a fair amount of the island's coast. Occasionally we'd steer into a cove of shimmering water, drop anchor and swim like birds fly. Suspended in the watery firmament we splashed about in the tepid sea and climbed back aboard just so we could jump back in, time after time. When the boat moved off it crashed through breakers; the plunging bow dipped our legs into the water repeatedly. Although our precarious position at the bow of the boat was unlikely to have survived a modern-day risk assessment, all I can recall is sustained laughter and my sophisticated and worldly sisters singing a rude song about a lavatory cleaner. I think my mother spent most of the cruise cramped in the cabin below where she suffered for her children's pleasure. This was just as well because my sisters' lyrics would never have made it through my mother's inbuilt decency filter.

I think it was on this same holiday that we joined a group of 'explorers' and made our way up through the Kyrenia mountains to a Byzantine castle at Buffavento. This was an extraordinary excursion which saw us climbing on horseback high into the massif. How, exactly, we came to book the adventure is something of a mystery to me, but I think it must have been via a private recommendation. It was so daring a journey that I cannot imagine any seafront tourism office advertising such a pilgrimage. Firstly, I can't recall ever seeing any seafront tourist booths, the like of which exist across Europe in their tens of thousands today. In those days, only a few holidaymakers visited Cyprus, and most of the well-known tourist destinations of today were then almost completely undeveloped for visitors. On our way up to Buffavento we lurched up steep goat paths and twisted and turned on dusty trails with the hooves of our mounts dislodging stones which fell down the mountainside and kept rolling until they were well out of sight.

Our guide was an elderly man who wore a tattered jacket of muted tweed and the traditional loose-fitting Greek trousers. He carried a long stick which he used to point out paths and maintain discipline in his team of mules and horses. He was attentive and endlessly patient as we made our way further and further away from civilisation. He also carried our food, along with the means to cook it. When the time came to eat, he chilled a bottle of white wine in a rushing stream of cool water. I was too young to be aware that, to our guide, our relationship was one familiar to every member of the rather embarrassing British Raj. The British Empire was eroding quickly; establishing control and introducing democracy across the globe was a recipe for eventual independence and rejection of the imperialists. Cyprus was no different. It had achieved its independence a decade before our journey into the mountains, but the relative wealth of Britain and the British still contrasted starkly with the economy of rural Cyprus. It was inevitable that, to some extent, we both played our roles as patron and patronised, though our origins were just as humble as those of our guide. It's likely that he thought we were better off than we were and we, in turn, had no idea about the life of the old man who fussed about us with all the demeanour of a mother bird.

The entire journey would have been perfect for an episode featuring Hercule Poirot. The landscape was a cinematographer's dream: sharp ridges of towering rock standing out against a deep blue sky, the relentless sun, the glistening backs of horses and their whiskered master. I could imagine close-ups of beads of sweat running down the foreheads of the hapless white

103

Raj... at any moment one of my sisters would scream and we'd discover a straggler slumped in his or her saddle. Fortunately, a plump Belgian would render the local police entirely redundant. However, because Hercule has always been the apparent common denominator in most cases of Art Deco homicide, we made it up and down the mountain without the need for any body bags courtesy of M. Poirot's absence.

Memories of Cyprus 1970–72

*

I had spent the afternoon trying to relax, but the challenge that lay ahead made me restless; my disquiet came from a slow acceptance of what I realised I had to do: prepare myself for a marathon walk! After about an hour I double-checked my toes, socks, boots and gear, and carefully distributed two litres of cold water amongst my rucksack and bumbag. I sorted my map and electronic equipment and used the last of my old water, now warm, to dampen my bandana and shirt. I carried out a failed precious-check and somehow left my white tube of skin cream behind, unseen against the white of the floor tiles I'd been resting on. I strapped on the rucksack very carefully, deposited a refuse bag of bivouac detritus in the park's bin and stepped out onto the hot road in pursuit of Nicosia. I knew I had to walk around twenty-five kilometres to reach the Cleopatra Hotel and confirmed that *if* I made it, I'd arrive just before midnight! I wasn't sure what the route would be like, but I hoped there would be plenty of places to buy drinks and snacks. I would need to take every opportunity to keep hydrated and nourished during the next five hours or so. I found a good road leading northwest to intersect the main highway leading west to Nicosia and, just less than one kilometre into my trek, I was relieved to see a shop. With a modicum of guilt, I made an early stop to buy a psychologically refreshing lemon ice pop; I was refreshed and had one less kilometre to deal with.

There was something deceptive about the dual carriageway which I was hiking along. Occasionally, enormous billboards gave the false impression that the city and its luxuries were immediately available or at least close by. Should I need a new bathroom, car or coquettish lipstick, Nicosia had it all, but to the pedestrian, these trappings of metropolitan life were still a marathon away and I didn't know when the Venetian gates of the old town would finally come into view.

As far as I could tell, my walking surface for the foreseeable future would be the hard shoulder of a very busy road, so I chose to walk facing the oncoming traffic, a strategy designed to afford me a few seconds to evade any stray vehicles by leaping over the road's metal barrier to safety. I thought this was better than trusting all the easterly drivers were awake *and* good at steering. I had a definite sense of literally going against the flow; the traffic leaving Nicosia was so heavy that I felt and looked to be a complete misfit swimming upstream against an insentient tide of smoking machinery. The easy gait of my evening walks of late was replaced with a brisk pace; just a few hours earlier I'd had time to let my eyes wander to distant horizons, but there on the racetrack out of Nicosia I had to keep my eyes on every approaching vehicle.

Over to my right, the Kyrenia mountain range was still a faded orange colour, but the sky was beginning to sharpen the outline of the mountains and increasingly darken them into a line of black pyramids stacked up against a brilliant sky and covering me in gloom. In the distance I could see the Turkish flag, laid out in painted stones, on the southern shoulder of what the Turks call the Beşparmaklar mountainside, facing Nicosia. Beside it, another ensign sat above a few Turkish words proclaiming, '*How happy is the one who says, I am a Turk*'. The words are attributed to a speech made by Atatürk in 1923, but on the hillside, it looked like hubris and provocation to me because I had heard the ghastly story of Palekythro. I had seen these enormous stone structures before but, until then, I wasn't aware that at night the outlines of the star and crescent are illuminated lest any observing Greek Cypriot should have an evening off hearing a message seemingly emanating from Ankara, Turkey's capital, flexing nationalistic muscle whether or not Turkish Cypriots wanted it.

I turned my attention back to the road and walked on. Looking around I noticed the land near the road showed an absence of grooming; large swathes of land between areas of housing were an unpleasant combination of *bondoo* and flowerless weeds. Occasionally, a dry riverbed was crossed, and sometimes roadside bushes invaded my path right up to the white demarcation line on the edge of the road. Whenever that was the case, I waited behind the bush for a gap in the traffic and hurried round the obstruction with an undignified rattle of water bottles and equipment. And so, the road continued on and on and on. Sweeping bends, which in a car would soon reveal a new vista, to the walker just very slowly unwound to show ever more kilometres of monotonous tarmac. My imagination was constructing footage of my son delivering a eulogy about a father who ended up under a bus in Northern Cyprus and this forced me to take further precautions. I stopped and took refuge over the road's barrier in the comparative safety of the litter-strewn verge to attach a flashing red headlight to my forehead. The idea was, that to oncoming traffic, this might look like the rear light of a cyclist or a moped and cause drivers to drift a little to their right allowing me more room. For most motorists it worked immediately and, courteously, I was given more space, but for some drivers it seemed to present a kind of target to aim at!

My bottles of water were getting warmer by the minute, which didn't bother me too much because they were for hydration more than refreshment. However, just then, on the other side of the cannonball run, I saw a minimarket and crossed the road to investigate. Bright neon signs adorned the outside of an immaculate store with an impressive deli counter and acres of ice-cold drinks. My attention was drawn to the water and ice cream sections, and I was about to pay for some provisions when two young Turkish girls approached and spoke to me. 'Hello, what are you doing?'

The innocent enquiry was probably the result of my looking like a one-man survey team with professional equipment and all manner of interesting gear like the curious red light blinking on my dripping forehead. I answered with sweat stinging my eyes. 'Ah, I'm walking across the island.'

'Why are you doing that?'

'Because I love Cyprus and I want to learn more about it,' I answered.

'Where are you going now?'

'Nicosia – *if* I make it tonight…' I sounded doubtful.

'Oh, you'll make it tonight,' said the first girl, looking at her friend for confirmation. Her pal nodded enthusiastically.

'Let me show you my map,' I said, switching to geography teacher mode. The line of black chevrons now resembled a stitched cut across fully half the island. I traced the line with my finger from Paralimni's coastal start point to the east of Nicosia. The girls sighed and spoke to each other. I observed the pair and suddenly realised they were both stunningly beautiful. They wore immaculate makeup and designer clothes which complimented their lovely figures, and each girl moved slowly and gracefully. In comparison to their uber coolness, sweat seemed to be running from beneath my bandana as if I were standing under a shower head. The girls were about the same age, in their twenties, and one was slightly taller than the other. The smaller girl addressed me once again.

'You're going to Nicosia now?' she asked.

'Yes,' I said.

'We could take you,' suggested the same girl with her brown almond eyes just inches from my face.

'I'm sorry but I have to walk,' I replied. 'I'm writing a story about my journey.'

'Where can we read 'bout this?' asked the taller girl, tucking strands of glistening hair behind a delicate ear.

'I'm not sure yet… maybe a paper, maybe a book or podcast?' I sounded uncertain. I wrote down an email address so they could make contact if they wanted to.

'Well, good luck,' they said, almost in unison.

'Thanks. Goodbye,' I replied and went to pay for my goods before stepping out to face Death-Race 2018 once again. I felt a little disappointed; those few moments of simple conversation were so welcome after hours of quiet on the road. Now for the first time I felt a bit sorry to be heading back to the loneliness of the highway. Perhaps my gloominess came from having to walk a depressing twenty-five metres in the wrong direction back to the road crossing. As I trudged back, my mind dealt with the beauty of the girls, and its neurons delivered a few moments of compounded loneliness. If this were a scene from a spy film this was the time to introduce the honey trap… I shrugged away the images and walked on, cool as a monk made entirely of cucumber.

My pace and rhythm returned to me as another lemon ice pop occupied my attention for at least three minutes. I was buoyed by the girls' encouragement that, I'd 'make it to Nicosia tonight', but this boost faded as depressing lengths of unpromising road emerged from every sweeping corner. I became tired of the road and its demand for complete attention, lest some motorist swapped concentration for reading a text message and ploughed into me. This made it difficult to enjoy the light changing on the mountains minute by minute; just one moment of distraction and I could be joining the various carrion along the road. Over the three days of my journey, I had seen: birds, dogs, cats, badgers, hedgehogs and snakes aplenty, all occupying only two dimensions on the surface of the road.

Just then, a white Mercedes passed me at around eighty kilometres per hour with less than a metre between me and its nearside; out loud I alluded to the driver being the very embodiment of a certain part of the male anatomy. I blamed adrenaline for the vulgarity and strode on, hoping that at some point the traffic would slow as the suburbs of Nicosia came upon me. Passing lorries displaced so much air that they moved me sideways whenever they thundered past, leaving a trail of black diesel smoke and a choking gall of fumes. Suddenly, a motorcyclist passed me doing about ninety kilometres per hour on just his back wheel; I considered getting off the crazy highway altogether, but the immediate terrain on both sides was unnavigable. After an hour and a half of this unpleasantness, I spotted a very smart garage and market complex and diverted to enjoy its relative calm. The entire site was colour coordinated in red neon livery and this carried with it the promise of an air-conditioned shop and the familiar sound of fridge and freezer machinery. The last few kilometres had seen me drenched in sweat and then repeatedly dusted by passing traffic. I had taken on the form of a grey ghost haunting the hard shoulder of the highway.

Inside, an assistant welcomed me. 'Hello, friend. Nice to see you.' Again, English... why not Russian or German? I returned the greeting and selected a Coke for salt and sugar purposes, a sports drink and several bottles of cold water from the rows of delight on display. Within moments of the transfer from the fridge to the shop's ambient air, the chilled containers were covered in condensation and yet the shop felt cool compared with outside. The evening was still suffocatingly hot. I sought some encouragement from the, by now, two young Turks serving at the counter.

'How far is it to Nicosia, please?' I asked.

'Maybe about half an hour?' suggested my friend.

'No, no, no! Not half an hour, much more than that... Nicosia is very far...' countered the newer man. I observed the disagreement, and the second guy reiterated his point. 'It is too far to walk – but you can catch a bus...' The man was pointing across the blur of traffic to a white shelter under which several disparate and ragged individuals were waiting for transport to the city.

'I can't take a bus, I have to walk, I'm afraid,' I replied. The two men capitulated and shrugged their shoulders.

'OK, OK, good luck,' they said.

I walked across the forecourt, finished my bottle of Coke in three swigs then drank half a bottle of water. I started a rhythmic consumption of the sports drink and water – one sip/ sports drink, two sips/water. I was confused by the nonchalant enthusiasm of the Turkish girls and the pessimism of the men in the garage. Just how far off was Nicosia? The bus crowd across the road were watching me like I was newly landed from another planet when a brightly lit bus pulled in concealing them from view and we lost sight of each other.

In front of me, the sun was still above the eastern horizon and the outline of a large building surrounded by four minarets, in classic Ottoman style, was starkly silhouetted against the evening sky. It was the Hala Sultan Mosque, its presence huge and somewhat controversial. The minarets are reputed to be sixty metres high and the whole structure is supposed to be a scaled-down version of the Selimiye Mosque in Edirne, Turkey. The brand-new place of worship was, at the time of my walk, due to open in a month's time, but not without some local Turkish Cypriot protest. Although exact figures are not available, the building might have cost more than thirty million dollars, with the money coming directly from the Turkish Government in Ankara. Protestors were arguing this money should have been spent on schools and hospitals first. Given what I had seen on the road from Pergamos to Nicosia, there was good evidence to support this argument. Turkish Cypriots with a leaning to the political Left claim they are an essentially secular society and have a natural affinity with Greek Cypriots, however tentative. Therefore, the new mosque is seen as a powerful statement of intent from Ankara which is not endorsed by many Turkish Cypriot people. With the Hala Sultan project some feel that President Erdoğan of Turkey might be impeding the islanders' (most islanders?) natural affinity for one another. The enormous structure now sits conspicuously on the outskirts of Nicosia acting as a reminder that Turkey is watching. Such actions might be interpreted as Turkey treating Cypriot soil as Turkish soil, and this drives a wedge between Turkish and Greek Cypriots, pushing the hope of a unified island, without mainland interference, out of reach.

The sight of the new mosque meant that I was now on the outskirts of Nicosia but still heading west and not south into the centre of the capital. I noticed the city's easternmost edge was clearly visible below me, occupying lower land and spreading out from the city's heart like the expanding rings of a stone dropped into water. Before I could turn left and head south, I needed to ensure that whichever road I took would not be a route leading to an impassable barrier of painted oil drums, barbed wire, soldiers and sandbags! As far as I could tell, I needed to take a road south from around the 'one o'clock' point or perhaps 'twelve o'clock' on my theoretical clock face. I would take careful note of any major road south and hope it would be clearly signposted as leading to the crossing point at Ledra Street. To my right, the Turkish star and crescent and their rectangular perimeter were now very clear on the southern flank of the Kyrenia range. The bright lights of the flag had an aesthetic quality which seemed to override any national point-scoring and just then it simply presented itself as an innocent illumination on a dark hillside.

I took some comfort when finally the main road had reduced in size to become suburban. On both sides of the now slower thoroughfare, I could see numerous car and van dealerships – the adjuncts of a city. Occasionally an out-of-centre furniture store appeared, but the path I was walking on was little used and poorly maintained and still had large areas of rough ground to walk over. There were many intersections too, and I had to navigate these with some speed because, by now, I was a gloomy, poorly lit walker with a vulnerability when viewed from side on.

I was pretty much exhausted but certain I still had about ten kilometres to go. I was concentrating so hard on just putting one foot in front of the other that I lost focus on my progress. How far round the clock face had I come? I suddenly realised that by now I must be ready to turn left and head south towards the crossing point. I felt a pang of sickness – had I gone too far west? Would I have to backtrack eastwards?! My joints ached and my sweat-soaked clothing had caused chafing in all sorts of places. I started to dream about a hot shower and clean sheets but denied these imaginations any longevity so I could remain focused on making progress towards the crossing point. I took bearings from the city's nightlights by waiting until a concentration of illuminations lay immediately south of me, which would be my cue to turn left. The seemingly relentless traffic had reduced to the point where there was now a little space between vehicles making crossing roads less deadly. Finally, I reached a junction which seemed to be a major road south, and a signpost indicated the road led to Nicosia's cultural centre. With an enormous sense of relief, I crossed a road with a little more spring in my step; finally I was heading south. I walked along a dark suburban street with several closed shop fronts and wondered if I was on the right road, just because it was so dark. Seeking encouragement, I stopped and asked a group of young Turkish men if I was heading the right way for Ledra Street. The youngsters were listening to loud music in a black Mercedes.

'Excuse me. Does this road lead to the border crossing at Ledra Street?' I waited nervously for a couple of seconds while a conversation in Turkish took place. An athletic-looking man in the front passenger seat turned to me and spoke to me with a London accent...

'Yes, bro... but it is far...' he said. I was delighting in the familiarity of his glottal stops when my heart sank at the news.

'How far?' I enquired.

'It's about a thirty-minute walk, bro. Do you want a lift?' he replied. I needed to make something of a paradigm shift; to an immaculate Turkish youth in sports clothing a thirty-minute walk in the evening heat was crazy – but to me... thirty minutes meant I was practically there!

'Thirty minutes! That's great. Thank you. I'm fine walking – I have to walk... I'm walking across the island.' The group in the car laughed and wished me good luck; I walked on with the sound of their laughter fading behind me. After a short distance a man on a scooter pulled up beside me.

'Hello, sir. Where are you going?'

'Ledra Street, border crossing,' I replied. 'How far is it?'

'A long way; maybe forty minutes,' he said.

The discrepancy in estimations of distances was something I was quickly becoming used to and, to me, a variance of ten minutes was still negligible. Even so, I was having to deliberately swing my legs like a man with some serious problem centred around the spinal cord, and every area of my body either ached or felt like it was chafing and sore. I thanked the guy on the bike, and he zoomed off into blackness. I watched him diminish into the night and imagined how pleasant it would be to make progress with the simple twist of a throttle. I discovered a very short pause of less than a minute restored the legs and feet enough to allow for a few minutes of good walking. This was the rhythm I maintained as I approached Eldorado, with the Ledra Street crossing as a prize in my imagined City of Gold! Soon

I found I was stopping about every hundred metres or so to adjust my rucksack; my gait was unbalanced and ungainly. For a moment I considered giving up and catching a taxi to my hotel from this side of the Green Line. However, that would involve a circuitous route further west to access south Nicosia at another crossing point open to vehicles. It would also mean having to return to a 'legal' starting point in Northern Cyprus on Monday, and that would involve a frivolous crossing and recrossing of the border point, which had no appeal at all. I chose to ignore the pain and press on.

The road leading down towards the border wasn't direct, it tracked west for a while, and I passed a few incongruous boutiques, flower shops and restaurants before I spotted something I thought might be a problem. I could see the old city walls and its lines of palm trees, but there was also a roadblock and diversion in operation. At a large roundabout with a circumference of black and white kerb stones I saw several police cars and a police motorcycle propped on its stand. I wasn't in the mood for a diversion. I decided to just walk through, stepping into the concealing gloom of the palm trees near a high wall to circumvent the roadblock.

As I drew near, I realised the road was closed to traffic but not pedestrians. The relief was immense, considering I was within a short walk of the Ledra Street crossing. My road in seemed easy to navigate, as if gravity itself were guiding me horizontally. Suddenly I saw a wonderful sight… A few yards in front stood a lovely floodlit Venetian arch. I was close to the dark Turkish streets I had explored just a few days earlier, but now it seemed like weeks ago. This was Kyrenia Gate, the ancient northern access point to and from the old Venetian city. It was easy to imagine laden mules entering or leaving the town burdened with silks, dates or spices centuries before I entered with my own more prosaic load. The stones of the gate were garnished with a vibrant green palm wafting lazily in the evening breeze.

If the stones could talk, would their stories be of romance and smuggling and spies, gold and girls and rumours of what merchants had discovered at the edge of the known world?

I crossed a deserted patio area and found myself just beyond where I had walked a few days before; a dimly lit minaret guided me towards the checkpoint. The streets were inky and quiet, and the warm air hummed with the sound of cicadas. My spirits were lifting as I walked on towards my goal. I allowed my mind to assess my body's status; I had a nagging blister on the inside of a toe, my joints ached, and my skin was probably vibrant red in places. I was wet through with sweat but… I'd done it! I'd made it to Nicosia and the border crossing was now just minutes away. I managed to navigate my way through the darkness and to locate the few, narrow streets that were familiar to me.

As I drew closer to the checkpoint, I hoped I'd be able to navigate the maze of tiny streets that make up the cultural Turkish Quarter. There were so few points of reference at street level; I needed to keep looking up at the green-lit minaret to find my way through the darkness. Suddenly, I emerged at an intersection of streets, recognising a circular bench which was occupied by a few shadowy figures all smoking Turkish cigarettes and drinking Coca-Cola. I nodded in place of speech and each of the smokers smiled and nodded back. To my left lay a brightly lit street with buildings on either side close enough to give the little road the feel of a corridor. Mercifully, I had finally arrived at the border control point.

I slowed to an amble and presented my passport to a smartly dressed border guard. '*Teşekkür ederim*,' I said. The guard smiled wryly and processed my document. After a few seconds I was able to proceed.

The space between the two control points in central Nicosia is fascinating. On either side, roads leading off, east and west, are barricaded. Yet, if you look up at the peeling paint on the shuttered windows or gaze through the barbed wire and steel of the blockades, a different world comes into view. The walls are pockmarked with bullet holes and mortar strikes, but the lovely houses, empty for nearly half a century, still possess a faded elegance. It is easy to imagine a wealthy, fifteenth-century Venetian merchant entertaining guests and regaling them with tales of the spice trails and storms survived at sea. There is an irony to the tranquillity found in no man's land; peace and quiet are the strange brood of war and disquiet.

There are about a hundred metres between the two control points, and I hobbled up to the less formal Greek border and saw I was being observed with some amusement by the officials in the booth, so rather defensively I said, 'I've walked from Dilekkaya today.'

My boast was met with an uninterested smile, and I was waved through without so much as a question.

On the other side, the vibrant Ledra Street crowd were all but gone. An Orthodox priest sat quietly dealing with the theological challenge of an ice cream, a skinny cat slinked around a corner and a few late diners sat outside bars and restaurants enjoying a still warm and very late evening. I knew exactly what I was going to do...

... The Cleopatra Hotel lay slightly south *and* east of me, so when I resumed my walk on Monday, strictly speaking, I would be further east than I was now. This meant, in my mind, I could quite 'legally' catch a taxi back to my hotel because I was, in fact, going the wrong way! I stopped at a road which crossed the pedestrian area of Ledra Street and took off my heavy rucksack. My body suddenly felt supernaturally light as I rested on an uncomfortable traffic barrier and waited... Sitting was an utter joy! I was watching for a vehicle with an illuminated sign on its roof, and after just three minutes I waved down a cab, shoved myself and my kit into the back seat and asked for the Cleopatra Hotel. The driver turned to me and smiled before saying, 'Cleopatra. Yes.' The taxi pulled away.

I sat like a remote tribesman in the back of a spaceship and marvelled at the speed of the car. I just sat quietly for the few minutes it took to reach the familiar frontage of the Cleopatra. I paid the fare and tumbled out of the air-chilled taxi making doubly sure, in my stupefied state, I'd not left anything on the back seat. The taxi had delivered me to a row of steps which were now all that stood between me and two days of indulgent luxury. I spent a second or two just staring at the short stairway before wearily climbing up and entering the cool lobby. When I approached the reception desk, I was relieved to discover they were expecting me! Before I started my journey, I had told the staff that I would be returning in *about* three days but, with so many unknowns, I wasn't sure exactly when. I had emailed my intent to make it late that day, but I hadn't actually guaranteed my arrival!

Before a word was said, the lovely receptionist held out my key card, and within seconds I was in the tiny lift and heading for my first proper wash in over three days of enduring dust, unrelenting heat and about a hundred kilometres of scorched road and baking trail. I noticed I was swaying with fatigue. I went back over the day's events; there had been twenty hours between dressing that morning, just south of Dilekkaya, and my arrival at the Ledra Street crossing. To reach Nicosia had meant a walk of at least forty kilometres or around twenty-five miles of strength-sapping and super-heated road!

I opened the door to my room and did exactly what I had been longing to do for the last several hours... I dumped my rucksack on the floor, fell backwards onto the bed and, with my dusty boots suspended over the end of the mattress, just lay there for a long time – perhaps about fifteen minutes, just staring at the ceiling and NOT walking!

I was just over halfway across the island, and it was time for a very long shower. Depriving oneself of the things we in the West take for granted daily should be a compulsory part of our education system. The luxury of hot and cold taps, showers, flushing lavatories and clean, dry towels become much appreciated when they've been absent from your life for a few days. There, in my room, I was as rich as Nebuchadnezzar, and the double bed was my hanging garden of Babylon with a mattress covered with four acres of smooth, cool linen. I stood adjusting to my new surroundings, wondering what to do first; I was newly landed on a strange planet. The bed looked inviting, and I was exhausted and sore, but I was also shaded grey from the repeated and alternating coats of roadside dust and my constant sweat. I showered and allowed the water to just flood over my aching limbs in an extravagance of cascading joy. I washed my feet and observed crusted lines of black dirt erode and vanish from the tops of my toes. I tidied the little shower room and walked into the air-conditioned bedroom, which looked to me like a marbled palace fit for Solomon or a bejewelled maharaja. The presence of the bed was all I needed in the room but here I had a desk and chair, TV, telephone and Wi-Fi. After the twenty-five miles or more of baking road, these adjuncts were of no immediate interest to me and so, finally, I slid into the vast, flat and deliciously cool bed. I fizzed with gratitude and fell asleep in seconds.

The Blue Berets

I found you by the dam, inappropriately dressed in full uniform,
wearing wrong berets,
I knew nothing of unrest or patrolled borders,
Strange soldiers; dis-camouflaged and crowned with blue,
Even I knew there was something juvenile in your behaviour,
I shared your finding simple joy;
Took comfort from seeing adults behave like me,
Your grown-up world a less-scary certainty,
You pulled carp from the crowded bottom of the drought-shrunk
waters,
You smiled at me and delighted in returning to your sport,
Now I know you were just boys too,
Displaced from Bury or Furness, Cardiff or Dundee...

M.J.W. Clark – *Memories of Cyprus 1970–72*

5

The Republic of Cyprus & Northern Cyprus

A Weekend in Nicosia – Part 1

Saturday 9 June 2018

I awoke the next morning with a luxurious stretch and the sensation of cool sheets, air conditioning and a flat bed of vast width. Streaming through my blinds were soft and golden beams which caressed the eyelids courtesy of the Mediterranean sun rising in an ocean of light blue sky. The next two days were to be spent recovering and assessing the lessons I had learned from the first half of my journey. I wanted to take a slow walk through the wonderful streets of the ancient heart of Nicosia; to imbibe its stories and try to fathom what lay at the centre of its multiple tenancies. I felt that in those quiet corners of Nicosia – just metres from the chain stores and tourist hordes – there must lie some answers. Was there an Excalibur not yet withdrawn? I had a longing to take the sword away with me, or at least grasp the handle and give it a rattle.

My day started with a profound appreciation of taps, toilets and towels. Travelling through many places across the face of the planet has taught me, as an adult, to deeply value things which might appear mundane. Showering in water supplied from a tall but open water tower in Uganda had taught me to shower with my mouth closed. To 'fully utilise' an African 'long drop' would have anyone singing the praises of a water closet – but there in my hotel room I had all modern conveniences at my fingertips, and I felt grateful that I was *already* grateful! I washed my outer clothes and sent my underwear to be cauterised by lasers. I enjoyed a shave to rid myself of an itchy early beard and hung my clothes to drip dry from the top of the shower enclosure. My legs felt stiff (diary entry says 'Painful') and reluctant to be of service again, but in the shower the muscles had started to lose what was left of the lactic acid associated with extreme effort. I dressed in clean clothes and, for some reason, felt guilty for the indulgence of clean sports socks which to me looked entirely suitable for a transfiguration. I was certain Moses and Elijah would be impressed.

My morning was infused with feelings of great accomplishment. I knew that I hadn't walked the Amazon or conquered the South Pole, but my weeks of planning and months of musing on the journey had resulted in my having to drag a dream into hard reality. I had gathered equipment, made arrangements at home for my absence and booked a hotel, car and flights. I had studied satellite images and pored over maps, but eventually I had to stand with my heels in the sea and begin striding west, not knowing what each day would bring. Apart from a slightly lop-sided final stage to Part One of the walk, everything had worked out well.

Although I don't suffer from a compulsive disorder, there was something a little retentive, yet irresistible, about enjoying an entire and neatly clipped weekend in the capital. It seemed 'very tidy' to break my walk in two, with the luxury of a complete Saturday and Sunday spent following my nose through the quiet and tiny streets of old Nicosia. I must confess that the capital-or-bust state of mind played a significant part in my completing Friday's gruelling marathon walk.

It was still early but, for me, 7am was a disgusting lie-in worthy of the most recalcitrant teenager. I went over the last three days and enjoyed the images as they formed in my mind. I recalled the quiet sand trail from the calm sea to the road near Paralimni, the hasty camp in the darkening field near Frenaros and my oven-hot bivouac en route to Xylotymvou. I considered Slinky the Dog, the night near Pergamos, the little Turkish coffee house in Türkmenköy with Ali the Red Falcon, Emine and the VIP Café. I thought about the lovely quiet villages that I'd passed through en route to Dilekkaya, the midnight farmer, the frying pan highway near Balikesir, the Turkish beauty queens and the tortuous walk into Nicosia. Underscoring the latter images were the plaintive cries of the muezzins; all these images were covered over by skies of passive blue, an unambiguous sun and hour upon hour of a peace so tangible, it thrilled the mind and lifted the heart. I was infused with such joy that I was sure my pores were oozing a gratitudinous light.

Before breakfast – a proper breakfast with a table and chair – I quickly separated my equipment into two distinct groups: essential and non-essential. With the benefit of three and a half days of walking 'in anger', I dispensed with various electrical cables and remote switches used for filming. I ditched my water pouch, two bottles of 'dry' detergent, a washing line and waterproof sandals, along with various other pieces of unused kit including a small, collapsible shovel. With the loss of the camel pouch and its contents, my backpack was suddenly lighter by several kilos. With these reductions I calculated that on Monday I would be walking out of Nicosia with a pack seven kilos lighter. This was a decision mitigated by a confidence that civilisation was never far away from my intended route west and, apart from my ascent and descent in the hills near my destination of Kato Pyrgos, there should be plenty of places to take on water a litre at a time.

Nicosia hasn't always been the capital of Cyprus and, given that Cyprus is an island, it's not surprising that the ancient port of Salamis once claimed that accolade. Apparently, it competed with Paphos as the most important port in ancient times. St Paul landed at Salamis and walked across the island to Paphos and, for some of my walk, I had probably been close to the route he had taken. It's probable that because Paphos and Salamis were vulnerable to attacks from the sea, an inland city or capital was something of a necessity. So, around the seventh century, Nicosia became the centre for trade and commerce. Later, in the sixteenth century, the Venetians established the town further by building defensive walls which ringed a now thriving inner city. I was interested to see what Nicosia had to offer for a mildly enthusiastic historian like me, but I was keen to concentrate my time in one small area of the old town. I wanted to take a detailed look at one site rather than attempting to briefly examine the numerous historic sites spanning the wonderful but sadly divided capital.

I was soon to discover that any visitor to ancient Nicosia has an advantage over most tourists exploring the great and ancient cities of Europe – where most fall foul of the postmodern 'privilege' of easy tourism. For example, anyone having visited Rome in the summer will have found themselves bewildered by the madding crowds of visitors all eagerly following a brightly coloured umbrella or selfie stick – topped out with bizarre collections of paraphernalia – to help them identify their guide. Like swarms of ducklings, they follow Mother Duck at a brisk pace and strain their ears to hear a monotonous patter which attempts to inform them about what they're speeding past. Ubiquitous Japanese students make equally ubiquitous peace signs to each other's cameras and hordes of street vendors try to sell you tiny Perspex Colosseums or other Romanalia, no doubt made in China. Ice creams and sodas can be purchased in exchange for bars of bullion, and the sound of jazz standards carries the full length of ancient colonnades, blending the images of Caesar and Sinatra or

Claudius and Cole, crooning their incongruous way through the Great American Songbook. Yet somehow Nicosia remains relatively unvisited, untarnished and ignored by the massing crowds of Euro-tourists. Even more remarkable given the fairly unrestricted access afforded to anyone interested in the ancient history of Cyprus. The same is true of the wider island, which is abundantly rich in Classical sites. In Rome you can queue for hours to visit Roman ruins, but in Cyprus the same might be enjoyed in delightful silence and isolation. For example, the bleached stones of the Roman curium near Episkopi offset the blue waters of the Mediterranean in spectacular fashion, yet any visitor to the site might sit alone for hours without so much as a hint of a selfie stick or peace sign.

After a healthy breakfast of fresh orange juice, yoghurt and honey, I swapped my walking boots for trainers filled with helium and floated, rucksack free, towards Ledra Street in central Nicosia. My route took me north, from the quiet location of Florinis Street up towards the border crossing which was a ten-minute walk away. I passed several smart boutiques and sports shops, and at a busy junction, I was delighted to see a fading advertising structure above a classic 1970s balcony. The shopfront below was a typical blend of metal and glass, but overhead, and unaltered for decades, an elaborate, patinated and vintage sign boasted the name ROLEX along with the familiar gold crown emblem. I would recommend all visitors to Nicosia to raise their gaze; any number of apparently uninteresting facades are often just a few feet vertically from lovely balconies and shuttered windows revealing a gentler, more lovely Nicosia. The buildings are often constructed close together with honey-coloured stones and terracotta roof tiles. In quieter streets, a glance through double doors might reveal a courtyard beyond, canopied with vines or lavished with flowers. The evening sun accompanies these sights perfectly as if the places were built just for the end of the working day which, of course… they were.

I crossed Eleftheria Square where major work was underway to link the old Venetian walls and moat with Ledra Street. This famous thoroughfare runs obliquely north and south and, approaching from the south, its northern end delivers the walker to a passport control booth. Above the street, triangles of yellow and white material had been strung from the buildings providing partial shade to the shoppers below, looking for all the world as if a giantess had hung her bikini up to dry. Ledra Street is the main tourist area and, in the evenings, numerous tavernas serve traditional Greek cuisine to the sound of traditional Greek music. I was making my way to the Turkish side of Nicosia, interested to walk the hundred metres or so between the two passport controls as slowly as I could. So far, I'd made two night crossings, one on my first evening in Cyprus a few days earlier and another late last night, but now I was going to be able to see no man's land in daylight. The name 'no man's land' is perfectly apt because once you have had your passport examined and its details logged, it seems the world has lost interest in you. Dwelling in the limbo of nobody's territory finds you momentarily dispossessed of a host. For a few moments you are not in any country at all, and a strange sensation of caprice takes hold, like those rare occasions when the teacher leaves a class alone and the students' suppressed spirits surface quickly shattering the usual order and quiet. Perhaps that's why, written on the walls of the long-abandoned houses, various miscreants have sprayed messages, ranging from, 'NO-ARMIES' to 'ONE CYPRUS'. Magnanimous, at least.

The short passage of no man's land has a few side streets which, prior to 1974, were lined with simple domestic residences. Here, Greek and Turkish Cypriots had once lived side by side; there are many stories about close friends being divided by a war each had no interest in. Indeed, most villages along what is now the Buffer Zone contained Greek and Turkish Cypriot communities with families whose children played together,

126

grew up together and for whom any ethnic differences were entirely invisible.

I took a few moments to gaze through the various barriers which prevented access to the disused side streets. Barbed wire, corrugated iron or more formidable railings allowed only a glance into avenues yielding to weeds and decades of settled dust. For me, the buildings were just as I remembered from when I'd lived here almost fifty years ago. To my yearning eyes the infrastructure of separation quickly disappeared, and I was an eight-year-old boy again, watching a warm evening come to life as my mind peopled the houses with their lost owners. These dwellings had shuttered windows to keep the inner sanctuaries cool and glassless doors opening straight onto sleepy streets. In the evening, after watering time, the occupants of these buildings would emerge and just sit silently to observe the conclusion of the day. Now their lovely dwelling places were deeply marked with bullet holes or damage from mortar shells. These streets must have been the backdrop for vicious fighting during the war of 1974. It seemed wrong that these silent thoroughfares were no longer open for the innocent wheels of a child's scooter, a breezy conversation about the progress of a vine or local gossip brimming with the fat of life. Should an infant squeeze through the bars of a barricade and run, shrieking with delight, down any one of these ghostly corridors it would seem entirely inappropriate to counter the action with talk of the UN or opposing governments. The child wins.

I entered the maintained area of the Turkish border control and presented my passport. I thanked the official and walked into northern Nicosia, but this time with the benefit of daylight. Days earlier, my passage into these streets had been a little disconcerting; the contrast with southern Nicosia was stark. Then, I'd noticed that the main streets were poorly lit, and any side street existed in complete gloom, a footpad's paradise. This dissuaded even the most arduous night adventurer from straying far from the relative safety of the high street, not least because it was difficult to see anything.

Even in the late morning sunshine it was obvious that I had changed countries. Here, the fashionable chain boutiques and outlets of Ledra Street were replaced with numerous private vendors, selling jeans and T-shirts made in the Far East. Several small grocery stores sold confectionery, Turkish Delight and brands of cigarettes unrecognisable to the average Western European. Local cafés lacked the commercial edge of their south Nicosia counterparts and had the bearing of the more rural coffee shops found in the small villages of Cyprus. A glance at the tables and chairs at one establishment revealed only a pair of moustachioed Turkish gentlemen drinking black coffee and smoking Turkish cigarettes; there were no crowds of Western tourists having a late breakfast. After a few metres I rounded a corner to find even these few lively places of trade faded rapidly to an array of deserted and scruffy shops. Outlets with dusty windows had floors littered with a detritus of scattered coat hangers or empty clothes rails, evidence of the difficulties of trading without the official recognition of the wider world. Even more shocking were a few buildings which had eroded to nothing. Where once a house may have stood there was now just a pile of mouldy rubble topped with weeds and open to the elements. After a while, once I'd found my bearings, I realised this was caused by the intrusion of the Buffer Zone. Some abandoned buildings within no man's land were attached to other structures nearby and this caused a domino effect, impacting neighbouring houses too. It seemed remarkable that such a dereliction should exist so close to the neon glare of modern Ledra Street residing just a few hundred metres down a dusty corridor.

My intention that morning was to locate the recently restored Armenian monastery in north Nicosia's Arab Ahmet quarter. This site has been the subject of extensive research thanks to a privately funded United Nations project. I was interested in this place for a few reasons. Firstly, presumably, Islamic authorities had been pleased to accede to the request to restore what is a site of *Christian* historic interest. Secondly, the restoration had been carried out with a view to seeking peace between those on both sides of the Green Line.

In contrast to the busyness of Ledra Street, the narrow passages and twisting walkways of the Arab Ahmet quarter were practically deserted. The old buildings on either side of me loomed above my head and shaded me from the rising sun. A black and white cat lazily crossed my path and disappeared through a broken fence; I wondered if the feline stalked the entire metropolitan section of the Buffer Zone and whether its furry ancestors had patrolled the same hunting paths back in 1974.

The paving of the streets was litter-less and polished by footfall; the sunlight reaching the road surface reflected back in shimmering sheets of silver. I rounded a tight corner and found the arched entrance to an open courtyard. Inside, a few trees gave dappled shade to a mixture of ancient and modern structures. On my right, as seemed perfectly apt that day, an ageing security guard was fast asleep in his glass-fronted office. I paused for a moment just in case I needed to pay an entrance fee, but the dozing guard didn't stir so I walked quietly across the courtyard to a series of arches bordering the far side of the compound. I was in a roofless colonnade of whitewashed walls and sandstone arches flanking the main sanctuary to my right. If this were Rome I would have been in an international scrum. In Nicosia, I could hear myself breathing…

*

One Day (4)

One day we visited Paphos. To reach the little port meant taking the old seaside road from Limassol and heading west. Today, this road has been replaced with an impressive coastal highway, but in 1970–72 the road was a single carriageway affair with acute hairpin turns. Between Paphos and Limassol the road is regularly flanked by high cliffs where enormous vultures nested and took to the air to soar overhead. Despite a disinterest in the living, the birds sailed and circled menacingly in a sea of sky, always watching, and waiting. Occasionally, the road surface might be strewn with fallen stones from the steep and arid hillsides bordering the tarmac. At night, the unlit highway hid from view the sheer drop which awaited anyone who might nod off at the wheel. The reason I tell this 'One Day' story is simple... Paphos was a tiny village with, as far as I can remember, hardly any buildings. You might see a few fishermen drinking coffee and mending nets and, most memorably... a pelican. That's about it! There were traces of the Ottoman Empire with the remains of an old fort, but Paphos felt literally like the end of the road, and to arrive in such an insular place felt like an intrusion into the home of a stranger. Anyone pulling up in a car was immediately conspicuous because I honestly don't think any locals had cars; they had boats, and should they want to visit the relative metropolis of Limassol they probably took a bus. I remember the faces of the fishermen bent over their nets and their downward gaze and our shared awkwardness. Within a few years the cranes would arrive, hotels would be built, new restaurants would open to feed the masses and the whole exponential exacerbation would happen. In my mind I erase the infrastructure, I remove the hotels and the shopping centres, and with every absent building an area of ancient Paphos is restored. I swipe away the swimming pools and the countless bars until only the fishermen remain – the fishermen and the pelican.

On our way back home, we would stop off at a mysterious necropolis called the Tombs of the Kings and run around the subterranean caverns enjoying the short echo of our rudely loud voices. Perhaps we might swim near Aphrodite's Rock in the early evening, and despite the goddess status of Aphrodite and the *aching beauty of her birthplace, we might have the entire beach to ourselves. There were no bars, nobody came looking for commerce and Aphrodite would have looked quite inconspicuous if she'd chosen to emerge from the lovely waters once again. No wonder someone had decided her birthplace for her… what else could have happened there? Beauty was the mother of invention.*

Time moves on and generations fade away taking their stories to the grave, buried stories of glorious mundanity. The old fishermen down in the harbour are gone, but somewhere, under the foundations of a modern hotel, lie stones once dislodged by the feet of ancient shepherds and mariners, or a hillside where lovers kissed or the foundations of long forgotten houses. How can we know exactly what we are seeing unless we look with two pairs of eyes? A pair to deliver an image to the brain and a pair to enlighten us enough to tattoo our soul with understanding. These are the only tattoos that matter – ones which cannot be seen. In my attempts to remember not *to forget, I take comfort from the words written near the graves of unknown soldiers: 'Known Unto God'. Every absent fisherman, shepherd or flower girl from yesterday's Paphos shares the epitaph.*

Memories of Cyprus 1970–72

*

I wasn't sure exactly what I was looking for that morning, but I suspected it would be part of the minutiae of the fourteenth century. It is the *minutiae* of any historic period that interests me most. To understand any particular period usually takes a great commitment to study the politics and geopolitics of a time and place; great care must be taken not to superimpose anachronisms of the contemporary mind. Yet the observation of small details can uncover a shortcut to better know the past. For example, with an entire afternoon on my idle hands, I once found myself examining a wonderful collection of ancient statues at a museum in Crete. Each was carefully labelled with a detailed description of where they were found, what period they were from and of whom they were a facsimile.

We are not all historians and few of us possess the discipline to really *see* a past era properly, but most of us *are* equipped with some degree of curiosity about the past. Why? Because we instinctively recognise it is part of who we are, and whether a Roman citizen or modern Londoner, we share things in common. Mark Antony certainly drank a cup of water and although it probably lacked fluoride, it would be a similar experience to our drinking a cup of water today. Should it be possible for any one of us to share a drink with the young general we might both gasp for air after downing the water and issue a knowing smile at one another. Mark Antony would know nothing of doing eighty kilometres per hour in a car or making a telephone call, but I am always on the lookout for what we have in common or *almost* in common. It's the similarity of our lives which fascinates me most, thus it's the *minutiae* of everyday life that I'm interested in.

To return to the statues in Crete... I had observed one diminutive likeness in a wonderfully preserved figure of a child aged about 10 to 12 years. I took the piece in quickly, noticing the Roman hairstyle and familiar Classical robe, but none of this really intrigued me; I was drawn to the extremely detailed carving on the subject's feet. There, in fine detail, were a pair of leather sandals with soles and strapping. To their owner they were just utilitarian and functionary, but should I have found myself in the Classical world then, just possibly, these would have been what I needed to wear; here was an amplified instruction manual detailing how to attach them to one's feet. Without knowing in-depth reasons behind the crossing of the Rubicon, or how and why Rome burned, I was immediately linked, albeit tenuously, to the great Roman Empire by looking closely at a pair of sandals.

So, there in the courtyard of the Armenian church in Nicosia, I was on the hunt for a hint of humanity; a tell-tale sign to join me to the practices of the fourteenth century; to open, as it were, a metaphysical doorway leading to a few moments in a vastly different century but perhaps not an entirely different world.

I made my way into the main sanctuary of the monastery and found many of the adjuncts of Gothic architecture: vaulted ceilings with exposed sandstone arches, clover-shaped windows, intricately carved stonework over shallow shelving and an impressive apse flooded with natural light from a collection of high windows. I attempted to filter out later additions: an icon of the Madonna and child, a candelabra, electric uplighting, modern coloured glass and a wooden cover over the altar area. Focusing my inner eye only on original features, which wasn't easy given the building's post-restoration state, I discovered areas of modern carving had been inserted into spaces where original work had disappeared over many centuries. Behind me, I couldn't avoid seeing what I suspected was a nineteenth-century augmentation; a large wooden balcony served to separate the 'great and good' from a more plebeian congregation below, in direct conflict with Christ's message of inclusivity.

An archway had been sealed up with close-matching stonework and I was alarmed to see what looked like hundreds of bullet holes in the more recent masonry. Were they bullet holes? Had a conquering Turk fired a machine gun at the wall to express his vengeance? Was there a more prosaic explanation?

I was about to leave the courtyard without any real discovery when my attention was drawn to a pair of Gothic panels either side of a decorative arch. I noticed there was no symmetry to a line of crosses which had been crudely carved into the stonework. On the left there were four Maltese crosses, usually associated with St John, and on the right, four thin, equilateral crosses had been scratched into the surface. However, it wasn't the design of the crosses that caught my attention, it was their rustic nature. Having witnessed some of the carnage exacted on Nicosia's architecture, I had arrived at the conclusion that for centuries, a laissez-faire atmosphere existed in the capital. Wandering amongst the town's various ancient structures it was commonplace to witness the most genteel of ancient arches crudely altered with coarse, square lintels. Entrances and exits had been sealed up with indecent haste and successive generations had made no effort to preserve any former venerations at all. There, in the Armenian church, some apparently unskilled rustic had taken a piece of metal and scored out lopsided and uneven crosses as his contribution to the aesthetic of the sanctuary. It wasn't much, but it was this sense of freedom to adorn a sacred building with one's own child-like art that most appealed to me in that hour of solace and silence spent in the old monastery. If I was right, much of Nicosia's ancient infrastructure seemed to have escaped the oversight and rigidity of strict authoritarian control, either sacred or secular. In the little Armenian compound, I imagined a benevolent and endlessly patient priest catching a junior monk at work with a rusty nail and just patting him on the shoulder whilst enthusing over the amateur artwork with all the passivity found in the countenance of a kindergarten teacher.

Despite its history of conflict, in times of peace, ancient Nicosia must have been quite laid back. Even as late as the nineteenth century, Luigi Palma di Cesnola had found Cyprus lacking the control and administration one might expect on an island with so many important sites of historic interest. He seems to have taken advantage of this innocence. Was Cyprus just a place where the joy of life came first? Had it always been a place of relaxation; where crusading knights passed through or rested from their long journeys; where ancient Romans escaped the power of Rome to build quiet villas in the foothills of Troodos? Has the location of Cyprus, between Europe and Asia, and its island status created a unique history and almost playground atmosphere? There is something different about this beautiful island; it's as if people change when they set foot on such a cosmopolitan place where traditions have been melded. Where, over centuries, people have lived and let live, making the entire island a haven for short and long-term visitors. Though in actuality, desire for control of the island has meant various invasions and a succession of overseers. Despite this turbulent history, the boats, the cargoes and the disparate peoples just kept arriving.

For the time being my shallow anthropological studies were over and my mind was beginning to form clearer and clearer images of poolside relaxation – with no musings on fourteenth-century carvings or their origins. I headed back across the border, slowly ambling through no man's land as was my custom. I retraced my steps to the relative quiet of Florinis Street and the cool interior of the Cleopatra Hotel. I spent the rest of the baking afternoon realising the earlier poolside images, battling through Aldous Huxley's *After Many a Summer* and resisting an ice-cold lager from the South Pacific-looking bar. I was still determined not to partake until I had successfully crossed the entire island.

The poolside wasn't crowded, there were just a few young Greek Cypriot families who were in town to visit relatives. The hotel's excellent food and quiet dining area attracted several large family gatherings. I was pleased *not* to have my suspension in Cypriot life disturbed by a plethora of Premier League football shirts and loud, beer belly behaviour. The bar was manned by Stelios, a handsome young undergraduate studying law, while Aphrodite herself was on lifeguard duty, going under the mortal moniker of Rafael. I was genuinely surprised there wasn't a queue of young men throwing themselves into the pool and feigning a dramatic drowning in order to have the very lovely 'Rafrodite' dive in to save them! Amusingly, the dining area around the pool presented Greek life in a manner akin to depictions of the world at the

Epcot centre at Disney World, Florida. Someone had created an entirely faux, Greek-style village in a metropolitan suburb. Rustic house facades, with closed shutters over the windows, provided an effective screen between the pool and an adjacent car park. There were several carefully arranged Greek urns and blocks of sandstone, probably made of fibreglass, which served to create the illusion the hotel's pool was actually situated in a rural Cypriot village. With Disney, their inauthentic Europe is thousands of miles from the authentic original, but here the fake village was a ten-minute drive from the real thing!

In the evening I spent a little time talking to a friend I had met in the hotel. One of Cleopatra's most cosmopolitan members of staff was the ubiquitous Costas, a multilingual and multifunctional waiter and bar confidante. Costas was a tall, middle-aged man who spoke fluent English with a sonic mix of Harry Enfield and Del Boy. He told me some fascinating stories and one in particular was quite incredible. Costas' Cypriot family were living in London in 1974 and one day his father announced that they were to return to Cyprus to start a business in Famagusta. In the large Greek Cypriot community of London, there was some disquiet about the future for their young republic homeland and not a few misgivings about the island's relationship with the Greek Government in Athens. His father was adamant, and flights were booked for the family's return late in July. Costas said they were due to leave on 16 July 1974 – just four days before the Turkish army 'invaded' or 'intervened' depending on your viewpoint. At the very last minute, Costas' father decided against the return to Famagusta and the flights were never taken. A very close shave! Heaven knows what would have happened to the family and eight-year-old Costas had they arrived in the middle of a vicious battle. Later, when Archbishop Makarios sought refuge from a Greek junta intent on his harm, a young Costas was taken to a venue in Camden Town where an impromptu and chaotic meeting was convened at which the

Primate was due to appear. Costas told me he could reme
a black-clad figure squeezing through an elated crowd of c..,
Cypriots, with Makarios shouting, 'I'M ALIVE! I'M ALIVE!'
Rumours were abounding that Makarios had been assassinated
or was being held in a martial jail but suddenly there he was – in
Camden!

Costas didn't return to Cyprus permanently until relatively
recently; he seemed delighted to be home and, during one
prolonged discourse in the Cleopatra's Baroque-themed bar, he
described Cyprus as paradise. I enjoyed listening to his stories,
all delivered in a wonderful Greek Del Boy, dulcet lilt. Knowing
that Costas was generally not far away whenever I was resident
at the Cleopatra, lent the uncomplicated and comfortable hotel
a more homely feel. Should I return there some day, I'm certain
Costas and I will pick up exactly where we left off. I was deeply
grateful that he went the extra mile for me on many occasions.

Back in my room the shocking indulgence of a wall-mounted
TV revealed that the FIFA World Cup was about to get underway.
I remembered the competition in 1970, the year I first arrived in
Cyprus; the bright golden shirt of Pelé and the iconic black and
white footballs of Mexico. Before long I was fast asleep – Fatigue
3 World Cup 0.

The Vultures of Episkopi

Wheel o'erhead your vanishing smoke,
Priestly plumes staining sleepy blue,
Spin ghastly black your feathered cloak,
High clifftop home from where you flew,

Darkly made – clearing befouled air,
Divine appointment – much maligned,
They flock to hear your final prayer,
Stock now stilled lain silently blind,

Signalled to land and hide the dead,
Episkopi's dark arts unfurled,
Loss turned to gain their gamey bread,
Overflown by the underworld.

M.J.W. Clark – *Memories of Cyprus 1970–72*

6

The Republic of Cyprus & Northern Cyprus

A Weekend in Nicosia – Part 2

Sunday 10 June 2018

I breakfasted and left my hotel at around 9am and made my way through the quiet streets near the Cleopatra. The previous day I had located the Turkish bath house on my walk round the cobbled streets of north Nicosia's cultural quarter and I was intent on a revisit. I navigated my way across the building site just south of Ledra Street and crossed the border into north Nicosia. Once more, I crept slowly through the corridor linking the two sides of the capital and realised that everything was as it was before; the changing world, which we are all subject to, does not exist there. Only the elements were at work to alter the buildings; no windows had been repainted, no doors had been renewed, weeds remained untreated. There was no vacant wicker chair awaiting the return of a wise elder who might sit and watch an evening's idle drama unfurl. Even a cemetery changes with every new resident, but there in no man's land *nothing* changed. The absence of man was, *ipso facto*, the removal of a body's vital organs leaving a hollow carcass, lifeless and dry as a mummy. This was why, for me, it was so fascinating; as if, when I was a boy, someone had blown a whistle, ushered everyone out and waited for the child to return as a man. Somewhere, just along the side streets, there are shops with TVs containing unused 1970s technology and classic-shaped Coke bottles resting on tables covered in an almost sacred dust. There are walls plastered with advertisements for cars long since out of production. The streets are a *Mary Celeste* of the world I remember so well; a three-dimensional, living photograph of boyhood haunts causing me a profound confusion of sorrow and joy.

I've never really understood why archaeologists need to dig whenever they want to find out about the lives, cultures and buildings of our ancestors. Surely not everything built in the past is slowly shrouded by an accumulation of dust or dirt. Presumably, the Parthenon didn't need its columns to be revealed courtesy of a shovel, nor, I suspect, did the Pyramids of Giza. However, on a recent trip to Rome, I visited St Clement's Basilica, which seemed to testify against my theory. The comparatively modern sanctuary had been built on the partly demolished remains of a fourth-century church, which itself had been built on what remained of an earlier, pagan temple. Anyone descending the steps into the foundations of the basilica would be able to witness a journey back through time with every few centimetres of descent into the earth's growth rings.

In Nicosia, the Büyük Hamam Turkish bath house was half submerged into its surroundings as if it were slowly submitting to a sea of quicksand. A long while ago, a UK children's programme featured their best ever presenter, John Noakes, having a Turkish bath. Poor old John was pummelled and dowsed in hot water until his skin was red. Although this looked to be an equal amalgamation of torture and ablution, it was also something I was interested in trying. It seemed, to me, a way of scrubbing away the aches and grime I'd accumulated between the coast near Paralimni and the ancient metropolis. Tomorrow's 'walkout' would at least start with a degree of cleanliness which no amount of showering could provide.

To enter the baths I had to descend a stone stairway beginning halfway up the building at ground level. A notice explaining the opening hours was ambiguous in its accuracy, as it attempted to outline men's days and women's days of operation. According to the notice, the place was due to open at 10am, but at five past the hour it was still shut and unpromisingly silent.

To kill time, I circled an irregular block of shops and cafés until I paused to buy a bottle of water from a stocky shopkeeper. He was lazily leaning on a peeling doorframe and thumbing his bright yellow *subha*. *Subha* are a set of Islamic prayer beads – in this case, thirty-three beads, each one representing praise to Allah. As I observed the process, I mused on the incentive behind the practice. To me it seemed to rely on the premise that God would be satisfied to be in receipt of a mindless petition. Presumably, one might fasten beads to the tops of one's shoes, whereupon every step would be a prayer – even if your feet were bent on evil. I questioned the shopkeeper about the meaning of his beads; he produced a gap-toothed smile and admitted he had no idea what the beads meant, which made us both laugh out loud as if we were old friends sharing a joke. As I understand it, after prayers, three phrases are to be repeated thirty-three times: 'Glorious is God', 'All Praises to God' and 'God is Great'. The beads make this ritual less of a monotony for the tongue. In much the same way, the Rosary of Catholicism was designed to aid the memory of the mysteries of faith, but if it becomes a fetish, it might also reduce sacred beliefs to mindless and impersonal superstition.

From what I had seen, the Muslims of Northern Cyprus were neither extremists nor fundamentalists. Cyprus, despite its mix of majority Greek Orthodox and minority Islamic peoples, has always been a secular society with religion being something of a private affair. Northern Cyprus, not being mainland Turkey,

COMPLETE ROUTE

MEDITERRANEAN SEA

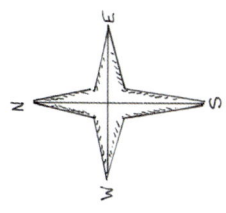

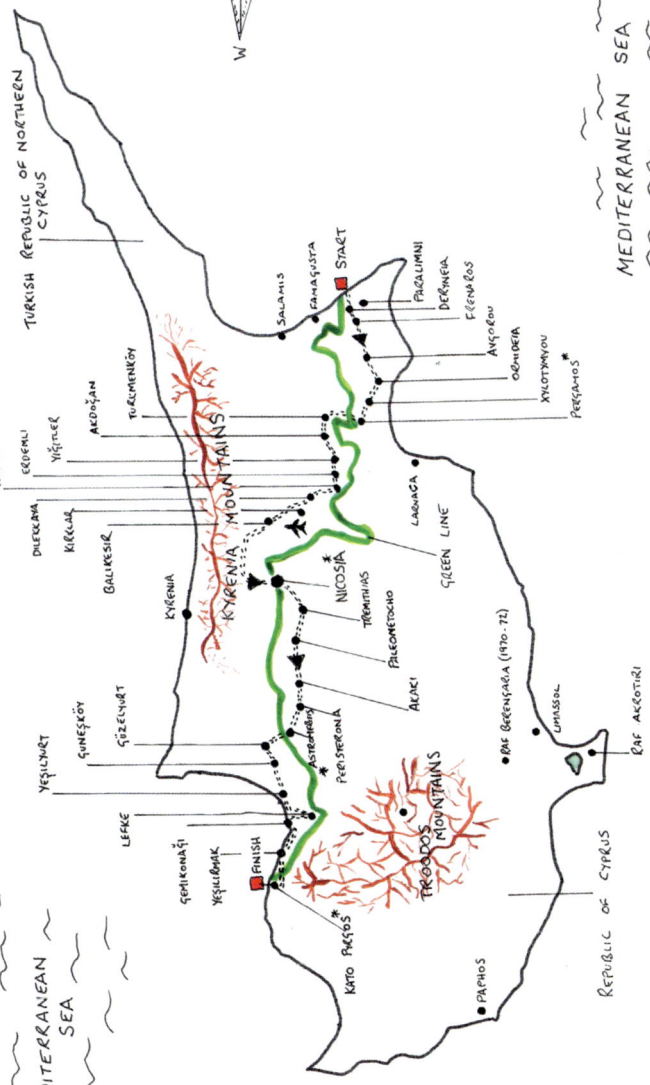

N · E · S · W

TURKISH REPUBLIC OF NORTHERN CYPRUS

SALAMIS
FAMAGUSTA
START
PARALIMNI
DEKHELA
FRENAROS
AVGOROU
OCHIDEA
XYLOTYMVOU
PERGAMOS
LARNACA
GREEN LINE

TURCMENKÖY
AKDOĞAN
VADILI
GEÇITKALE
KIRIKKALE
DÜZOVA
DILEKKAYA
KIRKLAR
BALIKESIR
KYRENIA
KYRENIA MOUNTAINS

NICOSIA
TRIMITHIAS
PALEOMETOCHO
AKAKI
ASTROMERITIS
PERISTERONA

YEŞILYURT
GÜNEŞKÖY
GÜZELYURT
LEFKE
YEŞILIRMAK
ŞEMIKONAĞI
FINISH
KATO PYRGOS

TROODOS MOUNTAINS

RAF BERENGARIA (1970-72)
LIMASSOL
RAF AKROTIRI
PAPHOS
REPUBLIC OF CYPRUS

MEDITERRANEAN SEA

KEY
* BORDER CROSSINGS
Green Line
My Route
Ercan Airport

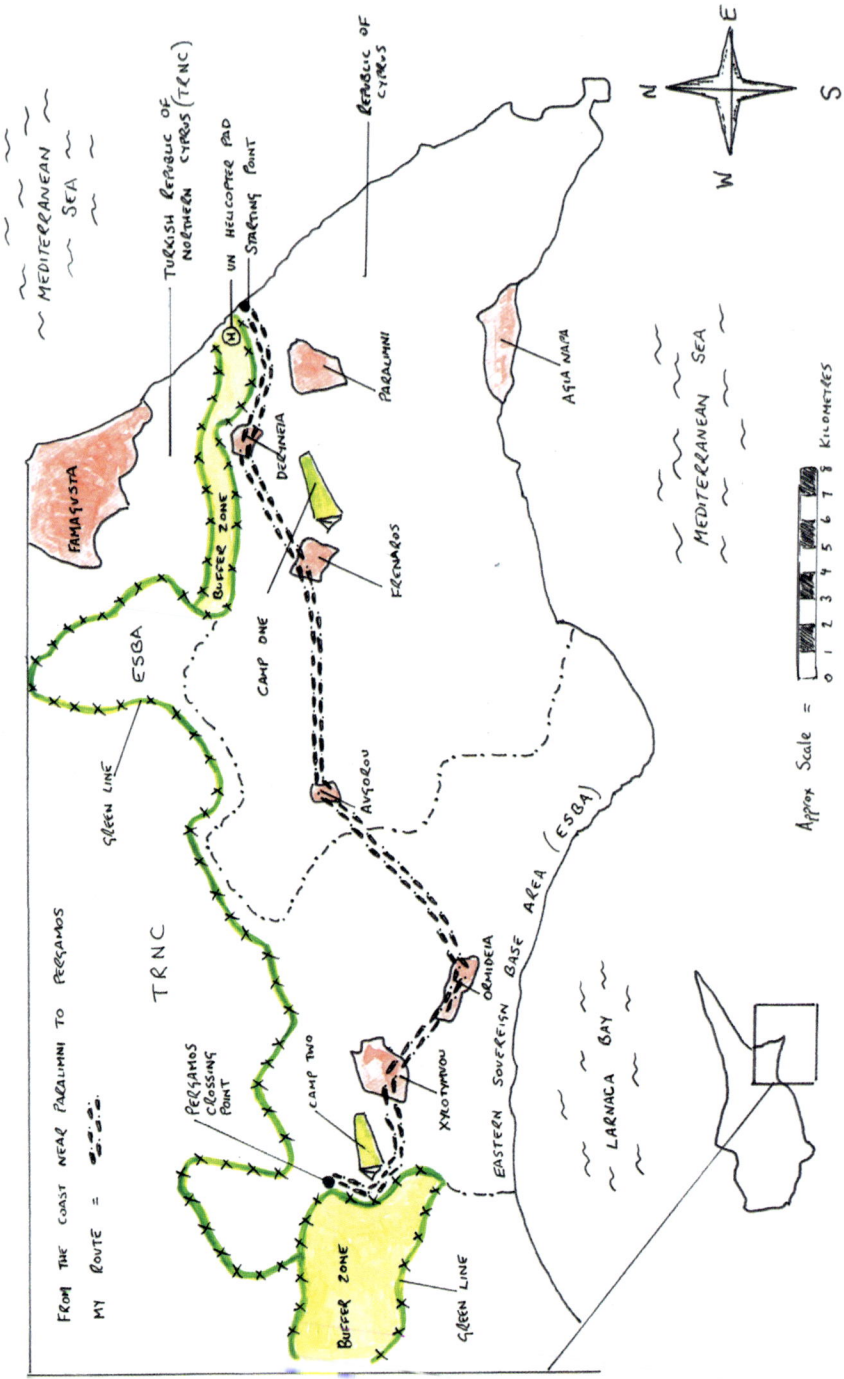

From the coast near Paralimni to Pergamos

My route = ·—·—·—

MEDITERRANEAN SEA

TURKISH REPUBLIC OF NORTHERN CYPRUS (TRNC)

UN HELICOPTER PAD STARTING POINT

REPUBLIC OF CYPRUS

FAMAGUSTA

BUFFER ZONE

GREEN LINE

ESBA

TRNC

DEKHELIA

PARALIMNI

FRENAROS

AYIA NAPA

CAMP ONE

MEDITERRANEAN SEA

AVGOROU

ESBA

GREEN LINE

PERGAMOS CROSSING POINT

CAMP TWO

ORMIDEIA

XYLOTYMBOU

EASTERN SOVEREIGN BASE AREA (ESBA)

BUFFER ZONE

GREEN LINE

LARNACA BAY

Approx Scale = 0 1 2 3 4 5 6 7 8 KILOMETRES

N E W S

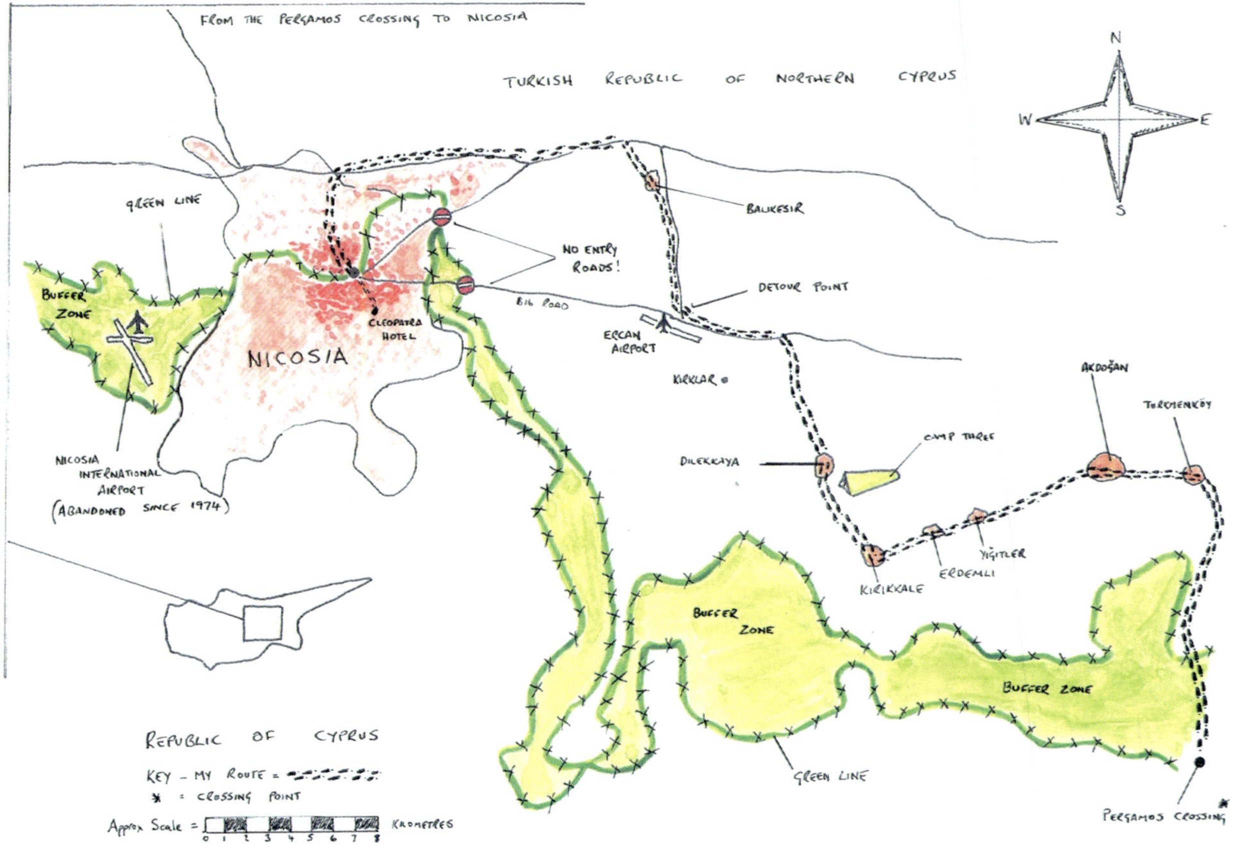

FROM THE PERGAMOS CROSSING TO NICOSIA

TURKISH REPUBLIC OF NORTHERN CYPRUS

N E S W

BALIKESIR

DETOUR POINT

No ENTRY ROADS!

BIG ROAD

KIRKLAR •

ERCAN AIRPORT

TAŞKENKÖY

AKINCILAR

HAMITKÖY

ERDEMLI

KÜÇÜKKALE

CAMP THREE

DİKKELİYA

BUFFER ZONE

BUFFER ZONE

GREEN LINE

PERGAMOS CROSSING

CLEOPATRA HOTEL

NICOSIA

GREEN LINE

BUFFER ZONE

NICOSIA INTERNATIONAL AIRPORT (ABANDONED SINCE 1974)

REPUBLIC OF CYPRUS

KEY — MY ROUTE = – – – – –
* = CROSSING POINT

APPROX SCALE = 0 1 2 3 4 5 6 7 8
KILOMETRES

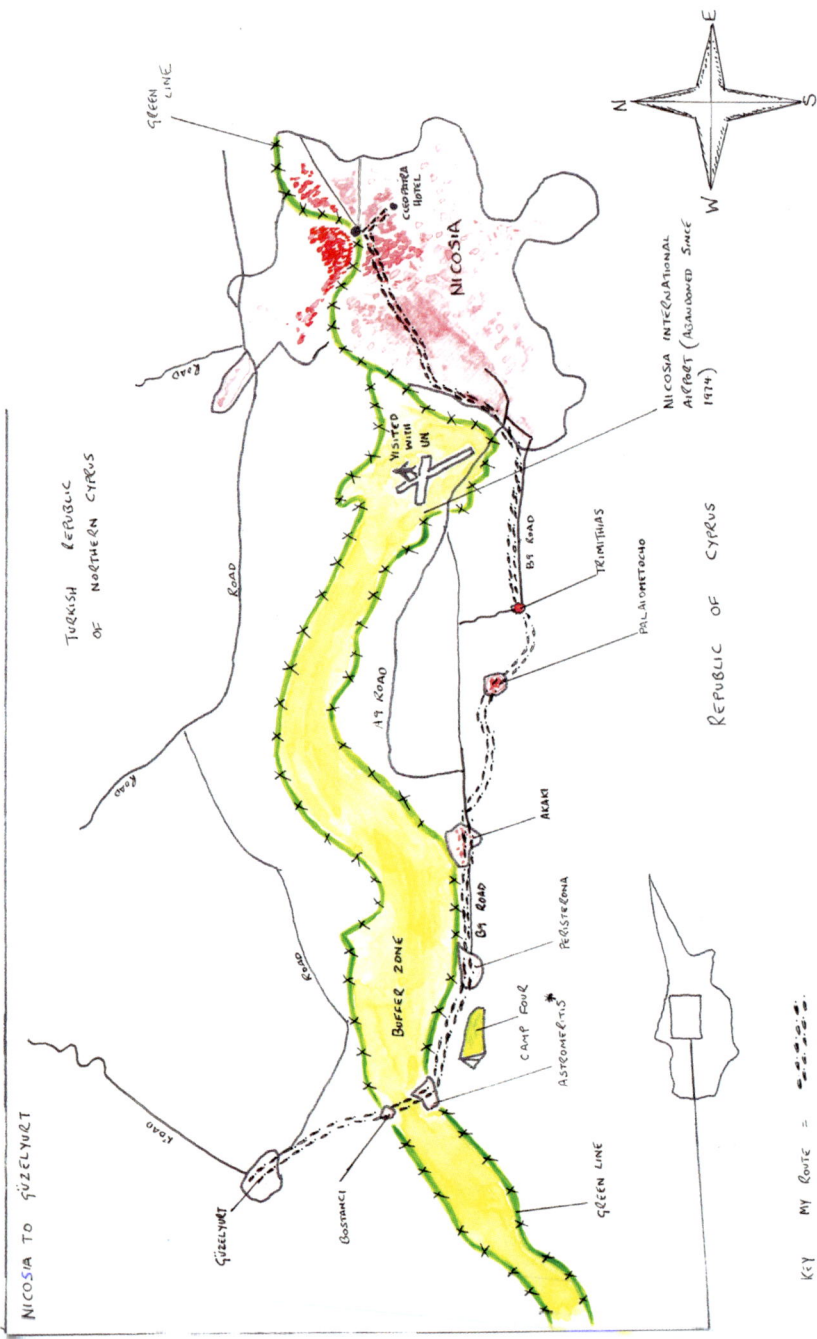

NICOSIA TO GÜZELYURT

TURKISH REPUBLIC
OF NORTHERN CYPRUS

GREEN LINE

ROAD

ROAD

CLEOPATRA HOTEL

NICOSIA

NICOSIA INTERNATIONAL
AIRPORT (ABANDONED SINCE
1974)

VISITED
WITH
UN

REPUBLIC OF CYPRUS

B9 ROAD

TRIMITHIAS

PALAIOMETOCHO

A9 ROAD

AKAKI

ROAD

B1 ROAD

PERISTERONA

ROAD

BUFFER ZONE

CAMP FOUR

ASTROMERITIS

GÜZELYURT

BOSTANCI

GREEN LINE

KEY   MY ROUTE = ·–·–·–·
       CROSSING POINT

Approx. SCALE = 0 1 2 3 4 5 6 7 8 KILOMETRES

N E S W

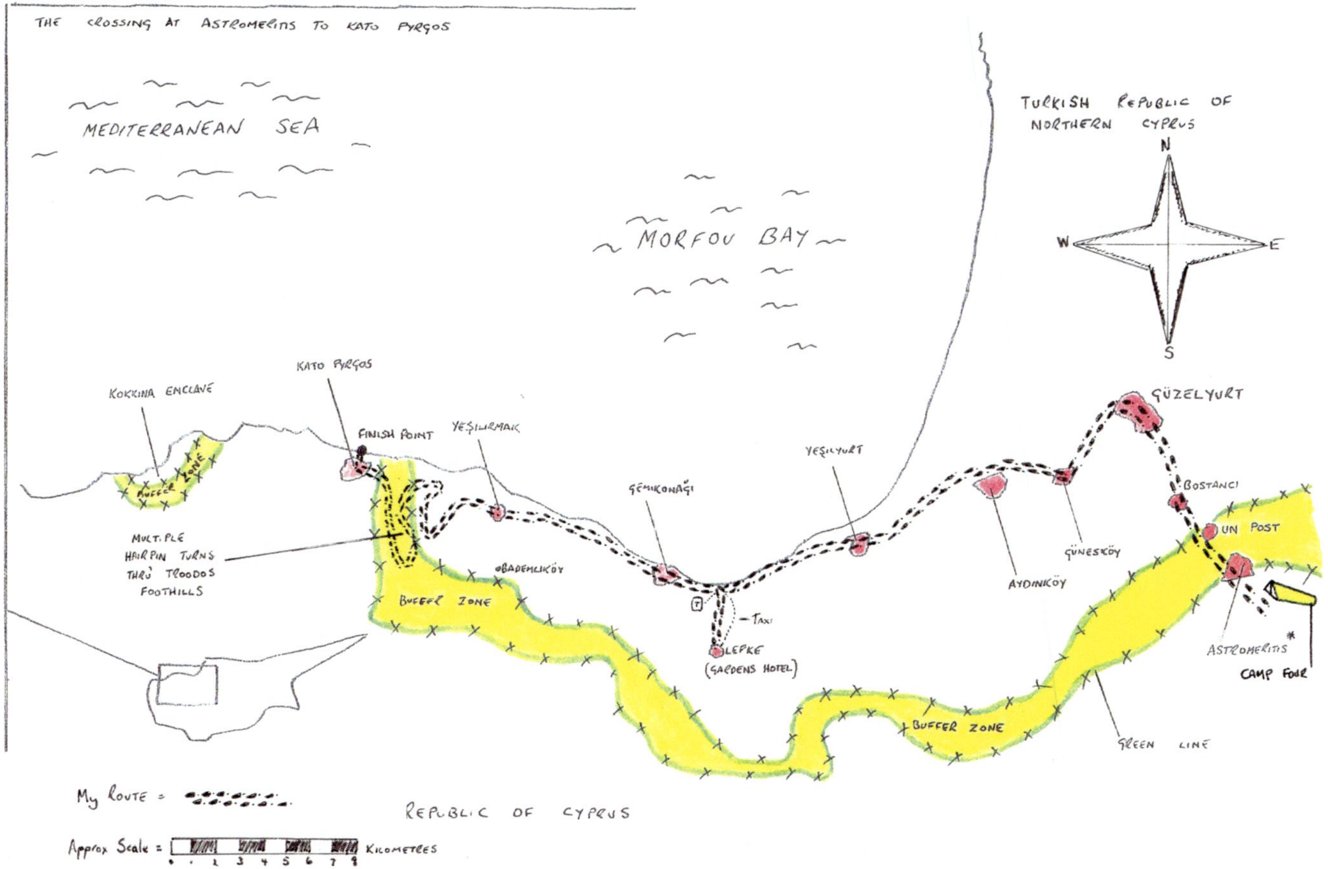

THE CROSSING AT ASTROMERINS TO KATO PYRGOS

TURKISH REPUBLIC OF NORTHERN CYPRUS

MEDITERRANEAN SEA

~ MORFOU BAY ~

GÜZELYURT

BOSTANCI

UN POST

ASTROMERINS

CAMP FOLE

ŞIRINEVLER

AYDINKÖY

GREEN LINE

YEŞILYURT

BUFFER ZONE

TAXI

LEFKE

(GARDENS HOTEL)

ŞEMIKONAĞI

GABRIELKÖY

BUFFER ZONE

FINISH POINT

YEŞILIRMAK

KATO PYRGOS

MULTIPLE HAIRPIN TURNS THRO TROODOS FOOTHILLS

KOKKINA ENCLAVE

REPUBLIC OF CYPRUS

My Route = ·—·—·—·

Approx Scale : |___|___|___|___|___|___| Kilometres
                0 1 2 3 4 5 6 7 8

*A tiny sparrow alighted on a branch just above my head – she was
so close I could have blown her feathers…*

The author - Berengaria - 1971

The author - Berengaria - 1971

Left to right from top:
1. *The author in training.*
2. *Kit check at The Cleopatra Hotel.*
3. *Air traffic control tower, Nicosia Airport.*
4. *The terminal at Nicosia Airport.*
5. *Abandoned Cyprus' Airways Trident.*

Left to right from top:

1. *Shackleton wreckage, Nicosia Airport.*
2. *'Disused' UN outpost, number 146 near Paralimni.*
3. *The starting point of my journey, the coast near Paralimni.*

Left to right from top:

1. Rustic artwork, Armenian church and monastery, Nicosia's Arab Ahmet Quarter – TRNC.
2. Memorial to the Morfou Heroes Astromeritis, Republic of Cyprus.
3. Old car, Republic of Cyprus.
4. My house.

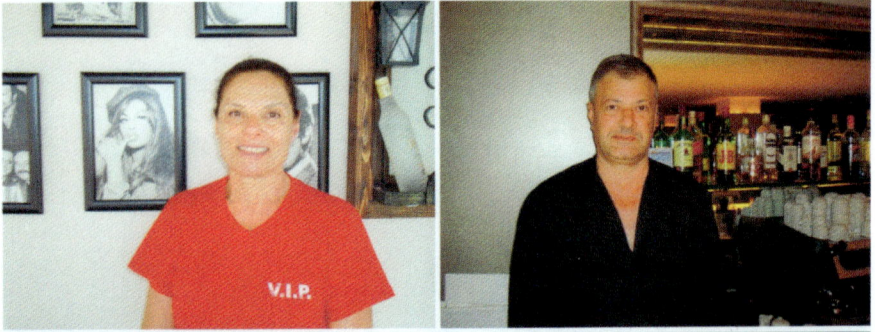

Left to right from top:

1. *Emine from the VIP bar in Agdoğan, TRNC.*
2. *Costas from The Cleopatra Hotel, Republic of Cyprus.*
3. *The Hala Sultan Mosque, TRNC.*

Left to right from top:

1, 2. *Graffiti within the buffer zone, Nicosia.*
3. *The illuminated Turkish flag near Nicosia.*
4. *A patinated door, Nicosia.*

Left to right from top:

1. *Lookout post, TRNC.*
2. *Turkish military warning.*
3. *Cengiz Topel Memorial near Gemikonağı, TRNC.*

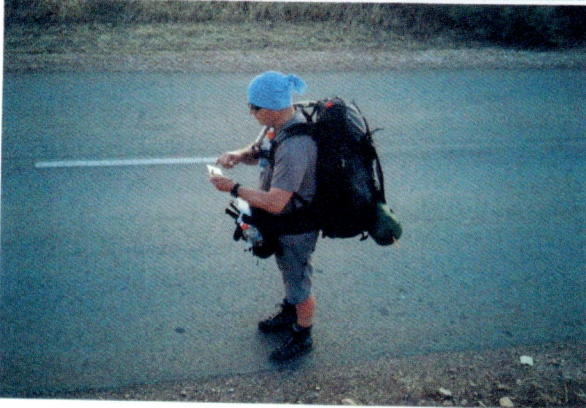

Left to right from top:

1. *Greek Cypriot military cemetery near Nicosia.*
2. *Turkish Cypriot memorial in Pergamos.*
3. *Ancient building in the TRNC.*
4. *Mosque and Orthodox Church in Turkmenköy.*
5. *The author en route.*

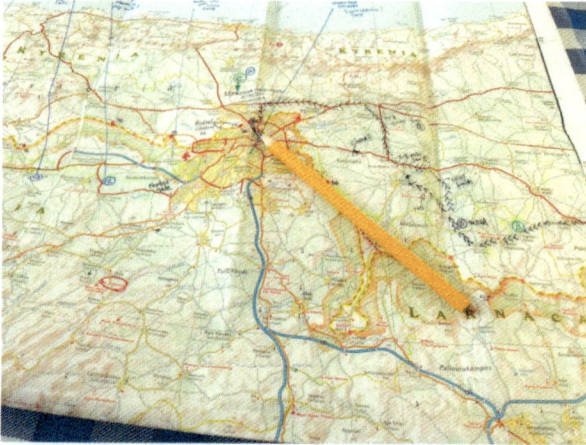

From the top:

1. My map.

2. Arriving in Kato Pyrgos.

3. Last few steps.

has a smattering of quite un-Islamic casinos and bars; the streets on the Turkish side of Nicosia have music and entertainment which portray a permissive society – if 'permissive' isn't too strong a word.

I returned to the bath house to discover the doors were now open. I remembered the rustic crosses of yesterday and my conjecture on the relaxed atmosphere of old Nicosia. Perhaps the same laid-back approach to life still existed today and extended to the flexible opening hours of the Büyük Hamam. Inside, I found the bath house to be exactly as I had hoped. The building had been carefully and sympathetically restored in deference to its original design. By retaining many of the building's original aesthetics, any modern visitor experiences a series of rooms familiar to the inaugural bathers of centuries ago.

Despite phoning ahead, a day earlier, I had a little difficulty communicating with the two mature ladies who were on duty. They were smoking Turkish cigarettes, setting up their desk and tidying elaborate cushions in the reception area. There was much ado and an extended conversation between the two matrons. After a while they turned to me and apologised for not offering me a cigarette; I politely declined, relaxing a little with the realisation that there seemed to be no male staff. Despite my positive recollections of John Noakes' experience, I didn't fancy being manhandled by a moustachioed Turkish wrestler with arms as thick as legs and legs as broad as the stone columns holding up the building's ancient ceiling. The no-nonsense ladies looked to be robust enough to deliver sufficient 'punishment'; this eliminated the dreaded awkwardness of intimate contact with a sweaty, Turkish bullock especially fatted for my visit and chomping at the cud for revenge in a role reversal of the sacrificial.

I received some instructions from the receptionists and took note of my surroundings: tall stone walls supported a high vaulted ceiling hung with coloured Arabian lanterns, and the space below was divided by dark wooden lattice work and coloured fabrics. These screens and curtains created areas of private repose decorated with bowls of fruit – disappointingly... plastic fruit. The whole place was festooned with Turkish carpets, conjuring up the western image of a harem. Fortunately, no eunuchs were on duty. A few wooden changing booths lined one side of the room with towels and waterproof slippers elegantly presented on wooden benches. I was shown into a tidy space and told to go through to the baths when ready.

I had been instructed to shower before I entered the sauna-like, wet area and complied, taking with me a ridiculously oversized key fob, a bar of soap and shower gel. These were all issued *gratis* by the Büyük Hamam, though it did feel a tiny bit like day one in a scene from *The Shawshank Redemption*. A few minutes later, one of the ladies, a tall, strong woman with dark skin and faded blonde hair, took me into a domed amphitheatre – a damp melding of a mosque and an enormous shower room. All around the central area, small anterooms jutted off and, occasionally, I heard a disconcerting whimper or shriek as if the place were a throwback to a time when questioning involved medieval torture equipment. In the middle, an octagonal plinth was topped with thick grey marble and my blonde 'grandmother' indicated that I should sit on it. Having obeyed, I discovered, in about one zillionth of a second, the marble was as hot as a frying pan. Worse was to come when I realised that Granny wanted me to lie on it! 'Here. Sleep,' she instructed. Considering my towel-covered bottom was already medium rare, placing my naked back onto the griddle was out of the question. I hoped the lady would go away, but she just stood there waiting to witness my discomfort with looks of disdain, disappointment and amusement. I lowered myself onto the surface, looking left and right to see if I was flanked by bacon and eggs. Having successfully delivered me onto the rack, mercifully, my torturer left. I could manage about five seconds before the heat became intolerable, whereupon I crossed the floor (also heated) and covered myself with ladles of cool water. Should a horseshoe be animate I now understood its feelings as it is systematically heated, beaten and cooled. I noticed that a thick mat was curled up and leaning on a nearby wall and realised, with the return of a little pride, that the Büyük Grill must also be a severe test for hardened locals. I quickly utilised the waterproof insulation and was feeling cleverly resourceful when my executioner returned. The mat was violently removed with the same vigour reserved for separating an innocent child from a bottle of boiling arsenic... out of the frying pan and straight back into the frying pan. My wrinkly bandit was now carrying something that looked like a wet pillowcase, and before long she was using the material to wash and scrub me with a complete absence of mercy. Time after time I was rotated on the griddle and battered with the soapy sphere, which inflated like a balloon every time Gran skilfully dipped it into a container of soap and water and twisted it violently to trap air. I was alternatively and repeatedly covered in white froth and then dowsed with water. Thankfully, the constant drenching in warm water brought the temperature of the marble down to about 'too hot'. I finally managed to relax into the experience; perhaps it was Stockholm Syndrome that allowed me to notice details in the ceiling above me. I counted nineteen coloured stars and a few clear circles set as tiny windows in a dome high overhead which let in a rainbow of natural light...

*

One Day (5)

One day I helped put out a fire. Our bungalow at RAF Berengaria was situated right on the edge of the camp and a wire fence separated our garden from a locally owned almond grove. A dirt path led from Berengaria camp up towards what we called Beehive Hill, and I frequently took to the trail in search of lizards and adventure. On this particular day I walked along the road outside our house to join the track as I'd done many times before, but this time I discovered that a large area of tinder dry undergrowth was on fire! I knew fires in Cyprus were a serious thing and warning signs about fire risks were commonplace across the island. I ran to tell my mother, who told me to go and raise the alarm with the camp's caretaker. I sprinted off and located the man who had an office near the entrance gate. I can't recall what we said to each other, but when I arrived with the news, I remember he was wearing a pair of trousers with braces hanging loosely around his midriff. The man, who was a little overweight, moved quickly, strapping his braces over his shoulders, grabbing a pair of fire beaters and jumping onto a tiny, gold-coloured moped before 'speeding' off towards the inferno. Barry Sheen's pole position wasn't in jeopardy because I'm pretty sure I overtook him and reached the flames before he did. By this time, my mother had extinguished much of the fire, robbing the poor caretaker of any kudos he had left. After a few minutes, the fire was out, and 'Barry' thanked my mother and me before slowly receding on his 25cc dream machine.

Later there was an in-camera inquiry by my mother... Being a boy scout meant I had participated at many a bonfire gathering. Not only that, whenever my father burnt garden rubbish, to stand and listen to the crackle of the fire, enjoying its warmth and the smell of woodsmoke, was an instinctive delight, after all, mankind has been gathering around the fireplace for millennia. Now, being a capable lad (I was cooking my own porridge at the age of seven), I soon discovered making a fire was a simple affair and that fires could be started not only for utilitarian purposes but also for entertainment. Consequently, various modest conflagrations had been created by myself and usually these were very quickly discovered by my mother; billows of thick, white smoke emanating from beneath a willow tree in rural Lincolnshire are quite conspicuous. Thus, my mother was justifiably concerned that her

146

eldest son was an apprentice arsonist, and the distance between my tiny collection of smouldering twigs and a towering inferno, with the loss of hundreds of lives, was just the shortest of steps (Oh, the humanity!) and all this despite the mitigation of my skills with the porridge pan and the advocacy of the 'Sixer' stripes on my scout uniform. After the flames were extinguished, the caretaker's braces were presumably back around his waist and the music from 'Bat Out of Hell' had faded, my mother sat me down to attach the sensors of an imaginary lie detector... 'Martin, did you start that fire?'

'No. I didn't.' Which, of course, was the simple truth.

'OK, well that's alright then. Well done for being such a good boy.' And that was it, the inquiry was over. Quite how my mother knew I was telling the truth is beyond me, but I guess it was just because she knew me so very completely.

Memories of Cyprus 1970–72

*

The human car wash at the Turkish bath kept spinning for another twenty minutes; I suspected the proceedings would conclude with my being spun dry or fed through a mangle! The soft cotton balloon was discarded in favour of a mitten made from a material more robust than wire wool; presumably, Brillo pads had been rejected because they were considered far too soft. The scrubbing was so fierce it was also a partial depilation of the chest. On one of my many revolutions I noticed tiny rolls of white material lying on the surface of the dark marble; I was alarmed to discover this was actually my skin! I was mightily relieved when my opponent finally relented, abandoning me with an air of 'no-further-torment-required'. I lay in the relative peace of the Granny-free torture chamber and before long I was sweating profusely. I noticed my assailant had left a tap running causing my mind to return to the great plain of Mesaoria. I had split my journey across the island into two roughly equal parts, with Nicosia as my halfway point. However, apart from a short passage through the Troodos foothills, almost the entire route involved crossing the Mesaoria plateau. If this tableland weren't irrigated then a great, arid and dusty landscape would soon emerge; water was a very precious commodity. But there, in the Turkish bath of Büyük Hamam, there was a veritable orgy of water, and I hoped that the US funding came with an insistence on a water recycling system. My thoughts were interrupted when the masochistic matron returned to finish the testing of my mettle with a wonderful and thorough rinsing in cold water. I was dried and led like a helpless and chastised child to the outer harem and rehydrated with cups of ice-cool water. I asked if I could buy one of the attractive Arabian lanterns as a souvenir of my near-death experience, but I was told they weren't for sale. After a little murmuring and a few giggles, I was kindly given one as a gift. If John Noakes and I should meet in the sweet by-and-by, we will compare metaphysical and physical bruises. The little lantern now resides in my bathroom to remind me that all my subsequent ablutions are seriously substandard!

With a cleanliness *well* beyond that required for surgery, I ascended the steps to the normality of Nicosia, wondering if anyone could actually see my glowing, antiseptic aura and bestowed halo. Surprisingly, at the top of the steps, there was now a small queue awaiting the chance to be roasted like a potato and sanded like a floorboard.

I recrossed the border into south Nicosia and registered that I would not enter Northern Cyprus again until the border point at Astromeritis, about forty kilometres to my west. I returned to the hotel via 'Pafos Gate' which is no longer used to enter the old city but still stands as a reminder of how the city's walls were navigated years ago. I was keen to see how the area looked in daylight. In the gloom of late evening, I had previously seen an intriguing mixture of ancient stonework, modern UN barricades, 1970s obstacles and tattered sandbags. Pafos Gate is a tunnel which passes through the old wall of the town and still has a set of archaic doors at its southern end. Centuries ago, this entrance would have been a busy thoroughfare, but today it sits quietly beside a junction with a redundant UN post. United Nations lookout posts and bases exist along the entire length of the Green Line; when I started my walk, I noted that the abandoned guard house at the coast was numbered 146. The ramshackle UN post adjacent to the old Venetian passageway was designated number sixty-five, so there must be eighty-one stations between where I was standing and the eastern end of the Green Line. The two that I'd witnessed up close had proved, as far as I could see, to be unoccupied. Unoccupied but perhaps not totally redundant.

I crossed the street to take a closer look at a 1970s shopfront which had probably been hastily barricaded in July of 1974. A tatty and sun-bleached awning shaded the peeling plaster of the shop's walls and a few palm trees had taken root in a shallow ramp of cascaded sand. Above, in the spaces where doors and windows had once opened, a wall of split sandbags proved to be the source of the sandy slope beside the pavement. The standoff in the areas where the Buffer Zone is of negligible depth must still be one of great intransigence and difficulty. When this shopfront's brickwork and roof became a hazard to passing pedestrians the remedy was to shore up the crumbling edifice with scaffolding and assemble a makeshift barrier to protect the public. Arranging repairs or demolition was, evidentially, not an option for property which so closely abuts the streets of no man's land.

7

Nicosia Airport

For my journey along the Green Line, I had arrived in Cyprus on the morning of Monday 4 June 2018, landing at Larnaca airport. The following day I had arranged to meet Captain Peter Vanek, a Slovak officer in the United Nations Peacekeeping Force (UNPKF). Captain Vanek had agreed to accompany me on a visit to Nicosia airport – closed to the public since the war of 1974. I have included a brief account of my visit here, within the pages referring to my weekend in Nicosia, though Captain Vanek and I met almost a week earlier. I also recount my arrival into RAF Akrotiri in 1970 – when I was eight years old.

Tuesday 5 June 2018

I had seen UN footage showing abandoned car showrooms in Nicosia, full of ageing Toyotas with only delivery mileage on their dusty odometers. I'd also seen photographs of a fading Trident jet sitting on the apron at Nicosia airport, so I had arranged with Captain Peter Vanek of the UN Peacekeeping Force to take a closer look. The airport is off-limits to the public and must be accessed through a very modern and very busy UN checkpoint called Foxtrot Gate. I pulled up at the incongruous, brand new checkpoint in my rented car and waited for Captain Vanek to arrive.

I was surprised at just how much traffic the checkpoint dealt with, taking note of the differing insignia on the uniforms of passing UN soldiers: Argentine, Slovak and British, amongst others.

The sky was cloudless and the dry grass next to the new tarmac road was bleached white and as brittle as glass. A gauge in my car informed me the outside temperature was 33°C – it was only 10am! Standing on the scorching asphalt, my mind vividly recalled my arrival onto the island in the summer of 1970...

*

When my mother announced that we were to be 'posted' to Cyprus it caused me some anxiety. This was because posting usually involved envelopes; I was certain I wouldn't fit in an envelope and expressly defiant that my family, which consisted of seven people, couldn't be accommodated by anything in the bureau whether it was made by Basildon or Bond.

My buoyant imagination had conjured up images of tent-sized, manilla envelopes before my mother abruptly punctured my thought bubble by explaining this was Royal Air Force-speak for going to live somewhere else. This led to the next question, 'Where is Cyprus?' My mother seemed overly excited about the prospect of living there, in fact I'd not seen her as enthusiastic about anything in all my eight years! She was suddenly, and uncharacteristically, bohemian, instructing me to attach a specific and very personal importance to the radio voices of Peter, Paul and Mary singing, 'Leaving on a Jet Plane'.

As it turned out, my mother had formed her own bubble of deception. When it came to leaving the UK, it wasn't on a jet plane, we flew from RAF Brize Norton at dawn on a damp, grey morning aboard a well-used, prop-driven Britannia aeroplane, but it was still very exciting. We were smartly dressed, as an officer's kids should be, and aware that something important was happening. The Britannia took, as I recall, about seven hours to rattle its way to RAF Akrotiri which occupied a southern peninsula of Cyprus.

En route my father took me into the cockpit where I was allowed to sit in the co-pilot's seat; I was a little disappointed when my attempts to barrel roll both plane and passengers were thwarted by 'George' the automatic pilot.

Eventually, we landed and taxied to our allocated section of scorching concrete. For some reason we were informed, with obvious relish, that the temperature outside was 110°F in the shade (43°C); this was met with manic enthusiasm by a fuselage full of 'Moonies'. This was not a reference to the arrival of a sect of obscure cultists from South Korea but rather to the white, translucent skin of the uninitiated, air-conditioned innocents awaiting their moment to disembark from the fridge and step into the oven. When I emerged into daylight, I had to half close my eyes to maintain any kind of vision in the overpowering glare of a much closer sun. In addition, I thought for a moment that an overzealous local had ascended the stairs and hit me square in the face with a hot water bottle, as was perhaps a Cypriot custom, but it was just Akrotiri, and I was wearing a dark blazer of English wool.

We were met by friends of my parents, and before long, five of us were squeezed into the back of a large BMW; my two elder sisters had been deposited in a North Lincolnshire boarding school. I have a vivid memory of being intrigued by the golden hairs on the very, non-Moonie arm of our driver's son. I had not seen suntanned skin like this before – ever; it was fascinating to behold and made me feel like I'd landed in the South Pacific. We were headed for the Continental Hotel on the seafront in Limassol. There, my mother insisted that we have a siesta, which sounded Spanish to me, and I felt this was inappropriate for Cyprus because, by now, even I knew we weren't in Spain. I reluctantly lay down in the artificial dark of the hotel room and listened to restless traffic bustling outside our shuttered window. The sun penetrated the shutters with a brilliant white light, striping the walls and forming a vertical zebra-crossing for my eyes to climb and descend. I wasn't tired. I wanted to get out and explore this alien world...

My mind returned abruptly to the present when a UN saloon car pulled up and parked upstream of my vehicle. An impressively smart officer made his way directly towards me and I knew I was about to meet Captain Vanek. My host had the bearing of a very professional soldier; as far as I could discern, he worked in an administrative role at the UN Public Relations Office, although he looked very capable of controlling armed soldiers. He was about six feet tall, thick-set with a kind face and immaculately trimmed hair, barely visible beneath his blue beret. His eyes remained invisible behind a pair of fashionable and very dark sunglasses. He was wearing khaki boots and fatigues covered in pixilated camouflage, looking more ready to tap the fire button of a rocket launcher as opposed to the keyboard of a personal computer. He checked my ID and instructed me to drive in a tight convoy with my hazard lights on. This caused more excitement than apprehension, and before long, an Argentine soldier lifted a barrier and we were driving onto the airfield's perimeter. We turned a corner, passing a long-deserted petrol station and, opposite, an equally abandoned photography shop. Both were replete with faded signage – MOBIL and FOTO PLAZA EXPRESS… both abandoned for fifty years!

Our first stop was a disused air traffic control tower. Captain Vanek and I stepped out onto a cracked concrete surface punctuated by lines of sunbaked moss. I was a little taken aback when Captain Vanek gushed forth with a very professional tour guide explanation of where we were and the significance of the bullet-holed control tower. I felt like a press crowd of one and began to take notes, frantically trying to keep up with the unfolding story. I was told the tower, opened in 1940, had been bombarded by Italian troops during World War II. Interestingly, Winston Churchill had given a speech to victorious British troops from atop the structure in 1945. Captain Vanek informed me that nowadays the airfield had become a venue for peace talks. This was not surprising given that the airport lies deep within the Buffer Zone and is therefore neutral territory.

My request to shoot drone footage of the tower was politely declined, with Captain Vanek suggesting that it was possible to mistake the drone for larger aircraft by misconception of scale and that it might get shot at. I understood. He pointed in the direction of some distant buildings and told me that the UN was still conducting inquiries into missing persons from the conflict of 1974. Almost fifty years on, skeletal remains were being uncovered, identified by forensic anthropologists and returned to their families for burial... all this, not far from crowded beaches.

Captain Vanek told me that included in the establishment of Cyprus as an independent nation, on 1 October 1960, part of the agreement was that no country involved in the negotiations should dominate the island, and this applied to Britain, Greece and Turkey. This article was designed to prevent any unification of Cyprus with either Greece or Turkey. Within three years though, there was serious intercommunal violence and, on 30 December 1963, Major General Peter Young, Commander of the British Peacekeeping Force, famously took his green chinagraph pencil and drew a ceasefire line across the island. It was a unilateral act that established the name Green Line and proved to be an effective physical and geographical division which helped curb the growing unrest.

At one time the UN had 12,000 troops stationed on the island, but at the time of my visit, according to figures available to me, there were fewer than 1,000 UN troops and military police stationed in Cyprus.

I was talking to Captain Vanek about the border when he corrected me. He made a distinction between the words 'border' and 'boundary'. 'There is no border,' he said. 'There is no fence running the entire length of the island, but there is a boundary and people know where it is...' I nodded but, at the time, I had no idea what to expect when I started with my back to the eastern sea near Paralimni and struck out west. It was clear that I would need to be careful where I stepped foot.

When the Greek military junta launched a coup d'état in July of 1974, it breached the article regarding the independence of Cyprus by delivering what was effectively a *de facto* annexation of the island. Therefore, the Turks refer to their response as an 'intervention' not an 'invasion'. Operation Attila was launched by Turkey on 20 July with the ostensive intention of defending Turkish Cypriots. However, Nicosia airport was a prime military target for both sides and the aerodrome bore witness to some of the most intense fighting of the entire campaign. During one disastrous action, around thirty Greek commandos lost their lives when their Shackleton aircraft was on the receiving end of 'friendly fire' which forced the plane to crash land on rough ground not far from the terminal – communication being a well-known and early casualty of war.

Captain Vanek and I drove towards the main terminal; as we neared the building the faded aluminium fuselage of the Cyprus Airways Trident came into view. We drew up alongside it and stepped out to take a closer look. The aeroplane was riddled with bullet holes and its engines had been removed – apparently to aid the air worthiness of another plane. Now the resting, empty hulk just sits slowly corroding into the ground and, today, the only things that fly from the apron are UN helicopters and the variety of birds which have taken up residence in the redundant airframe.

We arrived at the terminal. I looked through the glassless windows into the arrivals hall. Today the building is home to thousands of pigeons who have littered the floor with bird lime and broken nests. In 1974, this airport was only six years old and state-of-the-art – with pressure switches operated by anyone walking on

156

the welcome mats triggering a mechanism to open the doors to the terminal.

In those days, a line of fountains played in the forecourts, and their faded blue paint was still visible in bone-dry rectangles of weed-filled concrete. A rooftop café above the terminal building was known as one of the best places to eat in its day. The turnstile to the roof had rusted over time, yet its three chrome push-bars still gleamed in the sunlight. Fifty years ago, this machinery had been rotated by visitors to the elevated restaurant and viewpoint. The walls of the terminal had sustained some damage from mortar fire, and on one side of the building, a very well-equipped kitchen was now eerily silent, with its stainless steel appliances looking surprisingly good despite their half-century of respite. Once more the images all around me conformed to the unmistakable style of the 1970s. It brought back a memory of a similar building also trapped in time…

… A few years ago, I had steeled myself for a visit to a notorious Khmer Rouge prison in Phnom Penh, Cambodia. A school had been commandeered by the rebels and transformed into a foul and stinking torture camp known as S-21. Any mention of S-21 was enough to strike sickly terror into the heart of anyone unfortunate enough to be sent there because it was usually a one-way journey. Today, S-21 is a museum, but its sets of chains, handcuffs and restraining chairs are all set incongruously in the infrastructure of a 1970s school. There were the familiar, brightly coloured floor tiles of school corridors and the 'modern' angular architecture of the 1970s, but the windows were barred making classrooms into austere prison cells. Perhaps Nicosia airport hadn't borne witness to such an orgy of violence as that seen in Cambodia, but it did share the abandoned 1970s architecture. Hence the contrast between a period of inventive and hope-filled designs and the sudden rude imposition of gunfire and war. When the architects laid out their plans for a new school in the Cambodian capital, they couldn't have anticipated such a revolting change of use; similarly, no architect engaged in the Nicosia Airport Project had deliberated over the roof's suitability for the concealment of a sniper.

I asked Captain Vanek about the sound of explosions from across the Buffer Zone; he told me Turkish troops were often on exercise and the explosions were more a declarative statement of their presence than an essential part of military manoeuvres or exercise. Not far from the airport, the Turkish army had a firing range. I took the subject of ordnance to ask Peter about landmines. I knew that around 20,000 landmines were declared by the two sides after the war, of which 15,000 were anti-personnel mines and 5,000, anti-tank mines. I asked if there was any danger of treading on a mine nowadays and Peter replied that he *thought* they'd all been dealt with. I took this ambiguity onboard resolving to cross the island using well-travelled roads, trails or ploughed fields. Peter mitigated his remark with assurances that uncleared zones were marked and fenced off – '*You should be OK...*' No better guarantees were proffered. I just let the subject drop...

*

One Day (6)

One day we went to the wine festival in Limassol. As a child I found the wine festival a little bit scary. With such a relaxed atmosphere on the island already extant it wasn't easy to see why an even more relaxed atmosphere should be necessary. The idea of a festival or holiday is an ancient one and the word holiday is a catchall expression which can mean all manner of things are up for abandonment. It seems quite right to occasionally abandon the desk or plough in favour of the wine glass and music, but if the desk and plough are already worked in the close proximity of wine and music then why should a festival be required? As a boy it was ~~seemed~~ *to me that life in Cyprus was a kind of festival anyway.*

However, once a year, towards the end of summer, the wine festival was a two-week opportunity for locals to celebrate and to abandon their relaxed lives for a time of even more relaxation. The epicentre of the indulgences was a seafront park in Limassol and one evening we strolled along the promenade in the direction of its walled gardens. The seafront in Limassol was a delightful place to spend an evening. If the warm, twilight breeze wasn't enough to occupy the senses then there were street vendors who roasted sweetcorn over charcoal and served the cobs up in golden waves of salty butter. On this occasion we approached the entrance to the park, and beyond the low white walls I could hear the throb of loud music and raised voices. Every now and then a shout could be heard, then cheering, then the sound of breaking glass and general mayhem. My mother summed up the foreboding with two words uttered in the only way a disinterested matriarch can. 'Oh dear,' she said, and my mother's understatement elicited a fateful glance from my father. I had no idea what to expect; I was like Bambi in a bordello.

Inside the park the trees had been festooned with lights and the network of pathways lined with wine sellers and all manner of food stalls. The atmosphere was like the running of the bulls in Pamplona, but there wasn't a stampede of cattle, the locals' rampaging phantoms were not uncorralled, they were uncorked!

This, being the '70s, was a time when tie-dye T-shirts were popular. It was as if the random and organic colours and shapes, resulting from immersing a string-tied, white T-shirt into a vat of coloured water, produced an article of clothing that carried with it a random pattern benefiting from no intelligent design. It was a time for experimentation and freedom from restriction, a time for casting off restraint. The open air cinemas ran Coca-Cola adverts featuring the song about teaching the world to sing, though the 'global' choir of youngsters looked almost entirely European. Nobody questioned the idea that world peace might be ushered in by a soft drink rather than nuclear disarmament. The fascination with colour and chance extended to pop art too. Apart from tie-dye T-shirt stalls, a few outlets at the wine festival featured an adapted clay spinning wheel. The vendor would secure a piece of white card to the wheel and then the artist (the customer) would select washing-up bottles full of coloured paint and squirt the bright acrylics onto the spinning page. After a few applications, the artist would purchase their own work and no two creations were the same, with patterns as crazy as the carnival atmosphere. If Warhol's blazed trail of pop art was cooling in New York, the ignorant masses were now scorching their own artistic pathways in darkest Limassol.

There was a strange subculture on display too. This was the age of the 'Clackers' – consisting of two solid spheres suspended from strings held between finger and thumb. The idea was to cause the balls to ricochet off one another until they were forced to also rebound at the top of their arc; this set up a blur of hard ball and string, and there were numerous reports of serious injury including broken fingers and worse if the balls detached and flew like shrapnel into a crowd. As I recall, this was a pastime considered only suitable for reckless Cypriots in possession of a particularly strong death wish! The toy was banned in all RAF schools, but we'd gather round to watch locals show off and injure themselves with the deadly device. It was a certainty which drew morbid crowds at the wine festival, where a cocky Cypriot exponent would draw 'wows' as the speed of the balls increased, followed by wincing 'oohs' when his fingers got caught up in the blurry propulsion.

The limits for drinking were another notable absence at the festival, and I remember my shock at seeing grown men staggering around with open shirts and chests soaked with red wine. If Aphrodite had risen from the sea to educate us about love and beauty, then Bacchus was doing his best to remind us that alcohol was still toxic for mortals. At the wine festival the fruit of the vine was served directly from the barrel, warm, heady and wonderfully chaotic.

Soon I would be safely ensconced within the NATO fences of RAF Berengaria. Once we left the enclave of the camp, we

encountered a thoroughly different culture. It was enthralling and
spectacular and sometimes utterly exhilarating. RAF Berengaria
was self-sufficient with shops and village facilities providing
enough for an entirely independent existence. I might take a daily
walk to Mamma's Shop to buy sweets; whenever I entered the
shuttered shopfront, I would wait in the vacant gloom for Mamma
to appear. I'd wait in the sanctuary of confectionary and make my
selection from rows of unguarded boxes and often I would half-
heartedly plan a chocolate heist of Train Robbery proportions.
Mamma was a local lady who ran her shop with the business
strategy of an unattended, roadside honey vendor. There wasn't
an honesty box, you just waited for her to emerge for a smiley but
wordless transaction. We took exact amounts of Cypriot coinage.

Memories of Cyprus 1970–72

*

I looked across the airfield and, in the distance, through a
shimmering heat haze I saw the remains of another aeroplane
lying on its belly. I asked Peter what it was. 'This is the Commando
plane; would you like to see it?'

'Yes please,' I replied.

'OK. Follow me,' said Peter. He jumped in his white official UN
car (which I wasn't allowed to ride in) and cut across the apron
to where the edge of the concrete met a skirt of blonde grass. I
pulled up alongside his car and got out. Peter stayed within the
confines of his air-conditioned car and pointed to a trail which
curved towards the wreck... I was going to visit the war grave
alone. The Shackleton aircraft had been fitted with extra fuel tanks
and was lying with its nose pointing east, towards the terminal.
I circled the wreckage and noticed the steering column still had
parts which were free of rust and gleaming in the sunlight. The
war grave had been the victim of graffiti, as if the groupings of

bullet holes weren't enough of an indignity for the old aeroplane. Towards the rear of the fuselage the passenger door was missing, which left an opening shedding light into a dark interior. With as much reverence as possible, I climbed inside. The fuselage was interspaced with large bulkheads which needed to be stepped over to reach the cockpit. The pilot's seat had been looted, or at least stripped of its upholstery, and a pair of rusting foot pedals reminded me that people had died in this plane – at least thirty paratroopers and crew had perished – all as a result of terrible ignorance. Bravery and human error side by side.

I retraced my steps back to the cars and thanked Peter for his time, patience and kindness. A UN helicopter flew overhead, interrupting our final conversation; we both observed the fly-by. I asked Peter if he'd been up in one... 'No. Not yet,' he said. 'I don't like helicopters!' We laughed and shook hands. Peter gave some final instructions. He would accompany me back to a junction near the entrance to the airfield; he would turn right for work, and I would drive straight on, back to Foxtrot Gate and modern Nicosia beyond. Shortly after Peter turned off to head towards his office, I found myself passing the Foto Plaza Express and, unable to resist, I decided to pull in to take a closer look. Although it was obvious the shop had been abandoned for decades, inside it looked like it had been empty for just a few months. There were a few shelves with framed photographs of professional standard, but the images were faded almost to white. Several documents were visible on the counter, and I was certain that if I were able to read them, they'd be dated July 1974.

At the bottom of the road leading up to Foxtrot Gate I turned left and descended a hill to a roundabout. One of the exits was disused, but there was enough room to pull in. I stopped the car and stepped out in front of what was once the main road up to Nicosia airport. A padlocked barrier augmented with a UN-blue-and-white oil drum prevented further access, but the tarmac road beyond rose to a blind summit which must be close to the terminal with its empty car park and redundant fountains. Suddenly, in my mind's eye, and for some unfathomable reason, I pictured an RAF Mini heading towards me. The little car was replete with RAF flags of insignia flying from its wings. For a moment, the combination of airfield and 1970s buildings streaming through the synapses had short-circuited and returned me to Akrotiri where my dad was driving home as duty officer.[2] The vision faded and I took in my surroundings... Beside the disused entrance, a statue of a Cypriot soldier stood as a reminder that land here had been gained or lost at great cost.

---

2   Duty officer was a role rotated amongst officers and, as far as I can remember, involved a weekend (or other period of time) of answering the phone, accessing keys and dealing with any eventualities and emergencies that might present themselves while the station boss (usually a Group Captain) was on a deckchair-avec-G&T... It was, as far as I can remember, the only time my dad drove a car with RAF flags on it.

Mamma's Shop

Mamma's Shop was a temptation,
Mamma lived beyond the fly screen,
She emerged slowly – born thru coloured ribbons;
At least a minute after anyone stepped into her tiny store,
It would have been easy to take a chunk of chocolate,
And run like a shipless pirate,
But I just waited and paid.

M.J.W. Clark – *Memories of Cyprus 1970–72*

8

The Republic of Cyprus

Nicosia to Peristerona

Monday 11 June 2018

To maintain my early-start routine, I had deposited my non-essential items in my suitcase the night before and left this in the safe room at the Cleopatra Hotel; the only items in my room were those I'd be taking from Nicosia to Kato Pyrgos. Replace 'room' with 'tent' because, as far as I was concerned, I didn't want to start my day with anything other than a tent-style departure, despite the presence of a bed and the sheer extravagance of en suite facilities. In fact, I wanted to leave the hotel with as little fuss as possible and, if I could manage it, I wanted to slip away from the luxuries, unseen – like a thief in the night. For some reason I felt my return to the road needed to be unsullied with a conversation or interaction with another human. My three mornings east of Nicosia had all started at dawn and in complete isolation, dark and loneliness. Those solitary mornings had endowed me with such peace and tranquillity, an unforeseen imprinting had taken place. Now, to begin any section of the walk with a conversation was like impurifying myself with a sacrilegious impediment. Although it was a mystery to me, I knew my first steps should be made in monkish meditation. Walking the first kilometre or so in silence allowed for a kind of gentle surfacing from the deep; my mind was reluctant to admit any voice but one: the familiar tone of my thoughts about the world and my place in it. Was it an attempt to remain in a dream state? I wasn't sure – but I could breathe under these waters, I could see differently. Breaking the surface meant the water would drain from my ears, and my eyes would receive light without the special refraction of being alone in the dawn. Anything I could do to slow the surfacing process was attractive to me. I wasn't being antisocial; it took all my wits to deal with my faulty self as I was shown such beauty as that gifted by the burning up of a night and its replacement with a virgin morning. Everything appeared fresh to me, everything was renewed, restarted; I took to the road blinking at the world like a newborn. I had a longing for the loneliness of the open road and, although I had enjoyed my stay in the capital, I was yearning to be in the relative silence of the countryside as soon as possible. I loved my view of the world from beneath the weight of my rucksack. I was homeless again and I found the uncertainty thrilling and alien. It was as if, in my own earthbound way, I too had 'slipped the surly bonds of earth' because I was being afforded a quite different journey through this lovely island and, for the most part, my route was far from the commercial roar of the package holiday. My return to the island had been instinctive; I had come in search of words of comfort from the boy I had been. I was envious of the innocence of childhood, a time before decades of adulthood had exposed me to the darkness of the human condition and my own frailty. By middle age we all carry so much clutter... I love the scene in the 1986 film *The Mission,* where Captain Rodrigo Mendoza (Robert De Niro) undertakes a self-imposed penance. He gathers up the weapons and armour associated with his violent life so far and, having placed them in a net, drags them through miles of impenetrable jungle. Mendoza is attempting to pay a price for his murderous past. Father Gabriel (Jeremy Irons), a Jesuit priest, observes the relentless soldier climbing the jagged rocks of a waterfall with the weight of the net making an ascent impossible. Then we witness a profound piece of screenwriting; with Mendoza exhausted yet still aware of his ever-present guilt, a series of stark contrasts play out. A warrior from the Guarani tribe recognises Mendoza as the mercenary who had taken slaves from amongst his own people and the one who had murdered those who fought back. The warrior grabs a knife and holds it to the neck of a helpless Rodrigo; the penitent doesn't resist – he has submitted himself to what will be. Eventually it is Mendoza's victim who cuts the net away and the muddy sack falls into the water below, discolouring the water. Here Mendoza realises he *cannot* pay the price and he has been in receipt of grace and mercy. Mendoza weeps. The tribesmen laugh. The so-called civilised are schooled by savages. Rodrigo had come to the end of himself. Robert Bolt, the writer, observes an inverted world with its polemic peoples subjected to infectious love. One scene reveals Captain Mendoza reading 1 Corinthians, Chapter Thirteen, where Paul describes the true power of true love. Holiness is the opposite of repressive… it is irresistible!

… I didn't carry such a heavy load, but I longed for something to be cut away. I had come to the end of myself. All my achievements counted for nothing compared to the simple wonder of a boy's eyes. I knew who I was and what I had accomplished, and it had been an untypical life, but I was resistant to a form of surrender – a healthy giving up. Capitulation. The desire to keep living was still strong, but I was keen to cease trying to prove myself to an unseen jury. I was ready to relax after forty-odd years of herculean effort. I had toured the world, written, produced and directed plays and films, rehearsed with bands for tens of thousands of hours, maintained a full-time job, kept fit and raised a family – amongst other things. I had been utterly dedicated, but I had also had enough of being evidence of the Pareto principle, where eighty per cent of the work is done by twenty per cent of the people. I was no longer willing to shoulder that kind of burden; I had served long enough in that mode and was looking for less stressful pastures and I was eager to lie down in them – willingly. All these cognitions churned away as I plodded my way through my own version of Mendoza's jungle; these were long shadows pierced by stripes of brilliant light half a century old…

My less-trod trail led its way through glorious landscapes that changed slowly, where a broad, sweeping bend uncovered a new masterpiece with every step, where even fellow pedestrians didn't share the rhythms and vagaries of my day. These people might pass me amid the same beauty, but they were leashed to a domestic peg somewhere. Not too far away, they had invisible chains of residency and duty. Compared to me, they carried nothing, but on my back, I carried almost all I needed to survive, making my days unfettered and free. Though, strangely, my rucksack and daily effort felt like an entirely appropriate penance; progress could only be made with sacrifice. The burning of calories seemed like the settling of a debt. Just like Laurie Lee putting his boyhood Slad behind him in *As I Walked Out One Midsummer Morning*, his was a journey which *had* to be paid for in sweat, and the payment was instinctive. I was an unhorsed cowboy and low-plain drifter. I had the freedom to explore a roadside barn, or a silent lake, should I want to. I had no appointments, no one waited anxiously for me to arrive; I could stop when and where I wanted, and this *exemption* from the bonds of modern life shed magical light on everything I saw. Puddles on pavements became tiny seas with intriguing inlets and floating leaves morphed into boats carrying ancient Argonauts. If I passed under a tree, its canopy covered me with a symphony of sound. Fields of sheep occupied me for long enough to dream about being a shepherd whose only company was ovine, only breaking the spell of his loneliness to deliver fleeces to towny Venetians or Romans. Sometimes the intoxication of evening jasmine had me swimming out to meet Aphrodite or finding an ancient temple full of sirens with garlands of wildflowers and elegant limbs adorned with amulets of gold. All these were the hourly joys of my route whenever I was between villages or taking the cross-country option, but the concrete and infrastructure of suburban Nicosia produced very few such phantoms for my mind to enjoy...

My route out of the capital tracked obliquely west past small boutiques and then southwest alongside a suburban dual carriageway flanked with modern shops, car showrooms and large supermarkets. There had been a little rain overnight and the dampened pavement rid my boots of their usual accompaniment of disturbed dust. The broad road was still quiet as I approached the roundabout from which Nicosia airport would have been accessed prior to the war of 1974 and where I'd imagined my father's ensigned RAF Mini. I skirted the roundabout and ascended the same hill I'd descended following my tour of the airfield with Captain Vanek just a week earlier. I glanced up the new road to my right which led up to Foxtrot Gate and savoured my memories of the UN guards at the busy checkpoint and the contrasting quiet of the airport's apron with its sun-bleached airliner and decaying terminal. Why had I been granted so many years when just a few metres away an old aeroplane was a war grave?

I took a few moments to establish some kind of geographical regroup using the clock face as a directional aid. I had entered Nicosia from the north, at about 'twelve o'clock' and was now exiting the city at about 'seven o'clock', tracking southwest. I had to cross the A9 motorway or at least circumvent it because, as in most countries, pedestrians are not allowed on motorways in Cyprus. According to my map I should exhaust the suburbia of Nicosia about two kilometres south of the A9, which was marked as a broad blue line on my crumpled map. I pushed on up the hill, taking advantage of a wide hard shoulder punctuated with impressive bush-sized weeds which, occasionally, forced me slightly closer to the early morning traffic. Once more the sky was cloudless, and the promise of another glorious day was being heralded in song by quarrels of house sparrows. They were circling the air, landing on telephone lines or roadside bushes to watch me pass by with short-lived interest. A note in my diary informed me that at 4.50am the temperature was already 25°C and by 6am, it had risen by about two degrees.

I discovered I was drawing alongside a well-kept cemetery; I scanned the scene noticing the graveyard occupied a large hillside area and many of the headstones carried pictures of the people who were now resting there forever. I soon realised this was a military cemetery and the faces looking back at me belonged to Greek Cypriots who had lost their lives in the summer of 1974. The atmosphere changed as I gazed at the neat rows of hundreds of dead soldiers; it sobered me and brought back to me one of the reasons I was crossing the island. I had seen numerous cemeteries in Northern Cyprus, but this was the first Greek Cypriot equivalent and it quickly raised in me a deep sense of infinite cost. Once again, many of the fallen were extremely young – little more than boys. The hillside was a necropolis of acute loss – all those stories of first kisses and parties, school days and favourite foods, of dances and hopes and vocational studies, failures and successes, now silenced under acres of cold, white marble. A line of Mediterranean firs skirted the far left of the graveyard running uphill to a lone cypress tree which pointed to the early sky like a tall, green emblem of ancient Greece. Bygone battles mirrored here in modernity, the sword and the bullet both hungry for flesh. I looked back at the line of trees and realised, with a sickening feeling in my stomach, that beyond the dark fringe the cemetery continued with just as many graves covering ground further to my left. I took a photograph of two headstones, both of which recorded the date of the soldiers' deaths as 23 July 1974. Compared to the overwhelming losses of the world wars these were quantifiable in terms of numbers but exactly equivalent in terms of private grief. The parents of this generation of fighters will die out, and with them, the keenly felt bitterness and painful theft of their children's lives. If future generations share in the hurt it will be as siblings, younger relatives or friends – but not as *parents*, their bereavement is carried differently. A parent's loss of a child is a peculiar, choking gall of deprivation which never relaxes its grip.

I walked away in silence and for a while I didn't notice the landscape around me; it seemed to take a few minutes for my five senses to return and enable or allow me to enjoy my journey. How fortunate I was. How grateful for freedom and life and family.

In the distance I could see a pair of high towers rising from a large Greek Orthodox church with an impressive red-tile roof. This was the church of St Pantaleon, and it was sitting right alongside the busy road. St Pantaleon was a medieval figure of legendary status. A series of attempts to carry out a death sentence on him ended with just as many miraculous interventions; molten lead cooled and solidified when he was immersed in it, flames were extinguished when they tried to burn him and thrashing swords bent upon his neck in failed decapitations. All these miracles continued until the saint relented and submitted himself as a martyr. The saint's name means 'mercy to all' and the church's position seemed apt with the adjacent tombs of so many young men.

On a piece of dry *bondoo*, near an intersection, a popup shop was selling refreshments to commuters, but I avoided the melee and busy traffic by using a few reservations as stepping stones, skipping over to a quieter road heading directly west. After about half an hour it was apparent Nicosia was now fading behind me. I started to look forward to an immersion in the unknown landscapes of western Cyprus – to what I'd see, where I'd camp and who I'd meet.

My first distinguishable village was Agioi Tremithias, which stood on the B9 paralleling the newer A9 road to the north. I passed under a large flyover and marvelled at the motorists who seemed to be playing a game of who-can-drive-closest-to-the-hiker. A Mercedes approached me on the hard shoulder and just before it reached me, swerved back onto the carriageway. I had both boots on the dirt verge beside the road and he was *still* close – probably tuning his radio or having a nap behind the wheel. I was always relieved to get off busy roads; I'd discovered that you cannot rely on drivers to pay attention. This meant I had to maintain a constant mental alertness, and this had to be added to the expenditure of calories.

At last, after a few hundred metres, I was able to leave the concrete monstrosities of Nicosia's trunk roads and head off into the countryside. I rounded a sweeping bend which rose gently to reveal a welcome view of the pastoral. The ground to my right fell away to a sandy field fifty or sixty feet below. I saw a road sign for Palaiometocho where, according to the plans in my head, I would take to the shade until my evening walkout at around 6pm. I mused for a few moments on the different spellings of place names. There seemed to be no consistency and it wasn't unusual to see three different spellings for a village, as Time and the English and Greek languages combined to produce various versions of the same thing. Just then, my Polar watch buzzed on my wrist to inform me that firstly, it had taken me three hours to fully clear Nicosia, and secondly, I'd already completed my daily activity goal – pretty good considering the time was just 8.05am.

To my left and opposite the open land, a shop that seemed to sell everything looked inviting and suggested that along my route I could buy water and snacks with some regularity. Here I furnished myself with a couple of bottles of water and some energy bars before striding off towards Trimithias-proper. I noticed some seriously impressive houses beside the road. There were huge properties with security cameras, tennis courts and large gardens, some big enough to accommodate swimming pools. I'd heard stories about powerful Russians arriving to set up second homes on the island and wondered if one particularly gigantic and imposing residence was owned by a member of the Russian Mafia. Someone had told me that a similarly shady, Slavic character had taken a fancy to a house elsewhere on the island and had 'persuaded' the occupant to 'sell' the house to them.

I passed a bungalow which appeared to have migrated from St Mary Mead. Its gable ends were painted white with a few black beams running vertically in Tudor style. It was so typically English I fully expected to see Miss Marple spraying her roses in the front garden and wondered about the conversation my imaginary, elderly detective might have with some local crime magnate. Adopt Russian accent…

'Ah, Miss Marple, how lovely your floribunda look this morning…'

'Why, thank you, and how are your protection rackets proceeding? Not too violent, I hope.'

I rid my mind of the scene just as the Russian was laughing defensively and shifted my attention to the air overhead. Hundreds of chattering sparrows were flying in and out of a tall palm tree and stopping for a few moments on telephone wires across the street before returning to the safety of the palm leaves. Every time they flew into the air, they swarmed noisily like kindergarten children in a playground. It was so amusing, I took a few moments to enjoy the spectacle. Never mind Miss Marple, what were *they* saying to each other? Only God and Dr Dolittle can answer that one.

Most villages in Cyprus seemed to be quite small with little infrastructure beyond their older centres. Main roads emanating from the middle of the villages were often lined with houses along the highway but, visible through the gaps, I could see olive groves or the roughly cultivated fields of smallholdings. It was as if any building of new premises seemed to only take place along the road leading out of the village without further congesting the core of the hamlet. Typical of many Mediterranean countries, Cyprus had thousands and thousands of olive trees, and these ancient and hardy groves often came right up to the roadside. They became de rigueur to the eyes with their dusty, dark green leaves and gnarled and twisting trunks rising cleanly out of light red earth. Swathes of black netting were often looped around the trunks ready to be spread out at harvest time. I developed a love of the olive groves because they afforded me the opportunity to see a landscape unchanged for centuries. Whenever I could, I would detour through the quiet of a grove or sit in the shade of a tree to take a short break where it was easy to imagine what the ancient shepherds of Cyprus felt and saw during their days of yore.

As I continued into Trimithias I noticed something different from that which I'd witnessed in Northern Cyprus. North of the Green Line it seemed that landscaping was something to be avoided. I had noticed a love of cultivating plants in both republics resulted in any number of verandas and porches swollen with swathes of lovely flowers and shady creepers. Until then I'd not seen what I was witnessing in the outskirts of Trimithias; several houses had beautifully kept lawns. As far as I could remember the inhabitants of Northern Cyprus didn't seem to go in for grassy frontages but, there in Trimithias, neighbours appeared to be in an informal competition. The apparent aim was to produce and maintain an impressive square metreage of turf which needed to be of bowling-green standard. Even more impressive given the relentless furnace under which the grass had its existence.

An advertising sign beside the road was unreadable, its

paint peeled as if someone had taken a blow lamp to it. However, the colours and pigments had been scorched away by nothing other than the sun's power. I found myself recalling advice I'd received from a man in the UK who sold high quality sheds. He informed me, with sage tones, that the chief antagonist to the longevity of a shed was not rain but sunlight. He insisted no expense should be spared when painting protective coats onto a wooden garden building. He reiterated the point with a sigh and, in a Lincolnshire drawl, said… 'Yeah, it's the sun wot kills 'em! Y'need to paint 'em ev'y foo years…!' Clearly the road sign had been assassinated by our star years ago. Evidence of the sun's destructive power was everywhere across the island. Manmade fabrics were bleached and faded, sheets of metal had expanded and contracted into distortions of their original shapes. The paintwork of older cars had faded from, perhaps, a shiny red to a bloomed, matt pink, and any vehicle left in the sun with its windows closed would produce a vehicle on the verge of spontaneous combustion.

I was now amongst the houses and buildings which formed the core of Trimithias, but I decided to keep tracking west instead of taking a bend and heading north on the main road into Trimithias' centre. Although this meant that I would have to forego the delights of the village hub, it did mean I could take a lovely detour leading down a steep curve to a dry riverbed, where I found two more options. A new road, not on my map, had been built providing a more direct route to Palaiometocho; I opted for a more pastoral path and walked off into a rural idyll.

I was now so confident with my drone that I had it hover forward of me to my left and programmed it to track my progress as it backed away along the verge before me. When I checked the footage, I appeared as quite an ungainly character loaded with bulky equipment. The solar panels and various rucksack attachments made me look quite encumbered, but I had no option if I were to remain independent and self-sufficient for

176

all my needs in this intense heat. My load was now much lighter after the kit culling at the Cleopatra. I had learned not to skimp when buying equipment, so all my kit and clothing was the best money could buy. I was hydrated, nourished, solar powered and quite comfortable beneath my little tortoise-shell-house.

I passed another olive grove and watched carefully as an old lady hacked away at the ground with an antique scythe. She wore a white headscarf to keep the heat away and looked up at my approach. After a cursory glance my way she returned to her agriculture as if I were a figure of some contempt. I admired her. In England, most women her age – she looked to be well into her eighties – would never be seen chopping away at acres of weeds, let alone in temperatures like these. I wondered if she thought my accompanying drone was about to launch an air-to-surface missile strike against the peasant classes and that a stooped position would present a smaller target.

I ascended a gentle hill leading westwards out of the quiet little valley of fields. A vibrant pistachio tree presented its unripe crop as bright green pods about the size of broad beans but shaped like little rugby balls. The green pods had a red marking along part of their length, and they were grouped in several clusters of five or six nuts at the end of smooth branches.

The little-used road I'd selected was bordered with spear grasses and these produced a natural, hip-high skirt to the edge of the track. I walked along brushing my hand along the seed clusters, filming the action on my GoPro. The footage looked just like the scene in *Gladiator* when Maximus is dying, his mind filled with images of his wife and son who'd been brutally murdered by his nemesis. His hands were brushing the tops of the crops as he arrived to meet his slaughtered family who were waiting for him in the 'next world'.

At the top of a slight incline, I passed a long wall which looked like it had been built by a gang of drunken, first-year – or first-week – bricklaying apprentices. Whoever the builders were, they must all have been suffering from a combination of sporadic sight and debilitating vertigo, either that or an excess of kokinelli lubrication. Thankfully, the bleating residents on the other side of the wall didn't seem to mind the standard of bonding; if they had fodder and water, all was well.

At the crest of the shallow hill, I turned right to head north into the outskirts of Palaiometocho. The sun was near its zenith, and I was a little past the time I usually quit the road to seek out a shady bivouac.

I was about to enter the village through the back door as it were, entering via a side road. One of the first buildings I passed had an open garage full of junk resting on a lovely vintage car. It's not unusual to see old cars in pretty good shape in Cyprus; a combination of low mileage and the absence of corrosive salt on winter roads means the bodywork can last a long time. This survivor, a Peugeot 403, was sitting under a large, discarded TV aerial, several years of thickening dust and other oddments. Last produced in 1966, it was just possible that this old lady had been keeping the rest of the garage detritus company for decades. I walked on, past the mouldering ruins of mud brick buildings framed and offset with rows of youthful lemon trees. A growth of silverleaf nightshade with its deadly berries tumbled onto the road near my dusty feet, and gardens full of pink and white oleander provided a colourful reception.

History tells me that the village of Palaiometocho was a stopping point for pilgrims making their way up to the eleventh-century monastery of Kykkos in the Troodos mountains. The name 'Palaiometocho' means 'Old Inn' and, interestingly, Archbishop Makarios III started his ministry at Kykkos. The old place had remained so dear to him that he chose the site as his final resting place. Ancient pilgrims pausing here were still a good two days' walk from the revered monastery.

Understanding a little of the stories or legends surrounding the monastery at Kykkos lends information to the name of the village church, Our Lady of Odigitria or, loosely, Our Lady Who Knows the Way. The story goes that a righteous monk, Esaias, sought to have an icon of the Virgin Mary brought from Constantinople to Kykkos. He and a friend travelled to the great city of the emperor to collect it. The devious monarch had a copy made, which he intended to palm off onto Esaias, but the emperor's daughter fell ill with a mysterious disease. Esaias' companion suggested that the girl would be healed as soon as the original icon was released. So, the artwork – supposedly painted by St Luke – was sent by royal boat to Cyprus. The route taken by the icon passed through Palaiometocho, in transit from the coast to the foothills of Troodos. Legend has it that even the trees bent their trunks in reverence as the icon passed by.

I was now amongst a collection of neat bungalows, but just before I left the maze of small houses, I asked a late-middle-aged man, who was working in a garden, for the quickest way to a shop. He wore a pair of camouflage dungarees with a blue tool belt and looked up as I approached. He stood up straight to welcome me. 'Hello,' he said.

'Hello, I'm looking for a shop,' I asked hopefully, pointing to my left with the prospect it might be the right direction.

'Sorry, a moment...' The man disappeared inside and after a few moments emerged with a woman who looked the spitting image of '70s songstress and superstar Nana Mouskouri. The man relinquished the conversation to 'Nana' and stood back to enjoy the spectacle.

'Hello, I'm looking for the nearest shop,' I repeated, pointing to my left once again.

'Yes, you can go that way. Can I give you a drink?' she asked, quickly interrupting herself.

'I have water,' I said, holding up a crumpled water bottle which contained water above blood temperature. I must have looked ridiculously hot because it seemed I was being viewed as something of a casualty.

[old on please,' said the lady, and 'Nana' went into the
only to re-emerge a few moments later with her aged
mother. The older lady was carrying an enormous bottle of very
cold water and a glass. 'Please, drink,' instructed 'Nana', and the
old lady filled a glass and handed it to me. I thanked the little
party and took a sip. I must have looked like I'd just crossed the
Sahara. The taste of chilled water was heavenly, and I couldn't
help but down the entire glass much to the delight of my rapt
audience. I ventured forth with a little more nuanced English.
'A cup of cold water and may you receive your reward...' I said,
paraphrasing the famous passage in Matthew Chapter Ten. The
middle-aged lady caught on immediately and laughed. 'Are you
Orthodox?' I asked.

'Nooo,' she sighed, but with a tone showing no offence.

I was intrigued. The old lady wrestled the bottle, which
was almost as big as she was, to refill my glass which I raised
with a *'Kyrie eleison'*. My three friends repeated the phrase as
if it were a recognised alternative to *'Yamas'*, the equivalent of
our 'cheers'. I thanked 'Nana' and Co and made off towards the
unseen shop.[3]* Once more, I had to turn down the offer of a lift,
but meeting those people was a wonderful experience. It's a fact
that most people are friendly and eager to help, and this is all
clearly evidenced in meetings like the one I'd just had with three
complete strangers.

For some reason I started to recall a moment when I'd met a
retired American who was visiting the UK. He was a guest at a
house I was working in and positively loving his retirement, his
holiday and the complete absence of schedule and work duties.

For me it was just another day at work, with commitments
and responsibilities, but for him, it was an opportunity to just

---

3   When I returned to Cyprus a few months after my walk to say thank you
    to as many people as I could, I knocked on the door of the bungalow and
    completely confused the old lady with a gift of sparkling water and fresh
    lemons. She had absolutely no idea who I was!

enjoy everything about the day. Everything was refreshingly different: telegraph poles, letter boxes, shops and traffic lights. It was almost like a rebirth with quite different things to experience. My American friend was keen to find out about my job and my life; although mildly distracting, it challenged my cynicism and very British demeanour.

There, in front of a tiny bungalow in a small Cypriot village, I had been graciously welcomed and generously treated. The whole five minutes with the trio of strangers was totally inspiring.

The road down to the local shops seemed to follow gravity; the centre of Palaiometocho lay near the bottom of a shallow valley with a dry riverbed.

A few hundred yards from the centre I passed a rusting plough which was probably an early-twentieth-century device. The antique had two un-upholstered iron seats, iron wheels and a large manufacturer's badge revealing the appliance had been made in Uttoxeter, England.

A friend of mine told me, the world over, one could be sure of finding two things: Singer sewing machines and Coca-Cola. I think British-made plant is equally ubiquitous. I have seen British-made diggers and cranes rusting away in many countries, and often the railway engines or steamboats that carried technology deep into dark and undiscovered continents were knocked together in the white heat of British factories.

The village centre was quiet, and I began to look for a shady rest area nearby. There was a small play park, the usual war memorial, the very impressive church of Our Lady of Odigitria and, adjacent, a bus shelter which looked to be the perfect spot to while away an afternoon of recuperation. I found a shop where I bought two chocolate croissants, a lemon ice pop (deep joy!), a few drinks and savoury snacks to help with my salt intake. I repaired to the bus stop and made my bivouac on a wooden bench, taking the time to make myself as comfortable as possible. I laid out my self-inflating mat and pillow, arranged my various morsels in easy-to-reach places, swapped my boots for stocking-feet and settled in for several hours' rest. After a few moments of stillness, a pair of Sri Lankan boys were deposited by a 4x4 and they talked very loudly about bus times, or at least that's what I assumed they were discussing. My altruistic beatitudes of a few minutes ago faded quickly as these two young men were practically shouting at each other. I assumed they had jobs testing ordnance in an armaments factory and hadn't yet discovered the safety equipment. Now, ninety-nine per cent deaf, they were obviously headed into Nicosia to receive aural implants. After about half an hour the 'Def-Boyz' – my rap-group name for them – boarded a bus and left a delightful silence behind them. Bliss, the blitz was over.

I spent a while looking at the church of Our Lady of Odigitria, sending my drone high into the still air and having it circle the red pantile roof. Looking at the footage it almost felt like a trespass to have such easy access to places usually only accessible to those with plumage. I monitored the shots on my iPhone and the rushes looked impressive as the drone swept down onto the dome, heading for the arched windows circling the wall beneath the large terracotta cupola. Again, the front of the church featured two great square towers, like the church of St Pantaleon in Nicosia. As the camera scanned the village below, I wondered how the place might have looked in the days when St Luke's artwork passed by. In truth, I doubted Dr Luke was a painter.

Back at my bivouac I noticed that, on an area of tarmac beside the bus shelter, there was an interesting machine. Occasionally vehicles would pull up to the contraption and the driver would insert a few coins whereupon a liquid was dispensed and collected in a plastic container. I'm sure it was water, but why did locals need gallons of it in the town centre? I never did find out…

*

One Day (7)

One day I went to work with my dad. Back in my Lincolnshire village I wasn't sure what the other boys' fathers did for a living, but I knew they didn't go to work in a nuclear bomber. My dad was a navigator plotter on Vulcan aircraft which had a crew of five. The Vulcan was a victim of its own success. During the Cold War, a thing called Mutually Assured Destruction existed which created the acronym MAD. This meant that anyone pressing a nuclear launch button must be suicidally mad. Consequently, the defence provided by the RAF and its Quick Reaction Alert aircraft was never really tested in anger. A charity tried to keep a Vulcan flying long after all its contemporaries had been grounded for various safety reasons, but the cost of keeping an aircraft like the Vulcan airworthy proved unsustainable. Two World War II Lancasters still take to the air today commemorating the conflict and the bravery of the crews who flew the aircraft, but the Vulcan's successful deterrent against aggression means that its story is largely untold.

I had seen the Vulcan up close. I'd climbed the steps and sat in my father's seat – in the middle of a row of three and facing backwards. My dad was on the display crew and flew all over the world to perform low-level aerobatics for crowds in New Zealand, Australia, Canada and the USA. On one trip to New Zealand, far from prying eyes, my father's captain – who he described as a brilliant pilot – barrel-rolled the enormous bomber completely, despite the manoeuvre being beyond normal operational limits. The skills of the pilot ensured that all those onboard maintained 1G. That is, save beams of sunlight penetrating the portholes and rotating around the cabin, nobody in the back could tell they were actually upside down! For anyone in the Vulcan family, they can probably work out who this formidable pilot was; he ended up as an air attaché, so his Antipodean naughtiness did him no harm.

The Vulcan could be a traditional bomber too and this might involve low-level bombing runs. Somewhere near Episkopi there was a bombing range in the sea, and Vulcan crews would drop 'Flash Bang Smoke' bombs for target practice. To monitor the accuracy of the strikes an officer was given a pair of binoculars and sent off to a small hut conspicuously sited on a clifftop overlooking the target. As this was a low-key and solo assignment, my father took me with him to watch the ordnance landing in the water near a floating raft. My dad reported back to the crews their respective accuracy and so a very pleasant day was had with the two of us gazing at blue waters and blue skies.

I went into RAF Akrotiri with Dad once. I was intrigued that his day's work seemed to consist only of threading bright orange file strings into binders for students' folders; he also taught navigation. After this, the day was spent in an op's room where the only ops were the boiling of kettles and buoyant banter. I suppose those were the vagaries of doing a job where you were paid for a twenty-four-hour day. There were times when I didn't see Dad for weeks if he was abroad or when he might be on Quick Reaction Alert (QRA), which meant he was sleeping very near a fuelled and prepped aeroplane.

By and large the RAF was a wonderful family to be part of. Everyone made the best of their situation and families were well looked after. A more relaxed attitude existed in those days; I remember my dad's crew wanting to attend the wedding of a colleague back in the UK and the indulgent flight of 7,000 kilometres was recorded as a training sortie, which it was... of course!

Memories of Cyprus 1970–72

*

I spent a lazy but guiltless afternoon writing up my diary whilst the memories of my last few hours were still clear in the memory, and either dozed off or wandered around my bus-stop locale like a breezy-headed schoolboy.

After about four hours of rest, my Polar watch bleeped a message: 'It's time to move.' Being on a pilgrim's route I wondered if this was divine instruction. I slowly started to tidy away my impromptu camp. Before I replaced my boots, I checked my feet and treated a tiny blister about the diameter of a pencil. I carried out my precious-check before crossing the road to continue my trek west. Before I left the centre of the village, I noticed the local memorial to the conflict of 1974; it was well maintained and built with donated money. I read the details of one it memorialised; he had died aged just twenty. What do you know when you are twenty?

My road out of the village was a lovely one. A main road took less patient traffic out of Palaiometocho by heading more directly north towards the busy A9, which would have drivers in Nicosia in about twenty minutes or so. I enjoyed *not* going that way. I was slipping out of the little hamlet by way of a dusty and little-used lane, and it felt appropriate because, once again, the rhythms and near silence of the road seemed to require a joining of ghosts. My friends were my visualisations of the people who once trod where my feet were passing. My mind scraped away the tarmac and, in its place, laid a trail of soft sand or bare earth to walk along; my ears strained to hear ancient songs or the conversations of long forgotten farmers. In the late afternoon the warm sun, and its delicious rendering of all around me into a land of burnished woods and fields, made the air thick with whispered stories heard in the chorus of moving leaves overhead. It was as if the trees themselves wanted to tell me about what they'd seen, who had rested against their trunks and the centuries of loss – the loss of the knowledge of lives all as significant as any on earth but now gone from living memory.

I followed the dry riverbed west out of the village towards Akaki, which lay about a third of the way to Astromeritis where

I'd cross back into Northern Cyprus. I wanted to have my wits about me when I crossed the border, so intended to camp just east of Astromeritis near Peristerona and walk to the control point early the next day. This part of my walk would allow me to spend an extended period in the true hinterland of Cyprus, south of the Green Line. Even Palaiometocho felt like a satellite village for the capital, whereas from here on it looked far more rural. According to my map, a small track headed west towards Akaki, and though I was anxious I might not find it, in the end I assumed it followed the riverbed before the ravine turned northwest and the lane continued more obliquely west. Initially the road passed through typical Cypriot smallholdings with occasional assemblies of corrugated iron dotted about, making an unruly mix of shanty town and allotment – all very rustic.

Opposite an incongruous yet impressive compound full of solar-powered telecommunications equipment I saw a fenced-off enclosure and immediately recognised the verdant crop on the other side of the wire. It was an aloe vera plantation and the cactus-like leaves looked to be heavily loaded with medicinal sap.

The quiet trail kept on west, crossing another dry riverbed which, sadly, had been fly-tipped with discarded furniture and bags of rubbish. Apart from the rubbish, the meeting of road and riverbed was idyllic; tall trees shaded the junction and years of decaying leaves carpeted the floor silencing my boots as I crossed over. The dry leaves were lovely to walk upon and evocative of the hunting grounds of my youth… My mind formed images of my tiny, boyhood frame crouched and head down in search of the tiny lizards which might be caught in a handful of snatched leaves. My garden in Berengaria was an exotic zoo of fascinating creatures. Back home in England my village friends would still be in pursuit of sticklebacks and rabbits; none of them would bear witness to the silver flash of a speeding lizard or my little Cypriot safaris, carried out in the oven heat of summer,…

Just beyond the parched ravine was another of the early Cypriot buildings, something I was getting used to seeing. This one was made of honey-coloured stone; the structure was roofless and looked rather forlorn. It was a dwelling of pent design with a sloping roof to shed rain and a neat line of now glassless windows. Holes in the walls had lost their timber years ago and only the stonework remained. All the buildings harboured now were weeds and rubble. If I hid myself in the long grass at the side of the trail, might I see a farmer's apparition or hear the laughter of children born a world away from digital technology?

My lovely road continued its pastoral way west until it passed a deserted factory where I began to hear speeding traffic coming from the B9 main road linking the Morfou area (now renamed Güzelyurt in Northern Cyprus) with Nicosia. I stepped from the relative quiet of my country lane onto the busy carriageway which, further east, circumvented Palaiometocho to the north by means of the new A9 bypass. I watched a few vehicles whizz by and considered again how it wouldn't take very long by car to reach Nicosia, but for a pedestrian the capital was now some way off. I turned left and had something of a double-take… I was sure I'd just seen a wallaby! Sure enough, in a field to my left, I made out several of the Antipodean creatures along with deer, antelope and peacocks – not heat exhaustion, but an amateur zoo.

A road sign instructed me that heading directly west would deliver me to Troodos – and presumably the Kykkos Monastery. If I took a road to my right, it would take me to Mammari, which is one of just a handful of hamlets which lie deep within the Buffer Zone. I had read about an unfortunate incident which happened near the village involving a farmer and an undiscovered landmine. The farmer was unhurt; his tractor was not.

I was walking awfully close to the Green Line and just about everything to my right was pretty much *in* the Buffer

Zone. I wondered if there were any other landmines still lying undiscovered in the fields to the north of me.

I used my GPS system to double-check my position because the actual layout of roads seemed to differ a little from those on my map. I turned on my Montana 600 and waited for the device to locate a selection of available satellites; after a few moments a coloured map appeared on the screen showing my position and heading by means of a blue arrow. I discovered the track I'd taken from Palaiometocho was further south of the one I'd planned on using, so my intersection with the B9 had occurred slightly further east. With the confusion abated, I reassessed my position and noticed my originally intended route joined the main road just a few hundred yards ahead of me. As I passed the point where the trail met the road, I saw this route would have been an awkward slog across the soft soil of recently harvested fields. I kept on a westward track towards Akaki and before long I crossed what turned out to be the start of the bypass. I made my way over a very pedestrian-unfriendly junction to ascend a rising road into the village. I was hungry and tired, and it was about 4.30pm when I drew up alongside a very rundown supermarket. Large windows looked unpromising with long cracks repaired with sun-bleached duct tape. The automatic doors shook violently as they opened to welcome me in. Once inside, I quickly realised the exterior wasn't representative of the interior. The store was clean and tidy with several locals either perusing the shelves or engaging in light conversation with other shoppers. My rucksack and other equipment made it difficult to navigate my way around the store's narrow aisles without drawing unwanted attention from other customers and staff alike. I was looking for bananas and nuts – good energy food – a chocolate treat and fresh water. Time and daylight were always a consideration for me because I had to gauge arriving at a decent place to camp which was rural, away from prying eyes and not too far from my route west – all factors more easily realised in daylight. With this in mind, I decided to save time and ask where specific items were in the store. A man in an un-ironed T-shirt approached me. His top carried the ambiguous message 'Don't Blow It Go On', and broached a picture of a potted cannabis plant – which fell short of helping to clear up any confusion with the logo.

'Hello, can I help you?' he said, sounding very like Manuel from *Fawlty Towers*.

'Yes, thank you.' I spoke out my list.

'OK, OK, this way please,' said my host. Then, suddenly, and with theatrical relish, 'Manuel' took on the part of 'adult guardian' whilst I submitted to the role of 'overloaded and helpless child'. A bemused audience of Greek Cypriot ladies stopped their shopping and rotated like ample-framed mobiles to watch the spectacle of Manuel and me performing a kind of supermarket sweep or smash 'n' grab. I worried that the ladies' indignant frowns resulted from a belief that they were witnessing an unarmed hold-up and that Manuel's family were obviously in great peril and tied up somewhere pending a ransom of groceries.

'Here. Bananas.' My companion pointed at a collection of stunted, yellow fruit. 'This way...' I followed like a faithful dog... 'Here nuts,' he said as Ronnie Barker appeared in a thought bubble (*Your* nuts m'lord [sic]). I was led to a shelf of Cadbury's chocolate and, finally, a fridge full of chilled water bottles.

'Thank you so much,' I said. 'What is your name?'

'I am Marios,' he replied. 'I am from Romania.'

'*Mulțumesc*,' I said, which is about all the Romanian I know.

'Where are you doin'?' said Marios, with delicious syntax.

'I'm walking to Astromeritis today, but this morning I was in Nicosia,' I said.

'Nicosia? You walk?' He questioned this whilst puffing up both cheeks and widening his eyes.

'Yes.' I briefly outlined my quest and showed him some drone footage which he was very impressed with.

'Great pictures,' he enthused.

'I'm following the Green Line,' I said.

'Ah, yes. I see it on Discovery Channel,' he replied excitedly. I thanked him again and was about to pay at the checkout when he placed his right palm onto his chest, as if about to take an oath of allegiance, and said, 'No. Please to take, I pay. Good luck.' I didn't know what to say, I was genuinely shocked. I had entered the supermarket with some concern about its ramshackle appearance, but inside I'd found a very kind Romanian gentleman who may have lacked ironing facilities but abounded in generosity.

Outside, I turned left and walked deeper into the village along a broad pavement, which, like Xylotymvou, looked very French-provincial.

Akaki was still in the district of Nicosia, though it had taken me almost an entire day to reach it. The village was the ideal place to live if you worked in Nicosia but couldn't afford the city's property prices. Akaki has a long and interesting history, and after the war of 1974, a few hundred Turkish Cypriot residents were expelled only to be replaced by an influx of similarly displaced Greek Cypriots from north of the border. Such exchanges were a common occurrence resulting from the conflict.

Just recently, Akaki's historic significance received an enormous boost. In 2016, an archaeological dig in the village uncovered a large and truly remarkable set of mosaics dating back to the fourth century AD. The largest, a mosaic floor, depicts a scene from a Roman hippodrome. Colourful chariots can be seen with each carriage drawn by a team of four horses. The skill of the artisan involved was seriously impressive; the mosaic tiles are so small and so finely and subtly coloured, that great detail was made possible. The flanks of the different coloured horses were shaded as if they'd been finely painted, each adorned with an elaborate headdress and harness. The mosaics are thought to be a feature floor in what was once the home of a wealthy Roman nobleman. For the archaeologists, the location of the site has caused a significant rethink about Roman Cyprus. Assumptions had been made about the wealth of the island being exhibited only near the coast, but Akaki is well inland, and whoever owned these floors had obviously spared no expense investing in an incredibly special residence. It would seem reasonable to suggest this wasn't just an island retreat or simple workplace. This was a lovingly created home produced with a sense of having found a place beautiful enough to settle down in, perhaps for the rest of their life? For me, such discoveries confirmed my belief that in ancient times there was as much sophistication as any around today. Although ancient communities may have lacked antibiotics or the internal combustion engine, they were profoundly aware of the importance of aesthetics and had highly developed cultures. Even in the wilds of Mongolia, far, far away from any metropolis, highly preserved, almost prehistoric graves have been discovered in the melting tundra. I remember seeing the excavation of one grave on TV which yielded up the body of a female – thought to be a princess – whose frozen limbs still had visible and finely drawn tattoos. She'd been buried with her horse, and both steed and rider were adorned with gold accoutrements and elaborate drapery. If this young lady had ridden into town, back in her day, she would have looked every bit as striking as any modern-day royal rolling up in a gleaming limousine. I thought carefully about the *very necessary* differentiation between a people who lacked modern technology and so-called 'enlightenment', from a generation whose appreciation of beauty was profoundly sophisticated.

Looking at the excellence of the mosaics on display, I wondered why this wealthy Roman chose to build in this exact location. His villa was sited near a significant river that was seasonal and dry most summers. His home is almost equidistant between the Troodos and Kyrenia mountain ranges and about a day's journey from the nearest ports which lie to the northwest. Taking a northwesterly track would lead through a gap between the two mountain ranges and on to another area of even more ancient infrastructure. Not far from Kato Pyrgos, which would be my *ultimate* goal, lie the fascinating ruins of Soli and Vouni. These areas had their origins in the fifth and sixth centuries BC and both locations are something of a Cypriot's best-kept secret. The two places are archaeologically important and there are many tales about ancient Greeks and Persians and their fascinating military entanglements. From near these places, copper, mined in the hills of Troodos, was exported all over the Classical world. Was our rich nobleman a dealer in copper? Today the area around Akaki is agricultural, with acres of relatively small fields, so perhaps the mysterious owner of the villa was just an early landowner or successful farmer. Although the contours of the land and the river are probably quite unchanged, even after 1,700 years, the land around the villa may have looked vastly different if it had been deforested or developed by successive generations of farmers. Whatever the case, this residence was a very special place.

Interestingly, the Ashmolean exhibits of ancient Cyprus included a toy chariot, pulled by four tiny horses, and the details on the little novelty corroborated the features on Akaki's mosaic. Each toy horse also sported an elaborate headdress and extravagant harness. I wondered where on the island the model had been discovered and if that place was anywhere near Akaki and its equine, ceramic masterpiece.

Further on, at a roadside resting place, a statue of Makarios had been erected. The cleric, who looked a little out of proportion artistically, was leaning forward purposely, his left arm raised with a slender index finger extended. He looked like an unveiled version of the Ghost of Christmas Future, and he seemed to have spotted something interesting in the distance.

Yet his posture was metaphysical and I'm certain the observer was supposed to see the archbishop's digit pointing towards a different, better future. On the surface, Makarios had been a politically disinterested churchman but, privately, he was a representative of EOKA and an ardent supporter of the so-called freedom fighters. I'm not sure whether it was intended, but the statue of the archbishop also pointed directly to the Buffer Zone just a few hundred metres away with the hinterland of Northern Cyprus beyond. Perhaps I was reading too much into it?

Making my way out of the village, I came across an impressive stadium, seemingly quite out of proportion for such a small village. The sound of raised voices was emanating from within, so I crossed the road to take a look. On a well-maintained football pitch, a noisy training session was underway with a professional-looking team in bright yellow shirts. There is a thriving amateur league in Cyprus, probably because a local soccer team provides an important focus or welcome distraction for villagers as well as a positive outlet for youthful energy. Most villages and many towns in the UK would love facilities like the ones I saw in Akaki. To produce a quality pitch with an enclosed stadium, floodlights, tiered seating and changing rooms takes a community spirit and generous local funding. The very existence of this sports complex was testament to a strong synergy in the village and, according to the letters painted onto the stand, this team had been around since 1924.

On the other side of the main road stood the local police station where an abandoned car, 'parked' outside, appeared to be slowly sinking into the ground. I wondered if its presence was a kind of rebellious protestation. Perhaps it had been impounded after the owner had violated a minor traffic law? Then, seeking satisfaction, the driver had decided to burden the local constabulary with its crumbling hulk as retribution.

I still had quite a walk ahead of me if I were to find a suitable camping place before dark. I was hoping to set up camp just south of Astromeritis, so I pressed on, crossing a grassy riverbed, and passing a quiet collection of small, factory-like buildings as the road out of the village gently chicaned right then left. If the centre of the village was reminiscent of rural France, then the quiet buildings and dusty loading bays flanking the exit road reminded me of a scene set for an adventure featuring Tom Sawyer and Huckleberry Finn. The stillness and the warmth seemed to hang in the air like the drawl of a narrator from the Deep South – straw hat, shoeless feet and faded dungarees. There wasn't a soul around; a ghostly column of dust spiralled up from the verge and vanished into the branches of an overhanging tree.

Although the sky had clouded a little, the landscape around Akaki was illuminated with filtered sunlight making everything glow with hues of cream, copper and gold. To the west, and in the last quarter of the sky, the sun was veiled in long clouds of silver, light grey and white as a weather front formed a looming and distant diagonal. Occasionally, great, long sunbeams streamed across Akaki and into the Buffer Zone, coming to rest on the southern shoulder of the Kyrenia mountains to the north. The sunlight, like the birds in the air, didn't recognise the Green Line or any restricted zone; nature was blissfully ignorant of the construct. Even the statue of Makarios was rained upon with childlike innocence and scorched by the summer sun with a complete and delightful disregard for high office.

Just beyond the village I spotted something interesting. South of the Buffer Zone the Greek Cypriots seemed to have a lot less angst about the defence of their republic. In Northern Cyprus there were military outposts, lookouts, troop movements and all manner of army infrastructure but, so far, the only military compound I'd seen this side of the Buffer Zone was the serious-looking mirror post near Paralimni about a week before. However, just outside Akaki, not far from the road, stood a military structure the like of which I'd not seen in Northern Cyprus. Dug into the side of a small hill was a concrete bunker, very like the sort the Germans had built in France to thwart any allied invasion. It was a stark construction of reinforced and poured concrete, and its south-facing entrance had been well camouflaged with beige and green paint. Opposite the bunker, and offsetting the austere vault, a man was selling enormous watermelons and a variety of vegetables. A few people stopped to make purchases as I passed by his little stall.

The usual golden light of the early evening was becoming less spectacular as I trudged on towards Peristerona. The low cloud forced the retreating sun to shower its rays across a darkening sky, and the flat landscape was already surrounding me with lines of silhouetted and profoundly dark trees and buildings. The day was slipping away with shadows and light lengthening and fading respectively, the long shadows of Cyprus knifing the heart and ground and reminding me of my mortality; everything I was seeing would never be repeated exactly.

Although Akaki and Peristerona look to be two separate villages, their respective outskirts extend sparsely along the main B9 road to nearly touch. The village of Peristerona lies right by the Buffer Zone and the road to Astromeritis and its border crossing heads northwest to intersect the Green Line, presenting itself as a concave shape surrounding on three sides anyone intent on crossing into Northern Cyprus. Unlike my passage at Pergamos, which was accessed via the Sovereign Base Area of Dhekelia – softening the impact of the crossing – tomorrow, my route would head directly from the Republic of Cyprus, through the Buffer Zone and into Northern Cyprus. Looking at the map, this meant a walk of about two kilometres right through the Buffer Zone. The geography between these two republics would provide the starkest contrast for me to experience so far, other than when I had passed through no man's land in Nicosia. Here, either side of the Buffer Zone, two separated and opposing conurbations come right up to a UN-controlled corridor.

In Peristerona there is clear evidence of both Turk and

Greek having lived side by side prior to 1974. Along with a spectacular Byzantine church, dedicated to St Barnabas and St Hilarion, there is a fine mosque but, unlike the one just beyond the barbed wire at Pergamos, this Muslim sanctuary is one of the oldest on the island. Like some of the Orthodox churches in Northern Cyprus, which lie abandoned and unused, today the mosque is frequented only by pigeons – strangely apt given that Peristerona derives from the Greek word *peristeri,* meaning dove or pigeon. Like Akaki, Peristerona has a local river which is also dry most summers. Sadly, the island's intercommunal violence of the 1960s saw the Turkish minority occupants of the village fleeing to towns north of the demarcation line.

In what might be seen as something of a condescending act of 'diplomacy', the British Government once printed stamps featuring the almost adjoined church and mosque of Peristerona as evidence of 'understanding and tolerance' between the two communities – wishful thinking with a sticky back.

I had passed through most of Peristerona to reach my goal of camping just south of Astromeritis, when suddenly the thought of lying down, bootless and comfortable, overwhelmed me. I had made excellent progress that day, from leaving Nicosia at dawn and heading almost directly west all day with no lengthy detours to the north or south. With the capital so far behind me I decided to celebrate with an early night and pitch my tent at the next opportunity.

Just ahead, near the roadside, I saw what I thought would be a 1974 war memorial and decided to take a look. On closer inspection the marble construction was in honour of Flt Lt Andreas Papansozomenos, a Greek Cypriot pilot, whose helicopter had crashed in 2006, killing both him and his Russian instructor.

As per usual I wanted to pitch my tent out of sight to avoid a rude awakening from an overenthusiastic policeman or nosy farmer. I walked around the obelisk and noticed that the base of the structure extended to the rear, leaving a triangular area of flat stone almost exactly the size of my tent. It was out of sight, quiet and not too far from the road; should any intoxicated Cypriot steer clean off the road, they would have to plough through tons of marble before they reached my nylon bedroom. My portable home, an ultralight, two-man puptent, consisted of two featherweight aluminium poles and inner and outer sheets; the simple structure could be assembled in just a few minutes. If necessary, like that evening, I didn't even need to use tent pegs to pin it to the ground. I assembled the unit and it fitted onto the plinth behind the memorial as if it had grown there. The monument was surrounded by a cordon of green cypress trees which were about the same colour as my tent. A farm track passed close to my little campsite, but I was so well hidden I doubted anyone using the track would see me. For the first time on this walk I was camping on a flat surface, which made for a wonderfully comfortable bed. Within a couple of minutes, all my belongings were neatly arranged inside; I removed my boots and socks and lay in relative luxury with snacks and water at hand and an overhead light to read by. On my map I noticed that my direct route west had opened a considerable gap between me and Nicosia. I took great pleasure in adding a long line of chevrons detailing my progress that day. Overall, in just a few days' walking, I'd crossed around two thirds of the entire island. I now felt confident that I'd finish my journey well ahead of schedule and that tomorrow night would be the last of my journey.

For me, the long day's walking was over; tomorrow I would cross back into Northern Cyprus and continue west towards Kato Pyrgos. What would tomorrow hold? What would I see? Where would I stay? I soon felt sleepy with the comfort and confidence things would continue more or less as they had so far. I was lying remarkably close to the Buffer Zone; in fact, I was lying in a sleeping bag – or *on* one – just a stone's throw from no man's land. I thought about Andreas the pilot, his boyhood and all the stories he would have about Astromeritis. Outside I heard a car ambling up the farm track about two metres to my right… it passed me by as I lay, unseen, behind my perimeter of cypress trees. I thought about the Roman mosaics again and drifted off daydreaming about the meeting of a Cypriot horse trader and a man called Judah Ben Hur.

Berengaria's Tiny Lizards

You were swift and beautifully made,
Soft gills pulsating in sandy hue,
Striped like a fish – fast as an arrow,
To catch you meant a fistful of leaves… then,
Decanted into my hand you'd lose your rudder,
Tiny appendage twisting alone,
I meant you no harm and let you go,
To grow another tail.

M.J.W. Clark – *Memories of Cyprus 1970–72*

9

The Republic of Cyprus – Crossing into Northern Cyprus

Peristerona to Lefke

Tuesday 12 June 2018

The last time I glanced at my watch before falling asleep it had read 1.40am and then, in what felt like just a few moments, it was 4.50am – time to get up.

I packed slowly and carefully taking the time to treat my feet to a close inspection and liberal anointing of cream. It felt more urban than rural to be repacking my rucksack and equipment on such a stable base as that provided by the plinth and its local funders who, like many Cypriots, had raised money for a monument. It was just pre-sunup when I strapped on my Berghaus rucksack, tightened its straps and attached my bumbag. I carefully arranged what was left of my provisions so, during my first few hundred metres, they could be consumed easily. I tucked my 'trusty' map into a front pocket and made one more 'precious-check' before squeezing through a pair of cypress trees and emerging like an androgynous dryad into a cool and quiet dawn. Whenever I left one of my few campsites it felt a little brusque to move on without leaving a pile of stones as a marker or sign of thanks. To have been allowed to lay my head down for a while just inches from primordial soil was atavistic and pleasant. I was deeply thankful to something much greater than myself; I was twice blessed – once by seeing a new day, and again by living so freely and simply. Perhaps that's why birds sing when darkness gives way to light?

I walked back round the memorial plinth to rejoin the B9 which heads west out of Peristerona then northwest up to Astromeritis. I placed my feet onto a road surface polished by tyres, pausing for a second before turning right to walk away from Andreas Papansozomenos' little palace of marble.

It was very early and there didn't appear to be a soul awake except me. There were certainly no cars on the road and, apart from the distant sound of various manic cockerels, all I could hear was the sound of my own boots, displacing loose stones and rudely tarnishing the silence.

As I walked between the straggling infrastructure of Peristerona, I soon caused absolute havoc… I was passing an iron gate when suddenly there came the sound of metal chain running through a hoop, the abrupt and violent arresting of a rapidly moving body and a deep-throated barking. In a real-life re-enactment of a scene from *101 Dalmatians*, the doggie-jungle drums commenced *molto fortissimo*. Across the road another canine, with much shorter vocal cords, started yapping its little head off and, in stereo, a pair of dogs next door to the yapper barked in unison. By the time I'd passed about a dozen houses at least as many dogs were making their contribution to the choir of cacophony; I was the 'destroyer of worlds'. At any moment I could expect an angry and pyjama-clad Cypriot to emerge from their dwelling, clutching a firearm familiar to anyone who'd been brought up watching *Tom and Jerry* cartoons. Certain I was about to face the more dangerous end of a nineteenth-century blunderbuss, I became very concerned that all these rabid animals were securely tethered and that I wouldn't find myself bitten by a monstrous and slavering escapee.

Somehow, up high and to my right, a pair of pickup trucks had been parked on a flat roof, though there was absolutely no evidence as to how they'd got up there… Perhaps the owner also 'drove' a Chinook. Running along the roof's parapet, a pair of terriers yelped away adding not only a screeching soprano to the racket but also a kind of frantic choreography. Finally, as I entered a more built-up area the decibel level dropped to a volume which admitted other thoughts.

The grey-topped and empty mosque of Peristerona provided a sharp foreground to the indistinct and ghostly mountains of Troodos beyond. The early morning sky was coloured pink, courtesy of a few wispy clouds on the horizon which led the eye to a pale blue overhead. The village was, as far as I could tell, remarkably undisturbed by the dawn chorus of rattled, frothy guard dogs and the air had a lovely freshness to it. I drew alongside the hill which had provided the inspiration for the British stamp-artists of fifty years ago and felt a little embarrassed at the British condescension. At least the two buildings' closeness to one another was true. The five-domed, Orthodox church stood just below the silent mosque with just a few metres between the places of worship; from the road they looked conjoined. I wondered how long it had been since the voice of a muezzin had called the faithful to prayer from the tannoy speakers hidden in the minaret? The familiar shape appeared as a plaintive and lonely tower in the early sunlight with its unpainted stone reminding me of the fading Renaissance architecture of Italy.

The sun broke the horizon just as I crossed the dry riverbed of the seasonal Peristerona river. I looked behind me to the east; a few cypress trees and low buildings were lined up against the sky giving the impression they'd been cut from black paper by a silhouette artist, his handiwork being superimposed against

ground of gold, silver and pale pink. In the centre was
ing crest of bright sunlight and radiating warmth,
producing a scene far too beautiful for an audience of one. Not
being able to share the display with a companion caused me
to sigh; it was a moment which dispensed with the milk of life
and exchanged it for a rich cream of *joie de vivre*; too viscous
to imbibe quickly. My thoughts turned to my family and true
love's immunity from attrition no matter the distance between
its subjects.

Most of Peristerona lies south of the main road, so I had to
forgo the delights of the village-proper which covered a curved
hillside to my left; I pressed on northwest towards Astromeritis.

A roadside shrine drew my attention to the dangers of
speeding traffic on country roads. The tiny little structure
resembled a birdhouse on a short column, but inside it contained
only an oil lamp and a framed notice urging drivers to take care
with the words, 'It's very easy to take the life of a child'. There
are hundreds of these shrines all over Cyprus and, of course,
the wider Greek-Mediterranean, each remembering loved ones
lost in a fatal road accident or other tragedy. Sobered, I walked
on and noted, with some delight, that a road sign included the
name Kato Pyrgos, where I would complete my walk. According
to the notice, Kato Pyrgos was now just forty-three kilometres
away!

The border crossing at Astromeritis came into sight soon after
Peristerona and the road up to the checkpoint was unremarkable
until just before the barriers and guard house appeared. On the
left was an elaborate memorial to the 'Morfou Heroes'; it was
made up of a broad, white marble wall several metres long with
black iron reliefs of huddled refugees set into the stone. A soldier,
imprisoned behind bars, stood with an arm aloft as if pleading
for release. These ordinary people and their stoicism, despite
displacement and dispossession, have rendered them heroic for
posterity. However, this image might be seen as nationalistic,

because 'victims' were often made into 'heroes' by communities on both sides of the Green Line. In *The Politics of Trauma in Education*, by Michalinos Zembylas, I realised I was reading the memoir of a Greek Cypriot professor who, as a child, had never heard of a 'Turkish Cypriot'. In Cyprus he'd been taught there were Greek Cypriots and 'Turks'. He was a victim of a biased pedagogy from an early age. Any involvement by him in 'hot' protests (close confrontations with Turks) was hailed as heroic behaviour. Much later, after a university education abroad, he met a 'Turkish Cypriot' and their initial, fiery arguments were soon extinguished when increasingly historic references to acts of aggression by either side became tiresome. Eventually the attrition led to a close friendship, hopefully the future of Cyprus in microcosm. Professor Zembylas must be credited with great magnanimity, after all, as George Bernard Shaw said, '*Those who cannot change their minds cannot change anything.*'

There are, still, annual protestations by locals in Astromeritis; these tend to be about nearby 'occupied' villages which were once Greek Cypriot. Across no man's land, or the 'dead zone', as some locals call it, the main town, Morfou, has had its Greek name changed to the Turkish, Güzelyurt. The tiny village of Zodeia, now called Bostanci, lies at the end of a fenced corridor of road – cutting right through the Buffer Zone. Within this dead zone, an active UN base stands as a deterrent to any violence from locals on either side.

I approached the checkpoint and nervously handed over my passport. I'd read, in several guidebooks, that the crossing at Astromeritis was, '*Open to vehicular traffic only*'. Probably because the long, rural corridor between the two checkpoints might be too much of a temptation for would-be protestors crossing no man's land on Shanks's pony. Perhaps an ambling miscreant might pass an antagonist on foot and then there could be trouble. Pedestrians are more suited to breaking through the long fences running the length of the road and seeking out a fight. Why motorists were acquitted of all suspicion eluded me. As it was, my passport was scanned by a large, moustachioed Greek policeman and, a few seconds later, I was in the strange quiet of the Buffer Zone – on foot!

At Pergamos, the distance between the two republics is in the Eastern Sovereign Base Area (ESBA), which acts as a semi de-civilianised space within the Buffer Zone. Consequently, any possible intercommunal tension is more easily controlled because the ESBA is an active military base operated by UK Forces, twenty-four hours a day. In Nicosia, the two republics are separated by a short road through no man's land which has the bearing of an Aleppo avenue or Sarajevo side street. Yet the scarred, urban passageways stand in a now peaceful city with a heavy UN presence and a carefully patrolled and long-established Buffer Zone. But there, in Astromeritis, the two republics exist in plain view of one another across open fields. Every day, the sight of lost land and lost property was on show as a provocative reminder of how things used to be. If reunification ever happens, then the world's peacemakers and negotiators could pull up their chairs right here to observe exactly how the toothpaste might be put back in the tube.

Morfou, to use its Greek name, has been described as a lost jewel for Greek Cypriots. It was once a predominantly Greek Cypriot town, but then the war happened, and it became an entirely Turkish Cypriot conurbation. Greek Cypriots were dispossessed and displaced; their furnished houses were suddenly occupied by strangers. Of course, this was a scenario which played out in reverse south of the Green Line. Morfou might be a good place to test any process of reunification because it's neither too small nor too big a place. The solely Turkish Cypriot community has been in existence for well over forty years so how, exactly, do you remove 'illegal' tenants and restore properties to their rightful, Greek Cypriot owners? And how would you properly care for any late-dispossessed,

Turkish Cypriot community? One possible solution has been the suggestion of a new town being built nearby which might cushion the blow to any newly displaced. Whatever happens, the entire exercise of reunification is an engine requiring an extravagance of high grade, 'fully synthetic', political lubrication. In Güzelyurt, these difficult plans have been close to agreement but then there have been equally firm resolutions *not* to relinquish land. Just as political progress was being made, it was quickly found to be unworkable and redundant. The whole negotiating process is an unravelling of tight knots or seized and seemingly immoveable joints, but many of the younger generation are keen to see reunification. Perhaps then, *all* might benefit from a unified island without sanctions, and free trade might be restored. Members of both republics need to keep seeking a resolution, even if it turns out to be one requiring great sacrifice and mutually painful compromise.

My mind returned to the non-unified present as I contemplated the empty road in front of me. This short walk needed to be savoured. On either side of me, well-maintained chain link fences prevented anything other than progress directly towards the checkpoint in Bostanci. The first thing to strike me was the quiet. Just like the Buffer Zone I had stumbled into near Paralimni, this no man's land was eerily quiet. Interestingly, running alongside the road, from one republic to the other, was a row of pylons supplying power as well as telecommunications – presumably without dispute or complaint from either community. There was the occasional birdsong to emphasise the quiet, and in the middle of the zone I slowed to the pace of an asthmatic tortoise to soak in my surroundings. The fields on either side were well cultivated, though one had been left to lie fallow. I spotted a very impressive lookout building just ahead which had various aerials reminiscent of an air traffic control tower. As I drew closer, I saw this was UN post 32 and the lookout post was just an improvised addition to the top of a water tower. The UN enclosure I'd walked through near the east coast was 114 posts further east than this one. The ground around the compound's buildings was scattered with whitewashed stones; these either provided lines of demarcation around the buildings or spelled out the familiar acronym: UN. The painted rocks in the base were reminiscent of those one might find outlining an 'H' at some remote cattle farm in the Australian outback where visitors tend to arrive by helicopter. The whole place had the air of a homestead, and probably, for the penned-up soldiers within, that's exactly what it was. At first, I wasn't sure if the camp was active, but I soon realised the UN flag flying overhead gave warning that UN troops were indeed providing a small presence twenty-four hours a day. On the far side of the compound an orange windsock hung limp in a gentle breeze; all around was so still, there was a temptation to just sit and enjoy the tranquillity. A signpost in the enclosure offered a 'Welcome' from the Argentinian Task Force – its current tenants. I noticed the inner sanctum of the camp was screened from view with the same netting popular with most of the army bases in Northern Cyprus. A few UN pickup trucks were parked outside the main building and, wouldn't you know it, in keeping with local tradition, the UN also had a neurotic dog which barked loudly to let its owners know the end of the world was nigh.

It was still very early, and one or two urgent-looking pigeons flew with alacrity between the two republics. As I neared the checkpoint in Bostanci I spotted a few empty buildings. These were a more acute reminder of the events of 1974. Adjacent to the crossing point, to my right stood a long-disused, BP petrol station – slowly disappearing into a jungle of weeds and saplings. Once again, a glance at the building and its faded paint brought back distinct memories of my childhood in Cyprus. Adjacent to the garage forecourt was a small bungalow with an overgrown veranda and it was obvious that the little house was now unoccupied and, given its position, it was likely to remain so until after any reunification. I wondered what story would be told by the now-displaced occupant as they suddenly found themselves a dispossessed refugee; it was possible they'd been forced to relocate to a new home within view of their old one. How strange to have built a home and lovingly cared for it, only to be rudely transplanted – yet not far enough for you to be denied the familiar views of nearby mountains or fields. It would seem to be a peculiar type of torture to live just a few hundred metres from a place where you had put down metaphorical roots. To then watch literal weeds take hold, inexorably covering over your home and memory spaces with unchecked growth.

The actual infrastructure of the checkpoint was quite impressive. There were several temporary buildings and a covered area where vehicles were inspected and their occupants had their papers or passports checked.

I approached the first Portakabin window but was waved away languidly by a uniformed lady within. At the next booth I handed over my passport to a thin man and waited for it to be processed. Inside, about three or four border officials were sitting around with a studied attempt at looking 'necessary'. From what I witnessed, this checkpoint was a little over-the-top compared with the Greek, laissez-faire version just down the road. It had the slightly miniaturised look of the customs points familiar to those arriving in Calais or Dover. It must have been ten times the size of its humble counterpart on the other side of the Buffer Zone. The skinny official handed back my passport and nodded his approval; I was free to enter Northern Cyprus. As I emerged from beneath a gleaming awning, a fountain, set amid rows of enormous flowerpots, burst into life. Several tourist posters were on display, which I found encouraging; Northern Cyprus needs income from tourism and the more visitors crossing the border from holidays in the Republic of Cyprus, so much the better.

Leaving the border behind, I quickly found myself in a typically Cypriot village but with a difference: the lack of economic prosperity was immediately obvious. Stepping from the confines of the well-maintained control point into the village beyond was a move from monied infrastructure to the opposite. In the Republic of Cyprus, houses often had fairly new cars parked in their driveways, roads were well maintained and shops were well stocked. In Bostanci there was evidence of *some* wealth, but there was plenty of evidence of need. Many houses had the look of places which seldom threw anything away, as if economics mothered and engendered a wisdom not to discard old cars or appliances whose parts and motors could be donated and transplanted into other vehicles or appliances. One dusty roadside was covered in ancient and rusting farm machinery, and a similarly corroded car stood nearby, half covered by a stained tarpaulin.

I was slowly becoming aware of a disingenuousness which seemed to pervade parts of Northern Cyprus, hanging faintly in the air like an unfamiliar musk. There were hundreds of troops, proud mosques and a Kyrenian mountainside lit up to boast about a motherland and the happiness of its countrymen, but many of these amazing people seemed to be victims of want. Many millions of Turkish lira were being spent on, essentially, useless projects which didn't directly, or indirectly, help Turkish Cypriots. When I had met younger members of the Turkish Cypriot community they were obviously quite as capable as any of their Greek Cypriot equivalents but lacked opportunity. To me, some projects in Northern Cyprus felt like pride or hubris; I had seen how sanctions were affecting the people's lives and wondered whether the government in Ankara could do more or whether this was an unforeseen lasting consequence of the 'intervention'.

In 1974, the Greek junta had, to my mind, acted crassly and Turkey was forced to react. The Greeks had ignored the United Nations directive not to seek unification with Cyprus and disregarding it had cost the lives of thousands of young men on both sides of the divide. The aftermath is an island which has been locked in a state of limbo for decades. There was a time when these islanders lived together peacefully, and their differences didn't appear to be much of an issue. I'm surprised the leaders in Athens didn't fully comprehend what might and did happen to this beautiful island and its communities.

I stopped suddenly on the pavement at a verdant outpouring of summer jasmine cascading across the footpath in front of me. Before I reached the overgrowth the air was filled with the heady aroma of the blossom which is so evocative of the Mediterranean. It was still early enough for the nightly perfume to linger on with a delightful trespass into daylight.

All around, the little village was coming alive as people were waking to a new day. I'd been up for hours by the time I crossed the centre of Bostanci where, just like Pergamos, Turkish gentlemen were taking coffee and water in the shade of vine-topped verandas. I saw a garage shop and went in to buy two bottles of water. Both bottle tops came off with little resistance and I wondered if each container had been refilled from a tap and sold on for an easy profit. I strode off and passed under a glorious silk tree sunbathing its spreading canopy of bright green leaves and seed pods. At a junction in the centre of Bostanci I came across another 'standoff' between mosque and Orthodox church. Once again, both places of worship sat side by side though it was obvious which building lacked attention. The church and its elaborate tower, with intricate carving, were in good condition, but the walls of the building below were covered in peeling white paint. Yet, just a few metres away, the minarets of a pristine mosque radiated clean white stonework and gold design worked into various points along their length.

Soon I was entering Güzelyurt, realising immediately why the loss of Morfou, the Greek name for the town, had been so keenly felt. Güzelyurt was thriving, though it lacked any obvious commercialisation from tourism. Its geographical position has, so it would seem, been a blessing, with the town standing centrally in the gap which exists between the western edge of the Kyrenia mountains and the northeastern reaches of the Troodos range. The Turkish name, Güzelyurt, means 'Beautiful Place'. Anyone landing on the northwest coast of Cyprus would find an expansive, wide bay, and the first major place of civilisation inland might have been Morfou. According to archaeological discoveries, the land around Morfou has revealed the earliest traces of human habitation on the island including evidence that the island's resources of copper are what drew the first settlers.

As I crossed the town's wide and busy square, I was curious about how this lovely little town might have developed further had it not been restricted by over four decades of economic limitations. On the east coast, Famagusta had been decimated by the war of 1974 and, because of its position right on the Green Line, its thriving tourist industry had been abruptly halted. I was certain that Güzelyurt would have taken up an enviable position on any tourist map, had it been able to develop without sanctions and trade restrictions. To Greek Cypriots, this place would always be Morfou and, if reunification happens and restitution is part of the process, Güzelyurt is certain to be renamed, should land and property be returned to their original owners. Today there isn't much to see if you're looking for museums or historical sites; there are Orthodox icons on display at Agios Mamas church and a low-key museum of natural history close by, but the charm of Güzelyurt is found in its streets. For me, it was interesting to see a place in Northern Cyprus which was more town than village, and I was delighted to see signs of relatively healthy commerce. There was a large civil defence building nearby and standing guard outside in the forecourt was a very brassy statue of what I assumed was a typically sombre-looking Atatürk. His right arm was raised with a finger pointing at something in need of urgent attention. Perhaps Makarios (he

212

of Akaki) and Atatürk were pointing at each other across the Buffer Zone in a kind of fingers at dawn duel?

All around, Güzelyurt showed itself to be a great place to follow your nose for a few hours and wander on foot. However, I was following the Green Line, which meant foregoing the wonders of the town centre and heading west towards the villages of Günesköy, Aydinköy and Yeşilyurt before reaching Lefke where I planned to spend the night. I'd noticed that nearly all renamed towns or villages in Northern Cyprus were the namesakes of places in mainland Turkey.

On my way out of Güzelyurt I noticed a bus stop crowded with people heading to Nicosia and most looked to be in their twenties. I was suddenly aware of something hugely different about the town: it was the abundance of young people – and this posed the question, why? The answer came as I continued my journey west and saw a large building which revealed itself to be the Cyprus Health and Social Sciences University. I learned the university has a capacity for 10,000 students and that these scholars come from all over the island and indeed from all over the world. I was happier to see the modern campus than I was to witness the Hala Sultan Mosque on the road into Nicosia; this university was an obvious investment in people. I understood the desire and need for places of worship, but the building of such an ostentatious and expensive mosque, in a secular society, could easily be seen as more of a provocative pronouncement of nationalism. Such remotely controlled actions didn't seem conducive to peace and reconciliation. Were those young people, waiting patiently at the bus stop, the fallout from a decision made in Athens almost half a century ago? Weren't these kids deserving of a unified island, interacting communities and a homeland thriving under one flag?

As I journeyed across the island it was becoming obvious that the late standoff between Greek and Turkish communities is largely imposed by politicians. I'd witnessed great magnanimity between individuals on both sides of the Green Line, and most believed Turkey and Greece needed to let go of Cyprus for the benefit of all Cypriots. As I walked off, I could hear Ali the Red Falcon's words echo in my head… '*Not Turkey. Not Greece.*'

With Güzelyurt behind me, I found myself walking through fragrant citrus plantations; I decided to take some drone footage of the landscape because it was indeed a 'Beautiful Place'. The soil around this part of the island is reputed to be some of the most fertile on the island, and local farmers produce all manner of delicious fruit and vegetables.

I stepped off the main road into an unfenced plantation, dropping my rucksack onto a dusty track between neat rows of orange trees. A network of black water pipes disappeared under the little woodland to provide vital irrigation in dry seasons. I unpacked the drone and prepared it for flight, extending the machine's four arms and checking the four propellers at the end of each limb. Next, I ensured the wireless connection between my phone and the drone was working and registered its current position as 'Home'. This meant that whenever I'd finished filming, I could instruct the drone to return to 'Home' and it would automatically navigate its way back to the exact place it had taken off from. The drone launched vertically, and I watched my screen to monitor the drone's camera. The onboard gyro meant that all my footage remained steady despite any movement caused by my unskilled manoeuvres or gusts of wind; these were all cancelled out by the gimbal.

Despite hours of walking, it was still early and there was still a slight mistiness in the morning air. At an altitude of a hundred metres, the camera afforded me a magnificent view of the landscape. There were thousands of orange, lemon and lime trees in precise rows, and the whole scene looked as if it had been painted by Cezanne or a young and yet joyful Van Gogh. Below the drone, birds soared with complete freedom as they crisscrossed the farmland with flight lines rising and falling in the warm air. From on high I could see the various citrus groves interrupted by areas of open fields or copses of cypress and olive trees. Suddenly, a lone crow changed direction as it found itself heading directly for my camera. There was a busyness to the birdlife up there, though the urgency would have been centred on nothing more than the simple feeding of young or the feeding of themselves. In the distance, the Troodos range gave a hazy reference point and shady contrast to the verdant plain which was nearing its edge. The drone's camera showed the land as a broad, flat patchwork of a thousand shades of green and brown which halted abruptly at the wall of the Troodos range. I was an inexperienced drone pilot and didn't have the confidence to send it too far off but, as it was such a steady craft, I'd flown it out over the sea at Paralimni. If there wasn't too much wind, I was daring to send it a little higher with each flight. From such a vantage point the lack of topographical detail on my two-dimensional map, here, started to take on a three-dimensional form. Both the Kyrenia and Troodos mountains' tapering descent to the coast in the northwest could be appreciated easily when seen from a height which might normally involve a balloon, helicopter or tower of Babel. There was something otherworldly about the drone footage captured in those few moments above the orange grove.

I knew my journey was nearing its conclusion; my mind was filled with a fusion of boyhood memories and a sacred envy of my childhood. I understood I couldn't hope to regain my *'land of lost content'*; just as with A.E. Housman, it would always be out of reach. Yet the war of 1974 *had* produced a time lock, and, in various places like Nicosia, it did seem possible to reassemble faded images into a surreal reality, like opening a well-remembered book and feeling the thrill of the colours and the imagination they once triggered. It is a good thing to remember *not to forget* what you have put behind you; to stroll the corridors of your own museum of esoteric concentrate; to dwell in gratitude. In those unchanged locations my adult eyes scanned boyhood scenes, but beyond the retina, the brain had no precedent to cope with such confusion. Who gets to see the disturbed stones of youth still lying where you left them? Many get to see again a favourite toy or trinket stored in a parents' loft, but who has the chance to check their memory of an entire building frozen in time? Who finds the minutiae of half a century just as it was? The absolute preservation of the mundane – a coffee cup in the same spot, the contents evaporated.

Leaving Güzelyurt well behind put me on a southwesterly track as I circumvented the great Kolpos Morfou Bay which contributes a significant part of the coastal outline of Cyprus. As per usual there were several Turkish army bases which appeared to be a little more organised than those I'd seen east of Nicosia and there were certainly more troop movements. I noticed army trucks carrying uniformed soldiers between austere bases along the road and occasionally the lorries were loaded with off-duty troops who were out of uniform. Each lorryload of military youth resulted in an exchange of bonhomie as the soldiers issued me with frantic waves or thumbs-up, probably from an acute appreciation of my 'yomping' whilst they sat on their relatively luxurious lorry benches. Despite having had a father in the Royal Air Force, I have no experience of military life, but I do know a little about the physicality of walking with the weight of equipment on one's back. I also knew my load was about a *third* of the weight the average commando must lug about – and they often have to move at twice my pace; my experience had given me a renewed respect for these men.

I hoped to find shade in the village of Güneşköy and soon found a quiet road winding down to a little collection of houses which were nestled around an Orthodox church. As I walked through a scattering of rotting oranges, I disturbed a lounge of large, fringe-fingered lizards feasting either on the fruit or the flies hovering nearby. It was now extremely hot, and I was ready for a long drink and a longer rest. A glance at my watch told me it was now 10.20am, so I'd been walking for more than five hours.

In Güneşköy I was amused to see that a local store traded under the name of Borat Market; I smiled as I recalled the exploits of TV and film star Sacha Baron Cohen and his invented and hapless star of Kazakhstan. Unfortunately – or fortunately – Borat was out, and his shop was shut, so I went on a hunt for an alternative shopping experience. As usual, I was at the mercy of the locals when I entered the small village. There were usually just a couple of shops in places like these and the maze of roads always presented a dilemma. I was often desperate for nourishment and hydration by the time I reached my resting place, sometimes finding myself at a built-up junction, unsure whether to turn left or right. By turning right, I might find I circled back to find a store just to the left of where I'd just been – or vice versa. Thus, the easiest thing to do when entering a new village was to ask a local and hope they spoke a little English. However, in tiny villages, where most residents were older, English wasn't understood. This usually resulted in the use of sign language to convey my near starvation to some nonplussed local, whereupon my sweaty choreography was usually understood to mean, 'I have just crossed the Sahara and need water *immediately*.' That day's confrontation involved my peering into a white saloon car and asking the four occupants if they knew where a shop was. A young man in the back pointed to an open door about three metres down the street which made everyone else in the car burst into fits of giggles. This was the other possible outcome of my interactions with villagers; it was often the case that a shop in Northern Cyprus didn't come with the accoutrements of neon signage or any obvious identifying features. In this case the intended target of the boy's finger was a shop set up in the tiny front room of an otherwise entirely normal house. I thanked the gang in the car and took the three steps to the hidden shop where I discovered the only external indication of the shop's existence was a large open bag of potatoes sitting directly on the road near a concealed door.

Inside, the windowless store was cool, and there were a couple of fridges and cluttered shelves which sold all manner of unfamiliar items. Apparently, one problem that manufacturers encounter, especially of edible products, is that a name given to a chocolate bar in somewhere like Turkey might not *sound* quite so edible in, say, Spain. 'Plop' might present itself as a delicious chocolate treat in Istanbul but conjure up images of water closets for the Spaniard! This has meant manufacturers have had to come up with universally suitable names to maximise sales. Inside the little store my mind boggled at the names of the milkshakes, confectionery and other goods on sale. I registered such delights as 'Camel Balls' and 'Willy Gum', none of which had me reaching for my lira. I settled for familiarity whenever possible and emerged into the hot sun with a family-sized bottle of Pepsi, bottles of water, yoghurt for protein and a bubblegum-flavoured lolly which, though cold, was genuinely *awful* on the palate.

Adjacent to the shop, a dirty bus stop stood alongside a pair of stinking bins, each with a faint black smoke of circling flies. I was so tired and thirsty that I just leant against a stone wall a few metres from the bins where I swallowed the bubblegum suppository with the aid of neutralising water. I needed to look for somewhere shaded and quiet, so headed past the shop to the end of the road where the Orthodox church had been converted into a mosque. The front of the building was partially shaded, so I spread out in the quiet grounds for a while before realising that to have an afternoon of uninterrupted shade meant I needed to relocate to the other side of the church. To the rear of the building an area of flat concrete extended to a lawn where an adjacent ante building turned out to be a WC with running water. Luxury! I wondered if I risked arrest for indecency by applying cream to various chafed areas of my body in the grounds of a mosque, but its deserted atmosphere persuaded me to go ahead. I guessed the area of my temporary repose was largely unvisited, and so I took the opportunity to wash from head to toe, even rinsing my clothing, which I knew would dry in minutes. I set up my mat and pillow and lay in a delicious state of sock-free comfort with an occasional breeze further enhancing the experience. After a while, the wind started to gust, and my precious map suddenly took off before wedging itself in the bars of a nearby fence. In my haste to ensure that the map didn't reach Kato Pyrgos before me, I strained an injured finger as I leapt to my feet. I'd hurt the digit while mountaineering in Crete about two months earlier, where I must have been close to breaking it. Suddenly putting it under such pressure exacerbated the injury.

Later in the afternoon I revisited the clandestine 'potato shop', with all my equipment left quite safely in the shade at my bivouac. On this visit I found myself engaged in an impromptu Facetime conversation with the shop owner's relative back in London. By this time, word had got out that an extremely shortsighted British hiker was at large in the village; I was obviously considered to be some kind of minor celebrity...

*

One Day (8)

One day we went to St Andrew's Street in Limassol. St Andrew's Street quickly became an essential part of any trip into Limassol because it was a tunnel-like thoroughfare with all the atmosphere of a Persian bazaar even though, strictly speaking, its lack of a roof and location in Cyprus meant it was neither Persian nor a bazaar.

The thoroughfare was narrow with numerous shops stringing up their wares to crowd the space above your head with overhanging merchandise. On the pavement, assortments of

Middle Eastern goods spilled out like shining glaciers of leather. St Andrew's Street was all about leather, in fact, I looked forward to any visit just for the smell. Thousands and thousands of leather handbags, suitcases, camel stools, drinking pouches of goat skin, sheepskin rugs, sheepskin coats, black leather coats, tan leather coats, leather jackets of every description, embroidered leather waistcoats, soft leather moccasins or gloves. You could buy a handmade leather belt or a pair of leather boots, a wallet or a purse; the list was endless and extended by some items surprising by simply being covered in leather. You might spot a leather tray, a leather box, a leather hairbrush. All these wonderful articles joined together to produce the heady fragrance of newly worked hide. Surely the skilled and tan-stained artisans responsible for all these amazing goods were working at the rear of the emporia in tiny little workshops. However, I cannot recall seeing any leather craftsmen at work and I suspected some of the items, like camel stools, were probably imported from lands further east. I had yet to witness a camel on the promenades of Limassol.

To me, the whole of St Andrew's Street was entirely appropriate for Cyprus; long before Chinese factories were commissioned to produce 100,000 fridge magnets bearing an image of Aphrodite or the outline of the island, you could buy a more nuanced souvenir – one which did not reveal its 'source' with a tacky name or picture. In St Andrew's Street you could buy a handmade and hand-stitched bag that people might admire and ask about for years... 'Oh, this old thing? I bought it from a shop in St Andrew's Street, Limassol in... Oh... 1971 I think it was...'

Sadly, today, St Andrew's Street's glorious fragrance is long departed. At some point people must have chosen to commemorate their holiday with a Chinese fridge magnet after all. Perhaps the lure of an ultra-cheap T-shirt proved too strong, and people started going home with items having nothing to do with Cyprus at all. I'm acutely aware of the dangers of over-romanticising foreign parts, but who would exchange the organic smells and textures *of hand-worked leather and wood – with their scars of creation on view – for the impersonal and purely commercial adulteries of mass-imported and deafening plastic tat? Thousands of people – apparently. Herein is the plaintive essence of the so-called romanticism; perhaps it's a protestation or lament. A yearning for the golden age of travel when people went in search of stories and discovery. The age of the Art Deco poster with stylish locomotives leaning into the future or ocean liners steaming into the unknown. Even as late as 1970, very few people went to Cyprus for a holiday.*

Memories of Cyprus 1970–72

*

Back at camp I spent the afternoon resting, and at 1pm the muezzin, or a recording of one, issued a raucous call to prayer; after a few minutes, a number of faithful men answered the cry by arriving at the converted church. I found a low and glassless window and looked inside. I could see the mosque's floor was covered with russet prayer mats. Although every Orthodox icon had been removed – they probably now reside in a Güzelyurt museum – there were still various bits of Orthodox furniture converted for Islamic use but without losing their original, Greek aesthetic. A hardwood pulpit provided an exalted position for teaching, an Orthodox lectern now carried the Quran; it was an interesting melding of the two faiths through the agency of simple functionality.

The church structure had undergone running repairs over the years. Much of the surface area of the walls had been rendered which gave the building something of a bandaged appearance; even the few tall palms standing like fronded sentinels in the forecourt looked rather dishevelled. There were no extravagant domes of course, just a series of gable ends which broke up the line of the red-tiled roof. The only part of the church which might be described as ostentatious was the familiar Orthodox bell tower. I'd seen many of these and they all more or less followed the same basic design. They were cross-sectionally square and every few metres all sides of the towers were open to reveal a bell visible beneath carved arches. This arrangement was repeated in slightly smaller dimensions and stacked on top of the former, whereupon the process was repeated once more until the bell tower's tiers were of sufficient height; normally this meant three or four sections with the same number of bells. It was also usual to see crude tannoy speakers incongruously bolted to these towers for announcements to locals that services were about to start. I'd heard muezzins *and* Orthodox priests utilising the speakers with either regular calls to prayer or sung psalms, respectively.

It wasn't unusual to enter an Orthodox church and find a priest conducting a service to empty chairs or to see a muezzin's call unheeded. I'd taken the time, on a few occasions, to watch any comings and goings at village mosques if I was passing by at the moment the tannoy crackled into life. I rarely saw anyone answering the plaintive calls of the clerics, but I suppose the faithful might use the sung messages as an alarm clock and pray privately on prayer mats aligned to face southeast. Workers devoid of established points of reference might use a *qibla*, a modified compass, to help them point their prayer mats correctly towards the holy city of Mecca. Prayers in Orthodox churches were often sustained courtesy of votive candles which had been lit by someone too busy to be bodily present but concerned enough to buy a candle and leave it burning in fervent advocacy.

At around 5pm I prepared for my walkout; I treated my feet, packed up my rucksack and disposed of any rubbish in one of the buzzing bins near the secret shop. When I'd arrived in Günesköy my feet, hips and shoulders were all complaining, but after a few hours' rest I was surprised at how rejuvenated I felt.

It was still extremely hot as I made my way towards

Aydinköy, a village that very nearly joins with Günesköy. A small road took me slightly south and west towards the neighbouring village, whilst the main highway acted as a bypass to the north of both hamlets. I stepped out with a renewed sense of excitement for one particular reason; as I headed obliquely west, I was expecting, after well over 125 miles of westerly hiking, to finally see the sea! My map showed that somewhere near the village of Yeşilyurt I would intersect, once again, with the Mediterranean. Yeşilyurt was about five or six kilometres away, so within the hour I'd be looking for a distinctly blue horizon to my right.

Aydinköy sidled right up to the main road which linked Lefke efficiently with Güzelyurt and, from there, Kyrenia or Nicosia and, of course, all points east. However, heading further west from Lefke would mean winding through the northern edge of the Troodos mountain range which almost tumbles into the sea. There *were* roads which would take you first south to Paphos from where a coastal highway would speed you to Nicosia or Larnaca in no time – but they looked like spaghetti on my map as they snaked their way through hundreds of hairpin bends. If it were possible to lift the 'spaghetti' from the map and pull it straight, its length would soon provide evidence that mountain roads were only for those with good vehicles *and* plenty of time on their hands.

Aydinköy made no real impression, at least not enough for me to have made any diary notes or to take any photographs – apologies to the lovely inhabitants. A small car passed me carrying four young footballers to a match. The car slowed until it was crawling alongside me and matching my pace; we had a very brief conversation.

'Hello, where are you from?' asked the front seat passenger.

'England,' I replied.

The name of my country sent the boys into a scrum of great excitement and there were a few seconds of Turkish conversation before the nearside rear passenger leant out of the window and said, 'Liverpool, Tottenham Hotspur, Chelsea…' This caused more laughter and a free-for-all in naming Premier League football teams.

There was just a hint that BBC Radio 4's 'Mornington Crescent' game had started as the mention of West Brom was met with groans, but when I said, 'Manchester United', the tiny car went crazy, violently rocking on its suspension springs.

'You like Manchester United?' said the boy in the front.

'My son supports United,' I replied.

There was much hilarity in the car at this revelation and then the front passenger asked soberly, 'Where are you going, my friend?'

'I'm walking right across the island,' I answered.

'No!' exclaimed the boy.

'Yes!' I said.

'No!' came the reply, then the boys became convulsed with laughter again and it was suddenly time to say goodbye. The car lurched off with the four dark shapes inside still laughing and waving spindly arms out of the car's open windows.

After Aydinköy I rejoined the main road and realised that my evening walk into Lefke was going to be a joy. With the road west heading towards the quiet foothills of Troodos and the road east heading to the more populated areas of Cyprus, I felt I was escaping into an enclave of greenery. I was set to experience a delightful few kilometres. The sun was quite low in the sky, and as I lined up to walk facing the oncoming traffic a row of tall eucalyptus trees to my right filtered the sunlight, splitting it into bright lines striping the road ahead. The tarmac beneath my feet was wonderfully shaded by this high border; the dusty verges were covered with dry leaves which, over the years, had rotted to a pulp providing a soft carpet to walk upon. After a few metres a line of trees on my right mirrored a row on my left and I was grateful to dwell in the tunnel of shade it provided. Strips of tinder-dry bark had peeled away and fallen to lie like carcasses of dried fish at the foot of the tree trunks. All was dry and warm, and the zebra lines of brightness produced a light show high above my head where any dust disturbed by passing cars made beams of early-evening gold stream between the branches of the trees. Just inside the passageway a familiar blue rectangle announced that I was now in Yeşilyurt and, emerging into the daylight at the end of the tree-lined road, I was treated to one of the loveliest views I'd had on my entire journey. The eucalyptus continued on my right in a more stunted form, but on my left the road was fringed with lines of pink and white oleander. The coloured blooms seemed to have been planted by someone with an eye for contrast as the tiny flowers in the foreground placed spots of colour below a background of grey and distant hills. I was still a long way from any of the buildings belonging to Yeşilyurt, so I wondered whether the blooms had sprouted there naturally. Just beyond the flowers a harvested field led the eye to a copse of tall Mediterranean pines and another eucalyptus wood. Beyond these were the hazy Troodos mountains, now big enough to present themselves in some detail. The nearest range was dark and low, but two further, greyer ranges were visible and had started to claim more of the sky as I drew ever closer. The field was alight with sunshine, but I viewed the scene from the cool shade of the quiet road which stretched itself out before me like the arched back of a reptile. Suddenly I noticed the increasing presence of giant reeds, signs that I was now in an area of coastal marshland. Occasional signposts, standing in isolation at the top of tracks heading north towards the sea, started to advertise beachside hotels and bars. In the distance a few white structures appeared; I realised for the first time, discounting Nicosia or Ercan airport, I was in a tourist area of Northern Cyprus. The internationally unrecognised land, north of the Green Line, is very much the poor relation with regard to tourism, attracting around just ten per cent of the numbers visiting the island south of the Buffer Zone.

I entered Yeşilyurt, passing busy cafés and bus stops advertising local attractions. I felt very out of place kitted out as a hiker when any other visitors I saw were clad in swimming costumes and flip-flops. I passed a very arid golf course and then... finally... emerging through a line of cypress trees came a dark band of blue to my right. I was within five minutes of the Mediterranean Sea! The last time I had been this close to salt water was seven days and 160 kilometres ago! I felt a thrill deep inside me. I'd dipped my boots in the eastern waters, near Paralimni, and now the same footwear had carried me to an entirely different coast. I allowed a vivid memory to fill my mind... I was about a year into my life on the island when a few of us were taken to Ladies' Mile beach, near Akrotiri, where RAF children were taught to swim. I have always been the world's most inefficient swimmer and this particular swimming certificate – which I still have – was presented to kids able to complete twenty-five yards. I imagined a scene where a teacher in England is asked to oversee the swimming exam... 'Miss Brown? I wonder if you're able to recruit a few helpers and take this swimming class? Of course, it *will* involve a trip to the Mediterranean and an hour or two on a sun-baked beach... normal rates of pay... sound OK?' Then my old school's prefabricated, outdoor pool in Dunholme appeared with its violently cold water, surrounded by milky white children shivering without complaint like lambs near the slaughterhouse. I would love to know how many teachers in Cyprus pinched themselves as they paddled about in balmy waters and got paid for it...? My mind cleared and returned to the present.

I had travelled like men of old, slowly and steadily, just as the ancient pilgrims to Kykkos must have made their progress. Now I had some understanding and empathy with their journey, their commitment, and their joy.

Any anxiety over the unknowns of my journey had now vanished; I felt extremely confident my dream of walking along the entire length of the Green Line was going to be accomplished.

I passed a compound full of British trucks and vans, shipped to the island for re-registration and a Cypriot life serving local tradesmen.

I knew this coastal area had been an important landing ground in 1974 and large numbers of Turkish paratroopers had established beachheads and strongholds along this shoreline. I would soon discover just how important this area had been to the military manoeuvres of the Turks.

On the western side of Yeşilyurt, the road ran alongside a stone beach, and I didn't take my eyes off the enthralling, broad expanse of water as I walked towards Gemikonağı (Karavostasi in Greek). The village sits on the coast just below the hilltop village of Lefke. The wind was gusting, and I found myself feeling a tiny bit cold for the first time in a week. My plan had been to camp on the beach somewhere, but as I strode along the open beach road, I changed my mind. The shoreline was made up of large, round stones and all around was wildly exposed. On the other side of the highway there was a sandy verge but, again, it was exposed, and any tent pitched there would draw attention. I hatched a plan en route and decided I'd treat myself to a hotel stay in Gemikonağı, *if* I could find a vacancy.

To reach Kato Pyrgos required keeping to the coastal road which would eventually climb over the foothills of Troodos, meandering north and westwards, until reaching the border crossing just a short distance from the little fishing village. When I'd studied satellite images of the road through the mountains it looked to be quite a challenge. The passage through the hills involved an endless series of hairpins twisting and turning back on themselves. Walking these bends would mean quickly gaining altitude from Gemikonağı, then steeply descending into the village of Yeşilirmak, where I'd experience another rapid rise and descent to my final control point. The last few kilometres were going to be a test of tired legs and resolve. It would be hot, and the gradient looked to be far more than 1 in 3 in many places – a challenge even for motorists; the road is a real clutch and brake burner.

Beside the beach just outside Gemikonaği, I saw a very large and rather inelegant memorial to a Turkish pilot called Cengiz Topel. During a Greek–Turkish conflict in the summer of 1964, Cengiz ejected safely from his F-100 Super Sabre jet. He was captured by Greek villagers who took him to a British hospital, but EOKA guerrillas, operating under retired General George Grivas, removed him to Kykkos Monastery where he was subsequently, and sacrilegiously, tortured and killed. From a short distance away, the memorial had the likeness of three aeroplane tail fins formed in concrete and sunk into the ground. On closer inspection it showed itself to be an attempt to portray the descent of the pilot by parachute, the tail fin shapes painted light blue to represent areas of sky. One large central column showed Captain Topel with his red and white chute deployed overhead replete with a Turkish crescent and star.

The Turkish 'intervention' of ten years later was swift and successful and meant many Greek Cypriots suddenly found themselves in hostile territory. It was situations like this which provided a deadly kind of freedom for anyone with scores to settle, and, on both sides of the Green Line, mob rule resulted in several ugly confrontations. The Turkish military had, ostensibly, arrived to protect Turkish Cypriots, but their arrival also had the effect of removing protection from Greek Cypriots. In a similar way, the crass move of the Athens junta meant Turkish Cypriots were just as vulnerable to attacks south of the Green Line.

A war memorial, incongruously sited near a designer outlet in Gemikonaği, revealed another sad story. Two people, sharing the same surname, had died on 21 July 1974 – one born in 1948 and the other in 1973 – suggesting that on that terrible day a father and child had both lost their lives. The notices in the window of the store boasted that the delights of Hermes, Tommy Hilfiger and Lacoste were all available inside but, compared with the infinite cost recorded outside, the signs looked somewhat revolting and insensitive.

Arriving in Gemikonaği, I soon realised there was certainly a dearth if not a total absence of hotels. I made enquiries at the local taxi rank and was told I'd need to ascend the steep road to Lefke to find accommodation. Given that my exit out of Gemikonaği would 'officially' start tomorrow at the bottom of the hill leading up to Lefke, I accepted the offer of a ride directly up the steep incline to a hotel owned, of course, by a 'friend' of the taxi driver. A few minutes later I was deposited at the Gardens Hotel in Lefke where the largely deserted streets were now dark. The Gardens Hotel seemed to have been fashioned to an Alpine model. Its white walls were divided here and there with oak-effect doors and shutters. Inside, an enclosed courtyard completed the chateau effect with similarly dark doorways leading to rooms circling the central space. Before I collapsed in my room, I needed to make very important arrangements for my last day's walk. The young man behind the tiny reception desk was a Londoner, newly returned to Cyprus. I was relieved he was, effectively, a native English speaker. He introduced himself as Oscan and extended a thin, brown arm towards me for a firm and reassuring handshake. Oscan was a relative of the owners of the hotel and had spent most of his life living in south London, which might explain why he wrote his own name as Oscan – an anglicised version of the more usual Turkish form, Özcan. I explained to him what I was doing, and he was shocked when I told him I was walking to Kato Pyrgos. 'Man! I ain't gonna lie to ya, that is a loooooong way. And the road is vicious, man – steep! You sure you don't want a taxi?' I reassured the dramatic Oscan I'd be fine, but I *would* need to meet my taxi driver again, tomorrow, *after* reaching Kato Pyrgos. I told him I'd need the cab to deliver me back to the Gardens Hotel and I'd be returning to a prearranged meeting point in Northern Cyprus tomorrow afternoon. The taxi driver, who was still loitering with indiscreet nosiness, was called Arcan; he took an enormous amount of persuading that I *would* be at Yeşilirmak at 3pm the next day. After about thirty minutes of intense debate, Oscan managed to convince Arcan that I'd be waiting at the 'shop' in the little village. From there, I'd be taken back to the hotel and finally driven back to Nicosia. The reason behind my return to the Gardens Hotel was simple. The last leg of my journey would finish in Kato Pyrgos at around noon or slightly earlier. I would *not* be spending the night there, I would simply reach the sea, wet my boots in the water and have lunch in the little town before promptly returning to Yeşilirmak, where I'd meet Arcan. So, I did not need my tent or rucksack, nor its contents; I would leave these with Oscan at the hotel for collection en route back to Nicosia later that day. My battle with the twisting, scorching road through the mountains and down into Kato Pyrgos would be fought with the luxury of just a small bag and a few necessities like cameras, drone, water and map. After a few more attempts at confirming our arrangements for tomorrow via sign language and bloodletting, Arcan climbed into his Mercedes and shot off down the hill back to Gemikonaği. I hoped the promise of a good fare for a trip to the capital would see us meeting again.

Suddenly the hotel was quiet, and Oscan took me to my room. I followed my host across a shady courtyard taking in my surroundings; the hotel was reminiscent of the famous Baron Hotel in Aleppo, Syria. The 'Baron', as it was known, was typically colonial and boasted a framed, unpaid bar bill hanging on a wall which showed that T.E. Lawrence had neglected to settle up. Apparently, he had stayed in room 202 and, supposedly, either next door or opposite, Kemal Atatürk had resided in room 201. In some quiet corner of the Gardens Hotel, I half expected to see Somerset Maugham and Co playing cards and decided that the collective noun for a small group of colonials had to be a 'bridge' of colonials. I recalled the rare treat of staying in 'Maugham's' room at Raffles Hotel, Phnom Penh, several years before. In the hotel's Elephant Bar, you might hear stories of yesteryear: of visiting maharajahs, of tigers leaving '*the forests of the night*' to wander along a Raffles veranda. The Gardens Hotel seemed to have been designed to welcome Europeans terrified of staying more than twenty-five metres from the familiarity of an après ski.

Although, compared with the Cleopatra, my room was spartan, in relation to my tent it was an Alcazar of absolute luxury. I showered in a shower tray which proved incapable of draining the water away; within a couple of minutes the water overflowed profusely onto the floor, making its way in rivulets towards the door, heading for the bedroom. Noah's naysayers saw the same. I finished showering, dressed and headed back to ask Oscan about places to eat in Lefke. The little town has always been a well-known destination for those seeking out the famous lacemakers long associated with the area. Unlike Gemikonaği, Lefke had a very different feel owing to its elevated position. There were several decent-looking restaurants and bars, with the whole town having a north European atmosphere. However, in places, impressive houses and quiet streets lent parts of the place the look of the *Chitty Chitty Bang Bang* film set; would the ghastly child catcher emerge from a side street at any moment?

Oscan had advised me to try the amusingly named Vimpy bar (Wimpy?), where I was assured I could enjoy an excellent burger. He showed me a secret doorway in the hotel, which provided a discreet portal onto a deserted side street. I left the hotel turning left to walk up a steep hill towards the town square. Lefke looked a little like a French village in the Pyrenees with its labyrinth of shops and cobbled streets. It was also reminiscent of famous Bellapais, near Kyrenia, where Lawrence Durrell penned his memoir of the island in *Bitter Lemons of Cyprus*.

I located the recommended Vimpy where the owner, who spoke excellent English, politely asked me to sit. My host was a short man, aged around sixty-five, who told me he'd been a policeman before retiring and opening his fast food outlet. Behind the counter, three disparate females were very busy. The ex-cop told me the girls were from Nigeria, Zimbabwe and Turkmenistan. Why was Lefke so cosmopolitan, I wondered? I soon found out. Lefke has an international university; the campus, opened in 1990, now has around 9,000 students. I suspect it would be an understatement to suggest that a number of those young people provide a considerable boost to the local economy. The girl from Turkmenistan looked slightly Mongolian; she reminded me of a young woman, from that little-visited part of the world, who had carried out a pedicure for me in China. The girl in China was in her twenties but had the bearing and innocence of a schoolgirl; we'd had an entire conversation translated through an iPhone. The Vimpy girl from Turkmenistan had the same innocence about her. All three girls were shy but hard-working and diligent. It was something of a shock to reach Gemikonaği, which feels like the natural end to the coast road, and discover Lefke, a town just up the hill, full of life with people from right across the world. I was very impressed to see these girls, so very far from home, working to support their studies in a tiny town nestling in the foothills of Troodos – what amazing people.

After dinner I returned to my Alpine retreat and slipped in through the side door like a member of the French Resistance arriving for a wartime meeting. I crossed the silent courtyard and opened the door to my monkish 'cell'. Sitting on my bed, I set my alarm for 0430; this would be the last early morning of my fascinating journey across the island.

I carefully separated the essentials for my hike to Kato Pyrgos from those things I'd be leaving with Oscan. I took a few moments to gaze at the neat arrangement of articles that would be coming with me. There was hardly anything. I laid out clean liner and outer socks, a clean shirt and shorts. I charged all my batteries and phone, making sure any connecting wires were not forgotten. I studied my map and estimated the distance to Kato Pyrgos was about twenty kilometres, plus a few added kilometres for the many hairpin bends. I washed my light blue 'UN' bandana, hung it up to dry and cleaned my sunglasses before finally slipping in between the smooth cotton sheets of my alien bed. I felt very pleased that, so far, my walk had gone without too many difficulties. It had taken three days less than I'd calculated; I hadn't expected to travel so far in my evening 'walkouts', which had proved to be the most enjoyable part of a day. I took to the road each evening at about 5 or 6pm feeling refreshed, with treated feet and a washed face. I set out with replenished food and water and, best of all, a very relaxed pace in the knowledge that any progress west was a bonus. Whenever I felt like it, I could stop and take to my bed in less than five minutes. Freedom.

Readying myself for departure was something I have enjoyed and perfected over more than thirty-five years of travelling as a musician all over the world. Often, I'd find myself in some remote part of the planet all alone. Typically, the artists I travel with would leave after a tour and I'd stay on for a day or two, perhaps, to take a look at Angkor Wat, stroll around Prague, drive to the Grand Canyon, or explore Bangkok or Shanghai. I'd always have a guitar and suitcase and various artefacts that needed to be carefully packed and prepared for flights. By separating kit into either 'carry on' or 'hold', over the years I've developed techniques for taking quite a bit onboard aeroplanes, learning how to liaise with the purser and cabin crew to get them on my side as it were. Another essential skill is the preparation for a departure at silly-o'clock. I would often find my flight was the first out and that would mean setting my alarm for the very early hours of the morning. Many times, my watch has bleeped at what felt like thirty minutes after I'd nodded off. Leaving a hotel room with bags correctly packed, guitars prepared for flights and all documents to hand is best considered *before* you take to your bed. I would have my kit so well prepared that rising and leaving my hotel room could be achieved in less than five minutes. It's comforting to know, when you're in a stupor of disturbed slumber, all you must do is rinse your face, dress in laid-out clothes, grab your three items of luggage and go. On this trip, my early departures had been uncomfortable, but there was always the thrill of taking directly to the road which was typically within twenty-five metres of my sleeping bag. I needed no taxi, no shuttle, no bus, but only to rely on myself. In my room at the Gardens Hotel, my equipment was ready, my rucksack had been left with Oscan and, unlike Lawrence of Avoidance, I'd settled my bill earlier that evening. Tomorrow I would take to the road for the last time. Once again, I'd slip away unseen onto a dark street and head west for the last time. To resume my journey without interaction with anyone always seemed appropriate; to rise alone with my thoughts and maintain the silence of the dawn for as long as possible felt instinctive. I would take to the road in complete isolation; the loneliness felt spiritual and entirely correct and all of nature was mine to claim. It was as if being alone in the seeing and hearing of a sunrise and birdsong gave me the right to plunge a flag into the ground and call them 'mine' – but only for a moment before I realised my joy had been afforded for me. Nothing belonged to me at all; the world was on loan. When the poet Emily Dickinson wrote, '*That it will never come again is what makes life so sweet*', she was wonderfully aware of the cutting edge of a life caught in the unfathomable space between past and future. That the present is a kind of metaphysical 'God particle'. I turned out the light in my room and fell asleep shortly afterwards.

The Curium

Could it be true – I'm standing where you stood?
Ancient Roman lauding the tragedy,
Seas unchanged – warm waves bringing bridal water,
Doric groom-stones moon-silver; late unpainted,
'Neath shared Orion and starry friends,
Lean into the breeze – yearn to know your face,
Flown 'cross time on briefly borrowed wings,
Carried to Curium's lobe where we embrace.

M.J.W. Clark – *Memories of Cyprus 1970–72*

10

Crossing from Northern Cyprus into the Republic of Cyprus

Lefke to Kato Pyrgos

Wednesday 13 June 2018

My alarm sounded at 4.30am. I washed, dressed quickly, stowed my equipment in my bag and was gone from my room in four minutes and from the hotel in five.

Outside, the street was deserted and wonderfully silent. As I stood in the stillness, I dwelt in the predawn darkness for a second or two as if to allow my mind to catch up with my body. I felt like a thief who had stolen the keys to the day. The entire village seemed to be asleep, and to walk on the fabric of the street was like walking through virgin snow; to be the first to kick up dust and sully the world with the movement of my impure feet. Why did I consider my feet impure? I had been nurtured to be good, law abiding, yet by nature I was faulty. By nature, my life was always in need of restraint, control, discipline and a submission to some higher law. This was almost a moment-by-moment battle; to walk through life and to leave a constructive trail not a destructive one – consolation not desolation. I still wasn't sure where the impulse to complete this walk came from, but I felt a need to stock-take fifty years of experiences...

... I recalled the words of Robyn Davidson, the young woman who, in 1977, walked almost 2,000 miles across a desert in Australia. She said, 'I want to be alone.' She started out with an emotional load far heavier than the packs of provisions carried by her beloved camels. She bore, amongst other things, the loss of her mother by suicide. I wondered whether her mind's preoccupation with survival and navigation pushed more painful thoughts away. If, in moments of relative safety and solace, she had time to admit the untidiness of her cognitive dissonance she could bring all her mind to face the onslaught in the cleanliness of the desert – a blank landscape void of distractions. Perhaps, there, the combatant thoughts were more black and white, making reconciliation easier. My journey couldn't be compared in terms of distance or hardship, but I realised I was looking for an opportunity to spend some time alone. In 1970, my arrival in Cyprus was clothed in the innocence of childhood, but there had been almost fifty years since then. At the age of eight you know very little about the world. Most of us are protected; committees meet to certify films and oversights create watersheds. For the majority, people watch over us. However, half a century of life delivers a barrage of blows: we bury loved ones, we struggle, we get thrown under a multitude of metaphorical buses – often driven by 'friends'. Yet, despite all this, I knew who I was. I didn't come looking to 'find myself'. I thought, thus far in my life, I had treated both success and failure as imposters and had developed a love for the underdog. I believed I had trained myself to think objectively. Isaiah wrote: '*Review the past for me, let us argue the matter together; state the case for your innocence.*' I think every step of my journey was a stating of my case. Being alone in the dawn was akin to being alone in a temple of tranquillity where I knew I was both unworthy yet honoured – honoured with a new day. Honoured with opportunity As a child, these profound thoughts were unavailable to me, out of reach, but I had spent a very special part of my childhood on this island. Perhaps I was hoping to round a corner and come face to face with my younger self? A meeting that would be mutually beneficial. I could reassure the child and perhaps the child might remind the man about true wonder. I was beginning to understand my desire to immerse myself in the island's few remaining places frozen in time. Of course, it wasn't possible to physically meet myself, yet, in various locations, it *was* possible to catch sight of the unchanged places of the past and check myself in the rarest of mirrors; to set myself down in the familiar scenery of youth. I was looking for my boyhood-self in a phantom form, running through the streets of an undivided Nicosia – no barrier hindering my progress... Might I see myself walking alone in the almond grove behind my house in Berengaria and chasing the bird hunters away, this time the catapults are dropped, the sparrows are safe. I understand J.D. Salinger's *Catcher in the Rye*... the desire to gather up those at risk... I'm the ugly duckling who was happy being a duck. I was often ridiculous, and I knew it, but I realised everyone is ridiculous. If anyone suspects their plumage or shape entitles them to laud it over others because they think they're a swan, it's a self-defeating delusion because that kind of thinking makes you an especially deformed duckling. Everyone's feathers are gifted, nobody really earns them. These were the kind of thoughts which formed and faded as I plodded my way across the island; I was checking the wake of my life.

I hope the island's barbed wire and control points are taken away some day, but I'm glad I had baptised myself in the dust of no man's land before the barriers are removed. One day, the 'Titanic' of 1970s scenery will be sunk forever, but it will slip beneath the waves with my fingerprints on it. I did not want to recover the past, to be nostalgic, but I was desperate to be informed by it, so that my future would be cauterised by the heat of the past. Even if future generations recall my name, following generations will not. One day, I will be forgotten…

… Oscan had told me I could catch a taxi from the square in Lefke down to Gemikonağı, but, as usual, I didn't want to interact with anyone so early in the morning, so I took the gravity-aided road down to the junction where I had ended my walk yesterday. Finding my way back down to Gemikonağı wasn't as simple as I thought; I took a wrong turn before backtracking to the right road. I had buoyancy in my stride as I located the main road out of Lefke, floating along with the legs of an eighteen-year-old now that my rucksack was temporarily residing at the Gardens Hotel. There was even a temptation to break into a gentle run in celebration of my overall lightness, but, not knowing exactly what challenges lay between Lefke and Kato Pyrgos, I resisted.

Unlike yesterday evening, which was cool and breezy, the morning was warm and still. As I headed directly north to reach the road going west, the sky to my right was brightening with every step and all around shared a coating of early morning gold. I was at the westernmost edge of the Mesaoria plain. I'd spent the last week crossing its tabletop landscape of farms, olive groves and endless citrus-fruit plantations, but eventually the huge flat expanse just crashed into the Troodos range and easy walking was coming to an end. From here all roads west or south presented themselves as steeply ascending mountain tracks. The normally open sky and low horizons of the last week were gone, and in their place, a dark shoulder of hills and mountains looked to be queueing to cascade into the sea. In front of me lay the western side of Morfou Bay, its natural shoreline broken only by a long steel pier. I wondered if the structure had been built to enable large ships to collect cargoes of asbestos or copper ore, both mined, at some point, in the Troodos range. The beige-painted steelwork stretched out into the calm sea with no apparent purpose whatsoever.

I remembered seeing an asbestos mine from a trip into Troodos as a child. We had turned a corner to come face to face with a large, grey, dust-covered factory. It was a scene from *Mad Max*, with the factory as a dystopian background of ghastly infrastructure. Had an informed risk assessment taken place, we wouldn't have driven within miles of the place; such were the vagaries of health and safety awareness in the 1970s.

On my descent from Lefke I was impressed to see a few faithful Muslims had risen for early prayers. An elderly man, dressed in a smart grey thobe, touched his chest to offer me peace as I passed by. Moments later, an open-backed lorry hurtled by with a delirious puppy in the back, jumping up and down excitedly, in complete oblivion to his perilous position.

I savoured the walk down to Gemikonağı. The houses on either side of the road were a blend of smart-urban and totally dilapidated. I heard buzzing insects and looked up to where a seething wasps' nest had been built in the green fronds of a tall palm tree. On a small traffic island, I was bemused by what I thought was the local community's artistic expression; two large and amorous snails locked in an unhurried, loving embrace presented themselves as a kitsch and incongruous sculpture. Subsequent enquiries were enlightening; the artwork's actual purpose is to remind the observer that life in this village needs to be savoured – slowly.

Every shop or market I passed was shut up tight. Doors were barred and chained, indeed, the entire village appeared to be closed for business. On my right a pair of white minarets pointed to the heavens, half silhouetted against the rising sun in the east. By the time I reached the junction with the coast road, where I'd caught the taxi last evening, it was about 5.30am and it had taken me around fifty minutes to reach the point where my walk could be resumed in 'legality'. Yesterday's cab ride had gained me no distance west but *had* added a few kilometres of northerly walking to my day's requirement.

In Gemikonağı, the village centre gave way to an open area of seafront, a very smartly paved space replete with benches and elegant palm trees. However, something confused me: a sign proclaimed that the shoreline had been developed courtesy of funding from the European Union. Yet Northern Cyprus was not recognised by the world's economy and Turkey, the *de facto* overseer of this territory, was not yet a member of the EU. In fact, recent talks about membership had stalled with accession currently suspended owing to some of Turkey's political, geographical or military agendas. At the time of writing (October 2019) the United States had started to withdraw troops from Syria, leaving their Kurdish allies vulnerable to attack from Turkey – Turkey considers Kurdish fighters to be terrorists. The EU is a broad church with an inbuilt nervousness about member states, or would-be member states, with a track record of 'interventions' which might be seen as an intent to extend their borders as opposed to delivering democracy or ending tyrannies. Yet there, along Gemikonağı's seafront, the locals had been in receipt of many hundreds of thousands of euros to redevelop the esplanade to a very high standard.

Although it was still very early, I noticed a small group of Muslim clerics sitting on one of the seafront benches. I'd seen several varieties of clerical dress on display during my time around Lefke and Gemikonaği and wondered if an international conference was taking place. Each one of these gentlemen sported differing versions of Islamic headgear. I noticed a Kufi hat, favoured by the African contingent – a small, circular, cylindrical headpiece made of perforated material which sits on top of the head leaving a little space between the hat and the crown. One man wore the tighter-fitting Taqiyah or skull cap, and another, with an immaculate white beard, displayed a dark-coloured Pakol familiar to some of the Muslims of Afghanistan. I was unable to draw any significance from the men's union, but it looked to be an Islamic version of an ecumenical meeting in the Christian Church. I was impressed by their friendship and discipline to be up so early, the first prayers of the day already behind them. Just beside the little gathering, the Mediterranean was an enchanted surface of blue and silver, as if just under the expanse, great lungs were causing the water to rise and fall in a deeply peaceful sleep. The water, moved gently by an invisible moon, sounded like rhythmic breathing as it lapped against the walls of the walkway, gasping each time a shallow crest of water moved in to exhale on the pebbles. Out across the bay the surface of the sea was entirely unbroken, leading the eye north across a Dali-painted floor of wavy glass. If elephants on stilts had appeared walking across the waters, it wouldn't have looked entirely out of place. On the eastern side of the bay the sun was gathering the last of the dawn's mist to shroud itself in an enormous mane of white gold as it ascended over the shore, illuminating me like an amoeba under a microscope. Granted the time, I will often replay the scene from that morning.

I wrenched myself away from the surreal beauty, my mind returning to an altogether more boisterous activity which had intrigued me the night before. Local elections seemed to be underway and the most popular way of promoting a candidate involved much flag waving from, where possible, a speeding pickup truck. Where a pickup truck was not available and had, by necessity, been replaced with an economy vehicle, then speed compensated for size. I'd seen any number of tiny cars lurching from side to side with the appropriate flags wedged into their rear windows. Evidently the presence of a flag meant that speed limits could be ignored with impunity; passengers were also allowed to dispense with seatbelts and sit on the doors with only their legs inside the vehicle. The final accoutrement was an aural one; car horns were soldered into the 'permanently on' position and these semi-demonic canvassers zoomed about the place as if they were Brazilian football supporters celebrating the arrival of a sixth star on their famous yellow jersey. It was hard to imagine such enthusiasm was solely political; I had little doubt the ballot was also an excuse for the penned-in youth of Gemikonaği to blow off steam.

Along the seafront an old house looked to be about to lose its first-floor veranda. The wooden structure was rotten, unsafe and a risk to anyone walking either on it or beneath it. I thought about the many evenings spent by past residents gazing out to sea, enjoying a drink from the vantage point before the risk of falling into the street below became too great and the hours of idle conversation on the platform had to be curtailed.

At the end of the Brighton-meets-Northern-Cyprus promenade, the road out of the village climbed steeply, heading slightly southwest. A tiny Turkish army compound clung to its clifftop position where a female soldier was busy hanging out her washing. I mused on her posting – where was she from? What did she think of her base? What was her life like? She was akin to ancient Roman soldiers who had found themselves spread out across a sprawling empire in Judea, Egypt or Spain, making the most of a strange and temporary home.

Further on, a tumble-down house reminded me of a time long before 1974, before the European Union, before Cypriot independence, before the world wars, before... who knows what? Its fabric was made up of the now-familiar mud-and-straw bricks. Whoever had built this house must have sat on the hillside, looked out to sea, and thought this was just the spot to put down his load and build a home. I imagined the informality of house building back in those days. Perhaps there was reference to an elder or mayor. Perhaps you just levelled out the land and built your house without any such consultation. How I would love to know a little about the lives of the people who, eventually, hammered in the last nail or secured the last shutter, spread their food upon a rustic table and ate their first meal whilst enjoying the sun setting over a sea of liquid gold. Was the splendid pomegranate tree by the gate planted by the builder or seeded by an earlier gardener? Whatever its origin it was now laden with fruit and had long outlived the original owners of the house.

As I ascended further into the hills, I took plenty of time to photograph flowers, fruit trees, quaint houses and the sea descending below me as I climbed higher and higher. With only fifteen kilometres to go and no rucksack, I needed to suck the very marrow out of my last day. I hoped this wasn't a case of overconfidence, as I hadn't yet reached the part of my walk that would wind its way through the steeper contours of the Troodos hills.

Some of the houses lining the road out of Gemikonaği had lovely shaded verandas. I saw a small dwelling whose splendid front consisted of swathes of frangipani trees with yellow and white flowers and a lush green vine. To offset the generous vegetation a line of very inorganic, dusty cars occupied space at the side of the house. Each had various pieces of bodywork removed to, presumably, keep an organ-recipient model on the road.

For a short distance the row of houses stopped, and an uncluttered view of the sea returned with, of all things, a working well – complete with a metal bucket suspended from its winding machinery above. A telegraph pole stood immediately beside the walls of the bore hole as if to serve as a contrast between two differing technological ages. Some of the coastline was completely devoid of human interference and could have served perfectly as an undressed film set for any tale of ancient Argonauts or Roman galley ships. Below me the sparkling coast was a snorkeller's paradise.

Oddly, the outer reaches of Gemikonaği yielded up a few rather promising-looking restaurants. I thought these must be places surviving from well-earned reputations given their remote location. It was certain that anyone partaking of an evening meal in these places would enjoy an unrivalled view of the sun setting over the west of Morfou Bay, whether or not the food was up to par. One of the eateries even provided a short, covered pier broad enough to support a few tables for diners keen to be even nearer to the sea.

Before long I was into the rapid ascent I'd been expecting, and for two hours I climbed deeper into the Troodos range as the road followed the natural contours of the hills. With just a little altitude, the flora changed to a mix of Aleppo pine trees and bushes of acacia; these were the heated stage for a full chorus of very noisy cicadas. I remembered first hearing these mysterious and invisible insects when I arrived on the island as a boy. My ears would locate the approximate position of the noisy creature, but as I drew nearer to see the source of the humming, the sound would stop, and the location of the cicada remained unknown.

The sustained effort and relentless heat of the morning saw me reaching for my water bottle with alarming regularity. I knew immediately that I would need more fluid long before I reached the shops in the village of Yeşilirmak, which was hours away. I was surprised at just how quickly the altitude had increased. Below, the shining, natural harbours of the coastline appeared and disappeared as I twisted my way upward for a few hundred metres before dipping slightly then working my way up another steep length of highway. I had plenty of warning that vehicles were approaching; the high-pitched engines were audible at least a minute before anything passed by. Down on the Mesaoria plain, the roads were busy with cars making their way relatively easily from place to place; the traffic here was comparatively light. In the blurb for Lefke's International University, I'd read that Kyrenia and Nicosia were only about an hour's drive away, with Famagusta only twenty minutes further! I think the Famagusta claim was a little optimistic – unless you owned a helicopter – but nevertheless, a car could easily cross *most* of the island in about two hours – a distance that had taken me a week to cross on foot! But things were very different there in the Troodos range. It was obvious that anyone wanting to drive to Paphos or Limassol from this part of Cyprus would first take the speedier route east, even though the road would take you well northeast of Limassol before it allowed you to head south and *then* west. This hot and winding road unravelled slowly; it seemed to be a thoroughfare for commercial vans and army trucks with just the occasional private car.

There was something familiar in the landscape. The rocky hillsides had been blasted to make way for the road and this process had left broad, open scars in the rock face. Looking into the exposed strata showed wide areas of the bedrock were streaked with green. I was walking through an area still rich in copper ore. Many, many years ago, explorers to this island had discovered that when the green mineral was extracted and heated, the ore produced a bright pink liquid resistant to corrosion and easily fashioned into jewellery or armour. When added to tin, it produced an alloy of much tougher material suitable for sharpening into formidable weaponry. I remembered a large copper ingot I'd seen at a museum in Crete. Typically, these ingots weighed between twenty and thirty kilograms and, in Crete, the large square of rough metal on display had been shipped from Cyprus. It was thought to have been exported to a Minoan settlement on the island earlier than 1100 BC – possibly even up to 3000 BC! I wondered what these ancient mariners would have made of today's Ayia Napa? They may have found it a little tame had they ever dropped anchor at ancient Corinth.

I was still en route to Yeşilirmak, but after a few hours' walking there was still no sign of the village, and my water was almost gone. The road went on and on, up and up, and out there in the hills there were no shops or places of shade. It was a hostile environment. Whenever a noisy car went by and disappeared into the distance, a kind of eerie stillness returned, settling as if a DJ were slowly turning his music off. My eardrums ran out of any vibration to report, with my brain registering only my heartbeat or the rustling of my clothes. Fortunately, I was in for a pleasant surprise. I hadn't figured on the roadside presence of part of the village of Bademliköy, whose centre occupied a position high above the snaking pass. Near a road sign pointing up towards the village, I spotted a very welcome and remotely situated shop!

Inside, a mother and what I assumed was her adult son sat in the quiet of the early morning. The shop looked more like a kitchen than a store, and gingham-topped tables stood in the places normally occupied by the rigid shelving of more typical outlets.

'*Merhaba*,' said the lady.

'*Merhaba*,' I replied, as I tried *not* to look like a hybrid of alien and human, as visitors to this shop must *always* arrive on wheels. 'Do you have water?' I asked, switching like a true Englishman to my mother tongue in the assumption that I'd be understood by the pair of shopkeepers.

'Yes. Here,' said the lady pointing to a fridge about ten centimetres from my right hip.

'Ah, thank you… *teşekkür ederim*,' I said, feeling like a complete fraud with one of my handful of Turkish phrases. With a kudos rating in the negative, I selected a bottle of orange juice and two bottles of icy water, all the while being analysed by my rapt audience of two. Hikers were obviously rarer than gold hen's teeth in these parts and, once again, images of swinging saloon doors and abruptly curtailed piano music appeared in a thought bubble above my head. The lady rose to her feet and presented me with a steaming, freshly baked turnover. Obviously, the vendor had decided to present a kind of baked, *fait accompli* to her hapless customer. It looked delicious, sitting in my hand as a hot and heavy lump of carbohydrate joy. I gladly accepted her suggestion and paid what I knew to be absolute top dollar for my prizes, before wowing them with a few more Turkish words.

Outside, I strolled off onto a downhill stretch of road sweeping into the distance before turning right to descend deeper into an enormous void between two high and arid hillsides. At the foot of the first stretch of road, in a precarious position for any motorist with failed brakes, stood a small house with a long driveway. I conjured up a scene of a family at breakfast suddenly joined by a taxi bursting through a window and coming to rest at the end of the table. Shunning the daydream, I noticed a mother and young child were sitting waiting in the scorching heat at the end of the drive. I presumed they were expecting a lift to civilisation but, strangely, their backs were towards me and neither paid me any heed. Suddenly I heard a clattering noise; I realised to my horror that my GoPro had launched itself from my bumbag, landing noisily on the road. I quickly retrieved it, finding no damage other than a few superficial scratches. I admonished myself. Until that day, my GoPro had resided inside a sock as a contingency against just such an occurrence! I passed the waiting couple and smiled, hurrying by just in case they thought I might be a madman on the loose. But neither the child nor mother looked up – not even at a sight as rare as a clumsy hiker. The child, a girl of about four, was sitting on her haunches idly playing in the vegetation beside the drive, but the mother sat still, seemingly carrying some great weight of sadness. I wanted to carry her load of sorrow away with me and cast it down a hillside into the sea.

In the quietness that followed, I listened to the sound and rhythm of my footsteps; they sounded laboured and tired. For some reason my feet were sliding forward in my boots with the steepness of my descent, so I tried leaning backwards to retard my pace.

An aged saloon car slowed beside me and pulled over onto the verge. A woman in a headscarf and long floral dress emerged to open the back doors and boot. The car was stuffed full of flattened cardboard boxes and the lady, without any attempt at furtiveness, began to hurl the entire load over the edge of the hillside right in front of me. She hadn't waited until

I'd disappeared, nor had she chosen a more secretive spot for the fly-tipping, she just brazenly tossed about a hundred or more squashed and printed cardboard boxes directly onto the ground. I was appalled. Each armload of cardboard landed on top of the previous one with the boxes cascading irretrievably over the edge until the site of her littering increased to a size visible from space! I had witnessed an enormous amount of littering on the island with roadside collections of cans and food packets of every kind, but this was criminality on an industrial scale. As a visitor to the island, I felt utterly powerless, all I could do was fix the transgressor with a disapproving stare and wait for a response. I stood watching her, waiting for her to realise I had stopped to witness her actions. When she finally looked up, I shook my head in disgust, but she just shrugged in apathy, muttering a few words under her breath. I had no way of following her home at a discreet distance to record her address before returning to the hillside and tearing each box to pieces then taking great pleasure in feeding the strips of cardboard back through her letter box. If I had been in possession of the time and the right equipment, I would have given up the whole afternoon just to assuage my displeasure.

After the horror of my encounter with the tyrant woman, I fumed for at least a kilometre or two before vainly hopeful images of a district clean-up team came to my rescue. It might have been a fantastic and vapid hope for restitution, but the sight of so much rubbish in such a clean space was anathema to me. Until I observed the lady, I had taken delight in the unspoiled countryside – existing between the coastal towns and humped back of the Troodos edge. I found myself thinking about a scene in the film *Lawrence of Arabia* and what T.E. Lawrence said when he was questioned by the fictional journalist Jackson Bentley. He asked Lawrence what attracted him, personally, to the desert. Lawrence's reply was two words long… 'It's clean.' If Lawrence of Arabia had seen the lady, I don't think he would have been surprised, he wasn't a great Turkophile. I think he would have taken a jambiya to her tyres and smote her about the ears with his camel stick. Perhaps, to restore balance to the universe, he could have done this whilst I was posting the litter back through her mailbox – a Lawrence-Clark pincer movement! I settled for a childish prayer that she'd get a flat tyre and, whilst changing it, a large bird would relieve itself on her scarfless head. I tried to rid my mind of the silliness, but images of Lawrence and Attila the Cardboard-Hun fighting beside the road started to appear, so I decided to erase all the associated thoughts above with reluctant grace and walk on.

I set my eyes at a kind of eagerness to see Yeşilirmak. I rounded a few more hopeful corners expecting to see the picturesque village, but each corner presented another bend to be negotiated, muting my hope. After a few disappointments, a lush valley suddenly appeared before me; I thought of one name at the sight... *Shangri La!* If my hotel in Lefke had conjured up thoughts of mulled wine and après ski, then the glorious valley of Yeşilirmak would have me looking for a line of Von Trapps running down a mountainside and singing 'Edelweiss'. For a moment you could be forgiven for thinking you were in Austria. After the scorched, sun-bleached and arid contours between Gemikonaği and Yeşilirmak, the village itself sat in what was a mini version of the Mesaoria plain. The bottom of the valley was flat and almost entirely green. Skirting the fertile centre, various buildings competed for space on the hillsides with palm trees and dark green fruit trees scattered over an enormous amphitheatre of verdant growth. The valley floor was carpeted with neat rows of vines and low crops of berries. From where I stood it was obvious Yeşilirmak was gloriously hidden in hills; to reach Kato Pyrgos I would have to stumble down into its concealed wonder then struggle out of it on its western side. The little plateau wasn't quite at sea level; reaching the Mediterranean would mean first climbing a steep hillside to the north. Once crested, the sea is at the bottom of an acute gradient of stony hillside, with jagged cliffs abutting the water. The altitude at the centre of the village is recorded as a little above sea level, so I wouldn't have quite the climb I had suffered out of Gemikonaği, but an ascent was going to be necessary to reach my ultimate goal.

I completed an inelegant tumble down the last of the steep road into town, passing a roadside stall with the most colossal strawberries – straight out of Eschol. I found the Imak Market, which Oscan had told me to look out for, replenished my water supplies and, as per tradition, bought the essential lemon ice pop. I'm certain it hissed on my tongue with the exact sound white-hot metal makes when immersed in water. I took a few moments of glorious respite on a dusty chair in the shade beside the shop. Once again, I considered throwing myself into one of the freezers and snuggling up to a box of ice creams, but a tiny sliver of self-respect kept me rooted to my plastic throne.

Being so very near the end of my Green Line odyssey meant I was eager to resume my walk and begin the ascent out of town before I became too comfortable. At a tight and very steep turn in the road leading out of the village, my legs passed on a message of apprehension about the way ahead. Just at that moment there was a sign warning, 'Border 4km'. Four kilometres! Four kilometres was a negligible distance after having marked up about 200 kilometres. I was overjoyed! Though the acute climb out of Yeşilirmak seemed to bring the road surface to the nose, it was a mercifully short walk to my destination.

Although I was yet to walk into Kato Pyrgos, find the sea and dip my dusty boots into it, I felt I had achieved my goal already. Bar my being run over by an army truck – or an aged saloon with a headscarfed woman at the wheel – I had made it. Within an hour and a half, I'd be at the coast in Kato Pyrgos.

I was amazed at just how many Turkish army trucks were still passing me with regularity. They couldn't be crossing the control point, and they were running out of Northern Cyprus territory, so where *were* they all going? The answer came as I entered an area of cone-like hills, many of which were topped with camouflaged lookout posts. It was quite hard to tell where the Green Line or Buffer Zone were exactly, but the area was brimming with Turkish flags and various communication aerials. In the distance, I could make out the occasional Greek lookout to the south or west. The atmosphere reminded me of a standoff between Philistines and Israelites with each staring at the other from across arid valleys. Around one bend I saw a truck full of Turkish soldiers leave the road and take to a steep dirt track running up the side of a hill. The lorry disappeared behind a steep shoulder of rock leaving blonde vapours of dust swirling in the air. The troops were obviously stationed here in good numbers so, unlike many other army compounds in Northern Cyprus, these bases and their soldiers were more 'frontline'. These enforcements were remote and the only company, apart from other Turkish soldiers, were the Greek Cypriot soldiers staring at their counterparts through binoculars from across the chasm of a steep valley. I hadn't yet seen a UN post standing between the two sides, but I was certain I'd come across one before long. Sometimes, I passed a deserted sentry post immediately beside the road. One was just big enough for two soldiers and painted in patches of green, black and beige, but anyone wishing to use it would have needed to wade through dry grass about a metre high.

I was now on a section of baking tarmac which seemed totally deserted; I began to take the shortest line through any bends like an advanced motorist straightening out corners. Every few hundred metres a dirt track would disappear into the hills and, where the track met the road, a poor and nominal barrier was erected, sometimes consisting of no more than a painted barrel in the middle of the trail. A notice would instruct anyone nearby to '*Dur*' which was a Turkish order to 'Stop!' All over these dry hillsides there must have been many hidden military installations. Another lorryload of uniformed youngsters sped by, waving at me from under a canopy of brown canvas that shaded them from a violent sun. They all smiled at each other and laughed at the spectacle, the sight of a hiker slowly cooking in the heat providing them with a few moments of light relief.

A glance at my watch revealed I'd been walking for four hours; it was still only 9am. As I started mumbling to myself that the *supposed* four kilometres was feeling more like ten, the grey tarmac road suddenly broadened and a large, white awning came into view. It spread itself over the highway providing shade for a few temporary buildings. Finally, I'd reached the crossing point just a couple of kilometres from the centre of Kato Pyrgos. I ambled up to the border guard's booth and registered a look of surprise on the official's face; I can't imagine many arriving on foot from the scorching roller coaster that is the road from Gemikonaği. The Turkish official returned my passport to me, and I made to stroll off into the Buffer Zone, but another officer appeared and challenged me.

'Passport Control!' said the man. I pointed at the booth I'd just visited, but the second official instructed me to wait. After a few frustrating minutes the consensus was… I was free to go. A UN pickup truck was parked just beyond the checkpoint, and I sauntered over to ask the driver where he was from.

'Hello there, may I ask you which country you're from?' I smiled and hoped he wouldn't mind the inquisition.

'Bosnia Herzegovina,' said the man. I think my sense of elation at being just thirty minutes' walk from the end of my journey filled me with an overflowing sense of bonhomie. I found myself thanking the guy for all his efforts and briefly telling him about my journey right across the island. The UN officer raised an eyebrow and laughed before courteously getting out of his car to shake my hand. We bade each other farewell and I strode off into no man's land towards the Greek Cypriot checkpoint. There were several hundred metres of Buffer Zone between the two control points and the quiet road looked relatively new, testament to the fact this crossing was not yet eight years old. The available crossing points over the Green Line have increased over the last few years making travel from north to south far easier than it used to be, and this border control was one of the most recent additions. The Kato Pyrgos point opened in October 2010 and provides a much-needed shortcut from the northwest to all points east and vice versa. Although this was a 'reopening' of an existing highway, the fabric of the road in the Buffer Zone had to be repaired after years of neglect, with the two republics liaising to build the infrastructure of their respective checkpoints.

I swept round a tight right turn and a very different lookout came into view. Perched precariously on top of another coned hillock was a white structure with an aerial or two and a small satellite dish. A set of whitewashed steps led steeply to a tiny structure which was the image of a minuscule air traffic control tower. A low wall of white sandbags bordered the building's frontage and painted on the structure were the numbers 08. This was UN base number 8, and its location was twenty-four UN posts further west than the one I'd passed in the Buffer Zone between Bostanci and Astromeritis. This was an eagle's nest vantage point guarded by a contingent of Argentine soldiers seconded to work for the UN over 12,000 kilometres from home! The road below the sentry point had triangular warning signs to inform drivers a sharp bend was imminent, and when I slowly rounded the corner, I caught sight of the Greek Cypriot checkpoint.

A languid immigration officer was sitting behind a desk in an office with a few other officials. He was an out-of-shape man, aged around forty-five, and I averted my eyes from a protuberance of hairy flesh attempting a break for freedom through a gap between his shirt buttons. I thought about my father and his strict discipline as a military man. I wasn't quite sure what he'd make of a man requiring so large a uniform. It seemed de rigueur at Greek Cypriot control points to encourage a laissez-faire atmosphere, and my passport came back to me with a smile and an air of good-natured disinterest...

*

The following 'One Day' story is an adaptation of an early piece of Cyprus-writing. I've decided to include it for reasons I hope will be discovered in its reading. The reader should forgive elements of this story which might sound like repetition, but this piece explains the seed leading to my journey and the writing of this book. I don't understand *exactly* why my two years living in Cyprus became so fundamental to my being; even now, I very lopsidedly divide my life's memories into Before or After Cyprus. It might be because I was at just the right age for beauty to deposit itself indelibly in the ledgers of my memory. If I'm blessed with a functioning mind at the end of my life, I will think often about the day described below...

*

One Day (9)

One day I revisited my old house in Cyprus. Let me share one of the most, and almost literally, incredible moments in my life. Between 1970 and 1972 I lived in Cyprus. In those days Cyprus was seldom visited. Paphos Harbour was a tiny, seafront fishing village and very few people knew where the Tombs of the Kings were; this was before they were fenced off. Unsuspecting beach-strollers might just fall into the subterranean cavities that lie just a few yards from the coastal highway. High over the bleached hillsides, vultures circled menacingly. The toga-white Roman Curium looked out over a jewel of a warm sea where

RAF Vulcan crews practised bombing accuracy with Flash Bang Smoke bombs. Sometimes my father took me with him when it was his turn to monitor and record the strike data. It was work – apparently. Aphrodite looked on, lazily.

My school day started at about 7am but was over by 1pm. Almost daily, my mother drove our mustard-yellow Volvo estate through the wonderfully aromatic citrus fruit plantations to a deserted beach where I tried but never caught a flat fish. I had to walk about a hundred yards out to sea before it was deep enough to swim. The balmy evenings were spent in long and languid meals at kebab houses where, bathed in moonlight, the children of three or four families would produce hilarious third-culture laughter way into the night.

The cinemas were open-air, and we ignored the Greek subtitles and giggled at exotic depictions of life outside England. We had it better. Better by a country mile. I could catch chameleons in my garden. If you were quick, you might catch the tiny lizards or spider-man-geckos… Unbeknown to me, my wife was a girl at the matinee… so close… but I didn't know her! We were both Forces' kids. Funny.

I lived in Berengaria village – named after the wife of Richard the Lionheart. His ancient castle, near Limassol, could be explored for free in those days. Nobody had ring-fenced it or thought about making money from the ruins. Occasionally we'd stop on the way home from the beach and run recklessly through its ancient grounds.

In my MOD village there was nearly everything you needed – everything you needed if you were eight! Swimming pool, NAAFI, schools, football pitches, tennis courts, scout and cub huts, cinema, barbers, church, sweet shop, and endless trails through the dusty eucalyptus trees. It was the age of Chopper bikes, and these were freely loaned amongst friends without restraint or record; we were camped together in an alien world of heat and dust. The hot, brown faces of friends morphed into the likeness of brothers with almost *everything in common. We had dozens of dens and hideouts. It was the nature of the place for kids to roam like feral cats from house to house where ice-cold drinks were freely available; we drank so much and so frequently that bottle openers hung like trinkets from our belts.*

I lived in Cyprus for two years and I still divide my life into pre- or post-Cyprus, which is ridiculous and increasingly disproportionate; I don't really understand why. Actually, I think I know why, but it's so profound I've kept it secret for half a century.

Fast forward forty years. I was in Cyprus again and I'd located Berengaria village. It had been mothballed years ago and was due to be demolished; I'd seen videos of the place on YouTube. It's as if they had sounded an alarm and everyone had fled – leaving a Mary Celeste village. There were still children's pictures hanging in my old school. The scout house was still there – like a tombstone, saying, 'Here lies your boyhood', but the graveyard of memories was going to be demolished. They were going to erase the furnace where all my stories had been forged. My ancient altar, my pile of stones down by the 'riverside'. I had been blessed by an island and now my point of reference was being scuttled; there will be no trace of RAF Berengaria left on the surface of history's sea...

... My whole life I've been a bit of a goody two shoes. I'd be the kid terrified of the police. I stayed within boundaries. I'd be a safe bet for the teacher leaving the classroom and I always hated the sound of breaking glass... but this time... I stood beneath the MOD barbed wire and thought... I'm going in! I imagined facing a Greek magistrate explaining my trespass – totally worth it! He's going to love this story... I'm definitely going in!

I climbed the fence and dropped down onto the hot and oh-so-familiar tarmac. I looked about but I was totally alone. And so, I ran, back forty years. Past the little shop where I bought my very first record for ten bob, past the Church of Scotland notice board and the oven-hot corrugated iron of the NAAFI. Back through time... In between the buildings I caught sight of my life

– like snap shots in an album. Back beyond my children and my wife, my employment, too many guitars, the kiss of a girl, failure, vanity, summers, winters, births, deaths... Look! John Craven and Johnny Morris! Newbiggin-by-the-Sea. Scalextric. Birds' nests. Spangles. Jimmy Page. Bruce Cockburn. Henry V. Douglas Bader. 617 Squadron then 9 Squadron with the Bat, then 27 with Dumbo...? Van the Man...? The random and personal nonsense of the unfettered mind... Beside the school wall were crisp, bleached leaves, then images of my school days formed in my mind – hated them, pretty much all of them! Boarding school – a brown-painted trunk and weeks away from home... but school in Cyprus was brilliant – literally! A kiss for you, Miss Heathfield. Thank you so much...

Memories of Cyprus 2012 – One Day (9) to be continued...

*

I walked into Kato Pyrgos just before 10am on Wednesday 13 June. It had taken about nine days to cross the island with a two-day sojourn in Nicosia. I spent a few minutes capturing photographs of myself using the timer on my little Sony camera. I propped the device on a piece of perforated rock, pressed the button and stumbled across rough ground to a large, rectangular 50 km/h sign bearing the name of my ultimate destination... Kato Pyrgos!

Strangely, the actual entry road into the village was effectively a side street. The broad and relatively new road at the crossing point suddenly narrows to an uneven and quiet road typical of most remote Cypriot villages. Thus, the transition from the modern checkpoint into ancient Kato Pyrgos is a little discombobulating. Either side of the quiet road, dusty trees and low garden walls provided a very humble guard of honour as I ambled off towards the village centre.

I saw a petrol station across the road and passed under a truly spectacular evergreen tree to reach the garage forecourt. I bought fresh water and emerged to ask a diminutive Greek Cypriot where the local supermarket was. The man extended a hand and pointed down the street.

'Here! Here! One hundred metres...' I looked in the direction his finger was pointing and, amusingly, I saw a few shopfronts about 300 metres away.

'*Efcharistó poly*,' I said and headed off towards the town centre.

Kato Pyrgos, despite its nearby crossing point, is not easy to reach, especially from the south or west. The little fishing port is more or less the only Greek Cypriot village situated on Morfou Bay. It also resides to the east of the Northern Cyprus enclave of Kokkina, a place of historic significance for Turkish Cypriots. This tiny crescent of Turkish-controlled land had resulted, indirectly, from the intercommunal conflict of 1963–64. The UN had been forced to intervene, negotiating a ceasefire in the region when Greek Cypriots, impatient for enosis, attacked Turkish Cypriots with a view to driving them out of the region. The Greek Cypriot EOKA fighters believed Kokkina was a strategically important landing ground for Turkey; evidence of this was the presence of around 500 paramilitary volunteers. These men had been trained in Turkey and had taken up residence in the town. Ostensibly, these men were there to protect the interests of the Turkish Cypriot community, but General George Grivas saw their presence as the thin end of a Turkish-military wedge. The conflict was a foreshadowing of what would happen a decade later. For the Turkish, EOKA's aggression towards Turkish Cypriot communities was perhaps a foretaste of that which might be extrapolated across the whole island. In short, the earlier conflict around Kokkina was the war of 1974 in microcosm. Somewhere in the azure skies over Morfou Bay, in the summer of 1964, Cengiz Topel would have been floating gently to earth, with his canopy fully open, thinking he was safe.

Today the enclave exists within a disconnected section of Buffer Zone, presumably the location of UN lookout posts numbered 01 to 07.

For Kato Pyrgos, this enclave to the west, the Troodos mountains to the south, the Buffer Zone to the east and the sea to the north mean the village is hemmed in on all sides. But the place is still rooted in a rich history with fascinating things to see for anyone determined enough to seek out this little Cypriot gem. For example, according to local knowledge, the twelfth-century Chapel of Panagia Galoktisti (Chapel of the Virgin Mary) was built using cement mixed with milk instead of water. With my engineer's head on I wasn't sure what effect the fat content would have on Portland cement, but I was willing to give the mortar the benefit of the doubt, after all, 800 years testify to the successful combination of cement and dairy products.

I spent a few minutes trying to communicate with a local café owner by showing him my map and pointing at the village of Yeşilirmak across the Buffer Zone. I was attempting to find a way to catch a lift back through the oven-hot hills to meet Arcan the taxi driver at 3pm. The café owner was a large, moustachioed Greek gentleman who was almost as wide as he was tall. Had he been French he would have looked the very epitome of a cartoon Parisian chef. If food was his forté, geography was not; after a few fruitless minutes of map pointing and car impressions I decided I would walk back to the border and cadge a ride with the first benevolent driver I met. I had loved every second of my journey – even the marathon stage into Nicosia – but the pool and bar at the Cleopatra Hotel were rapidly becoming the subject of irresistible desire.

I shut these delights from my mind, returning to consider my yet uncompleted walk. Nine days ago, my boots were immersed in the gentle waters of a placid Mediterranean near Paralimni, and I intended finishing by dipping my footwear in the same sea – albeit about 200 kilometres further west.

I walked north, knowing that the sea was just a five-minute stroll from the centre of Kato Pyrgos. I found a soft, sandy trail chicaning past a few dust-covered houses and saw the milky-blue waters of the sea. Standing between me and the Mediterranean was a copse of tall eucalyptus. Each massive tree stood like a natural pillar in a little forest grouped around to form a lovely temple of tranquillity. Under the trees, years of shed leaves provided a faded red carpet of welcome, and my feet made no sound...

... I was twenty-five metres from the water. To my left, a few silent beach houses returned me to the lovely haunts of my boyhood. The beat of cicadas, the warmth of the sun, the fragrance of blossoms overloading the senses, the caress of an evening breeze, a classroom full of light and friendship, coloured marbles, the music of the bouzouki, the hard-bleached curium and the gorgeous blue of the sea, warm sand and ice-cold drinks. Day after day of the above...

*

One Day (9) Continued...
Memories from 2012

... I was walking in Berengaria, back through time, I rounded a corner and there was my house! It was 2012. I was fifty-one years old. A few steps and I'd be standing in that same garden, the sacred scenery of a child's playground, unchanged for forty years! Amazingly the house was open – ready for demolition! I wandered through the halls and rooms. I pictured phantom-gifts and a Christmas in 1971. A leather football. A father younger than me. Odd. Beautiful. Second chances to express deep and sincere thanks... Surely I was cheating time. Someone had pressed

pause when I was ten years old and waited for my return. I'm time-travelling. I'm the returning salmon come to die in my own headwater but to live again in a cauldron of appreciation, charcoal embers still supernaturally glowing...

... This is, expressly, not nostalgia! Nostalgia is pathetically weak. It shrinks from the present and retreats. This is the checking of the wake of a life. The determination of how to proceed. The observation of churned waters. A musing on direction. The gathering of good arrows. My reunion of carried friends. The repetition of sacred names. The savouring of goodness. The recollection of sorrow, the sadness which is good for the heart. An understanding of mortality.

Memories of Cyprus 2012

*

I took the drone from my bag and set it to fly just three metres from the forest floor, programming it to follow me as I completed my last few steps. The little aircraft hovered as still as a hummingbird and waited for me to move. I turned to face the sea. The surface of the water was an inverted sky of cloudy blue and I just stood gazing at it for a few seconds. I took a step and the drone moved faithfully behind me. I walked between the ashen trunks of two towering trees and looked down at my feet moving slowly beneath me. The sunlight penetrated the canopy above and dappled the ground with areas of light as bright as flashing silver; even the shade had a lightness to it. Five steps and the trees were behind me. *Behind me.* Behind me like Paralimni and its evening sun, behind me like my first dawn in the field near Frenaros, like Slinky the Dog and the Red Falcon. Like Emine, Costas and Oscan, like the olive groves and dry ravines, like all those golden sunsets – only truly making sense when deliberately observed. Like the song of the muezzins and the mournful bell towers caught on the wrong side of the

Green Line, like the minarets and the rustic cross still resting and testifying in a hidden corner of Nicosia, like Lefke and 200 kilometres of barbed wire. Like the silence of my mornings. Like boyhood. Like the tiny sparrow – a feathered olive branch, evading the hunters in the almond trees and sent across decades to sing about forgiveness. I walked a little to the left of a deserted lifeguard tower and stepped onto a line of large boulders which acted as a sea defence. To defend against the sea – the ancient, primordial ocean washing this island long before they came looking for copper. Nobody can beat the sea. I hopped onto a lower stone and the water did not shrink back from me; it shrinks from no one. It will not retreat from Turk or Greek.

My secret is this: I needed to align myself with the sea or something like it. Something or someone unchanging and everlasting, like chiselled memory, immovable and faithful like the constant sun. I thought I was returning to a land of childhood innocence to bury the man, to start again. I yearned for the Eden of my garden in Berengaria; to stand perfectly correctly on the earth, where everything around you is a friend and no impediment has found its way into the folds of the mind. To be at one with nature. Then came the epiphany: I was still the boy, carried deep within and treasured like any child of my own. Harboured in my own paternal womb I bore myself, not twinned nor superimposed, we were One. Without the eyes of the boy, I would have seen nothing on this journey.

The surface of the sea was below me and disinterested in my story… merely a bending of the knee and my soul was wet.

Acknowledgements

Thank you to Mick Moore and Claire Jackson for early criticisms and a keen eye, and to Simon Fox.

My gratitude to: The Cleopatra Hotel, Nicosia, especially Costas (He's alive, he's alive!), and Angela. The VIP Restaurant, Akdogan, and the lovely Emine. Oscan from the old Gardens Hotel, Lefke. Ali the Red Falcon, for coffee and water at the football club

Captain Peter Vanek of the UNPKF — for very special access into the off-limits Buffer Zone.

My mother, for rightly believing I didn't start the fire! D, D, Dunholme Parish Council and, 'Well done, Bus Driver!'

John Sutton and Rosemary Brooks for encouragement. Catherine Williamson the Victorian Muse.

The Royal Air Force.

My Teachers: Miss Heathfield (RAF Berengaria Junior School) and Dr Peter Emmens (Cordeaux, Louth)...you may have forgotten me, but I will never forget you x.

Gill (well, try…), Edward, Evie and Maddy, for understanding my battles with Art — you make me immensely proud. We have seen some amazing places: from Raffles to The Rockies. From The Far East to The Yeti Ride (Not again!?).

To everyone in my music world: St Ephen of Richmond (Little Bubbles), Chris Bowater, Andy Bromley, Mark & Carrie Tedder and Claire 'Robinson' — for all you have taught me. Thank you.

Everyone at Troubador Publishing, especially Holly for patience aplenty.

Finally, to anyone who honours me by reading this book. Escape with me. I hope you become childlike enough to see the treasures of a world hidden in plain sight.

To Cyprus…peace, perfect peace.

Thank you